35 CLASSROOM MANAGEMENT STRATEGIES

Promoting Learning and Building Community

Adrienne L. Herrell

California State University, Fresno, Emerita
Educational Partnerships, Panama City, Florida

Michael Jordan

California State University, Fresno, Emeritus
Educational Partnerships, Panama City, Florida

PEARSON

Merrill
Prentice Hall

Upper Saddle River, New Jersey
Columbus, Ohio

Library of Congress Cataloging in Publication Data

Herrell Adrienne L.
   Thirty-five classroom management strategies : promoting learning and building
   community / Adrienne L. Herrell, Michael Jordan.
      p. cm.
   includes bibliographical references.
   ISBN 0-13-099076-0
   1. Classroom management. 2. Active learning. I. Jordan, Michael. 1944-D Title

   LB3013.H475 2007
   371.1024-dc22   2006045313

Vice President and Executive Publisher: Jeffery W. Johnston
Executive Editor: Debra A. Stollenwerk
Assistant Development Editor: Daniel J. Richcreek
Editorial Assistant: Mary Morrill
Production Editor: Alexandrina Benedicto Wolf
Production Coordination: bookworks
Design Coordinator: Diane C. Lorenzo
Cover Designer: Candace Rowley
Cover Image: Susan Bailey Harris
Production Manager: Susan W. Hannahs
Director of Marketing: David Gesell
Senior Marketing Manager: Darcy Betts Prybella
Marketing Coordinator: Brian Mounts

This book was set in Garamond by Laserwords Private Limited. It was printed and bound by Banta Book Group. The cover was printed by Phoenix Color Corp.

Pearson Education Ltd.
Pearson Education Singapore Pte. Ltd.
Pearson Education Canada, Ltd.
Pearson Education—Japan

Pearson Education Australia Pty. Limited
Pearson Education North Asia Ltd.
Pearson Educación de Mexico, S.A. de C.V.
Pearson Education Malaysia Pte. Ltd.

10 9 8 7 6 5 4 3 2 1
ISBN 0-13-099076-0

To all the hardworking teachers across the nation,
and especially to our models of classroom expertise:
Susan McCloskey, Diane Leonard, Vince Workmon,
and Jody Salazar. We salute your dedication.

ABOUT THE AUTHORS

Adrienne Herrell, retired from California State University, Fresno, was a professor of reading/language arts and taught classes in early literacy, assessment, and strategies for English learners. *35 Classroom Management Strategies: Promoting Learning and Building Community* is her 10th book for Merrill/Prentice Hall. Her previous books include *Camcorder in the Classroom* with Joe Fowler; *Fifty Strategies for Teaching English Language Learners* with Michael Jordan; *Reflective Planning, Teaching, and Evaluation: K–12* with Judy Eby and Michael Jordan; and *Teaching Elementary School* with Judy Eby. Dr. Herrell's writing and research are built on her experiences teaching in Florida's public schools for 23 years and teaching and supervising student teachers in California for 15 years.

The authors are currently engaged in research in public schools in California and Florida.

Michael Jordan, also retired from California State University, Fresno, was an associate professor in the Department of Curriculum and Instruction and taught classes in curriculum, classroom management, and social foundations. He has taught at many levels, from the primary grades through high school, in Georgia, Alabama, Florida, and California. *35 Classroom Management Strategies: Promoting Learning and Building Community* is his 10th book for Merrill/Prentice Hall. His previous books include *Fifty Strategies for Teaching English Language Learners* with Adrienne Herrell; and *Reflective Planning, Teaching, and Evaluation: K–12* with Judy Eby and Adrienne Herrell. Dr. Jordan is also an actor, a musician, and a former B-52 pilot. His work in live theatre is dedicated to providing children and youth with access to the arts. He and Dr. Herrell incorporate many dramatic reenactment strategies into their joint research working with English learners. This is Dr. Jordan's fifth book for Merrill/Prentice Hall.

CONTENTS

SECTION IV

BUILDING RESPONSIBILITY FOR THEIR OWN ACTIONS AND WORDS IN THE MEMBERS OF THE LEARNING COMMUNITY

SECTION V

INTEGRATING ACTIVE LEARNING EXPERIENCES, AUTHENTIC PRACTICE, AND ASSESSMENT

SECTION VI

BUILDING COMMUNITY THROUGH COLLABORATION

SECTION VII

BUILDING A SUPPORT SYSTEM: CELEBRATIONS AND PARENT INVOLVEMENT

SECTION VIII

SUPPORTING ONE ANOTHER: SCHOOLWIDE STRUCTURES TO ENCOURAGE INTERACTION AND COLLABORATION

TEACHER RESOURCES

STRATEGIES ON VIDEO

The DVD included at the back of this book illustrates 12 classroom management strategies in real classroom environments. The Strategies on Video demonstrate selected techniques that can be implemented in the classroom. Each Strategy on Video appears in a feature box that includes a brief synopsis of the strategy as well as a set of questions to help the viewer focus on the important points being demonstrated.

Strategies 1 and 2 *Arranging furniture and materials* Diane Leonard, first-grade teacher, explains her decisions regarding furniture arrangement and materials storage in her classroom. She presents some inexpensive storage solutions and ways to use everyday items in organizing the classroom.
Focus questions listed on page 22   Video running time: 4:58 minutes

Strategy 7 *Modeling and building respect & establishing routines and transitions* Vince Workmon, fourth-grade teacher, demonstrates ways to build mutual respect in the classroom and methods for establishing and practicing classroom routines.
Focus questions listed on page 52   Video running time: 5:35 minutes

Strategy 10 *Implementing class meetings* Susan McCloskey, first-grade teacher, and Jody Salazar, middle-school teacher, demonstrate class meetings. The first-graders work collaboratively to establish classroom rules, while the middle-school students brainstorm solutions to a disturbing classroom problem.
Focus questions listed on page 68   Video running time: 10:00 minutes

Strategy 13 *Empowering students to resolve conflicts* Vince Workmon, fourth-grade teacher, demonstrates the use of active listening and conflict resolution as he works with two of his students to resolve a real-life conflict.
Focus questions listed on page 88   Video running time: 6:02 minutes

Strategy 14 *Eliminating bullying in schools* Jody Salazar, middle-school teacher, discusses the definition of bullying and the students' experiences with this difficult problem. Included is a problem-solving session with the school principal, counselors, and teachers as they make plans to address the problem of bullying schoolwide.
Focus questions listed on page 96   Video running time: 11:45 minutes

Strategy 18 *Using the learning cycle to enhance academic success* Vince Workmon, fourth-grade teacher, illustrates the steps in planning an active-learning lesson, with the class participating in a science lesson in which he builds on students' prior experiences.
Focus questions listed on page 124   Video running time: 7:36 minutes

PREFACE

In *Beyond Discipline: From Compliance to Community* (1996), Alfie Kohn describes his visits to the classrooms of effective teachers in surprising terms. He talks about being struck not so much by what the teachers were doing as by what they were not doing.

> They were not concentrating on being effective disciplinarians. This was because they had better things to do, and those better things were preventing problems from developing in the first place. (p. xii)

To quote Susan Ohanian (1982), "There's only one true technique for good discipline and that's good curriculum." That quote sums up the theory on which this text is based. Teachers must be fully aware of the impact of what they are asking students to do. When students are fully engaged in the teaching and learning in a classroom, their behavior and decision-making skills improve dramatically. Thus, the reader may find many techniques in this text that are not typically labeled "discipline" or "classroom management."

In our years of supervising student teachers we have noted that many beginning teachers are reluctant to challenge students and get them actively involved in learning. Student teachers often tell us, "I would have liked to have done so-and-so, but I was afraid I would lose control of the class." They seem willing to sacrifice excitement about learning for quiet classrooms, and we believe that cheats our children.

In this text we challenge both student and experienced teachers to learn techniques for developing good decision-making skills throughout the curriculum. We believe that if students are given challenging daily curriculum, they will become engaged in their own learning and accomplishments. When students begin to experience the excitement of personal accomplishment, they become more focused on active participation in their classroom.

Effective teachers can create an auspicious circle rather than the more familiar vicious one (DeVries & Zan, 1994.) If teachers give students opportunities to practice making decisions, most students will act more responsibly and be more committed to their learning.

 ## RESEARCH ON EFFECTIVE SCHOOLS

In the past 25 years, research on effective schools has identified several correlates that are present in successful school improvement initiatives (Patchen, 2004).

Clear School Mission Effective schools have a clearly articulated mission, and all school staff members accept responsibility for student learning.

High Expectations for Success All faculty and staff members have high learning expectations for *all* students and a commitment to helping everyone master essential content and school skills.

Instructional Leadership   In effective schools the principal functions as the instructional leader and persistently communicates a school's mission and goals to parents, students, and staff members.

Frequent Monitoring of Student Progress   Student progress is monitored regularly in effective schools. A variety of assessment instruments are used, and the results of those assessments are used to improve individual student performance.

Opportunity to Learn and Student Time on Task   Teachers use time wisely to engage students in learning tasks. Students are involved in small-group, whole-group, and individual learning activities for a large percentage of their school day.

Safe and Orderly Environment   Effective schools have an orderly, purposeful, and businesslike environment that is conducive to learning and free from threat of physical harm.

Home–School Relations   In effective schools the parents are knowledgeable about the school's mission and play an active role in their children's education.

The strategies included in this text are structured to support these correlates of successful, effective schools. By defining classroom management in its broadest sense, teachers can design and implement a classroom and schoolwide mission that ensures optimal learning for all students.

 # HOW THIS TEXT IS ORGANIZED

This text is organized into sections related to the important elements present in a successful community of learners. In each section, strategies are explained, and steps for implementing them are given. We offer two classroom examples for each strategy to show how use of the strategies may differ according to the ages of the learners and the content of the curriculum.

Some of the strategies are demonstrated on the DVD that is included with this text. Those strategies will provide a platform for class discussion and a model to make the strategy more understandable. (See the description for Strategies on Video on pp. ix–x).

In each section we introduce the theory base for the management strategies discussed. The seven sections consist of the following:

Section I	An Introduction to Classroom Management and Discipline
Section II	Setting Up an Environment That Supports Engagement in Active Learning
Section III	Establishing a Classroom Management System Built on Mutual Respect and Caring
Section IV	Building Responsibility for Their Own Actions and Words in the Members of the Learning Community
Section V	Integrating Active Learning Experiences, Authentic Practice, and Assessment
Section VI	Building Community Through Collaboration
Section VII	Building a Support System: Celebrations and Parent Involvement
Section VIII	Supporting One Another: Establishing Schoolwide Structures to Encourage Interaction and Collaboration

Each section of the book includes a series of strategies that will enable the teacher to build competence and responsibility in students. These strategies are introduced sequentially in each section—some building upon the other, some developing from simple to more complex.

Because it is vital to understand the theory base of this approach to classroom management, we integrate figures summarizing important theories throughout the book. We also offer suggestions for further reading in this important area.

SPECIAL FEATURES OF THIS TEXT

Step-by-Step Instructions   Each strategy is explained with step-by-step instructions to make implementation easier for the teacher.

Connections for English Language Learners   Margin notes are included with strategies to help the reader understand the connections to effective instruction for English learners.

Strategies on Video   Many of the strategies in this text are demonstrated in real classrooms on the accompanying DVD. The classroom demonstrations characterize use of the strategies in some of our most diverse environments. Active learning, opportunities to acquire good decision-making skills, and the unique support found in classroom communities support both English and academic development.

Teacher Resources   Additional teacher resources, forms, and blackline masters are included at the end of the text, with the goal of making use of the strategies outlined in the text as accessible as possible.

ACKNOWLEDGMENTS

We would like to acknowledge these very special teachers who invited us into their classrooms for videotaping: Susan McCloskey is a first-grade teacher at Greenberg Elementary School in Fresno, California. Diane Leonard is a second-grade teacher at Balderas Elementary School, also in Fresno. Vince Workmon is a fourth-grade teacher at Muir Elementary, also in Fresno. Jody Salazar is a middle-school teacher at Martin Luther King Middle School in Madera, California. As you will see on the DVD, these four teachers exemplify the approach we discuss throughout this text. They enjoy exciting results from their students in addition to working in supportive communities.

Deb Stollenwerk is our outstanding editor at Merrill/Prentice Hall, and we acknowledge her contributions and her patience as well as the stimulating questions she asked to keep this project moving forward.

We would also like to thank the following colleagues for their suggestions and reviews as they read drafts of this text: Becky Birdsong, LeTourneau University; Karen A. Bosch, Virginia Wesleyan College; Karen Kusiak, Colby College; William R. Martin, George Mason University; Jane McCarthy, University of Nevada, Las Vegas; Betty J. Morrell, University of Maine, Orono; Eva Weisz, DePauw University; Amy White, Walden University; and Sherie Williams, Grand Valley State University.

▶THE TEACHERS FEATURED ON THE DVD

Diane Leonard is a first-grade teacher at Balderas Elementary School in Fresno, California. Diane holds a master's degree in curriculum and instruction with an emphasis on English language development. She also teaches part-time for California State University, Fresno, and is a fellow of the San Joaquin Valley Writing Project in Fresno. Diane's students speak Spanish or Hmong at home but learn to read and write English following the Reading and Writing Workshop approach. In her spare time, Diane enjoys participating in hot-air ballooning as a chase driver.

Susan McCloskey is a kindergarten/first-grade teacher at Greenberg Elementary School in Fresno, California. She holds a master's degree in early childhood education from California State University, Fresno, where she teaches classes in teaching reading to kindergarten through third-grade students as an adjunct instructor. She is also a fellow with the San Joaquin Valley Writing Project and leads workshops in teaching writing for that organization. Susan's primary students come from diverse homes where a variety of languages other than English are spoken. She begins with her students as kindergartners and moves forward with them to first-graders. Susan feels that having the same students for 2 years allows her to learn their strengths and interests and build their skills more solidly before they move to second grade.

Jody Salazar teaches reading development at Martin Luther King Middle School in Madera, California. She holds a master's degree in reading from California State University, Fresno. Jody teaches six periods a day of basic reading skills to students who are reading below grade level. Most of her students are learning English as a second (or third) language. She focuses on study skills, personal responsibility, and working collaboratively with her students in addition to building reading and writing skills in English. Jody's initial teaching credential was in early childhood education, and she feels that the skills she learned in that program greatly enhance her ability to effectively teach seventh- and eighth-graders using active learning approaches.

Vince Workmon teaches fourth and fifth grades at Muir Elementary School in Fresno, California. He "loops" with his class, teaching the same group of students for 2 years. Vince is currently working on a master's degree in reading at Fresno Pacific University. He has served as a district reading trainer for Fresno Unified School District but prefers to teach in the classroom. His students speak Spanish or Hmong at home, and Vince develops their English and academic skills through active learning. He finds that he must focus heavily on social interaction skills and concentrates on building his students' love of learning and personal responsibility.

References

DeVries, R., & Zan, B. (1994). *Moral classrooms, moral children: Creating a constructivist atmosphere in early education*. New York: Teachers College Press.

Kohn, A. (1996). *Beyond discipline: From compliance to community*. Alexandria, VA: Association for Supervision and Curriculum Development.

Ohanian, S. (1982, April). There's only one technique for good discipline. *Learning, 82,* 12–14.

Patchen, M. (2004). *Making our schools more effective: What matters and what works*. Springfield, IL: Thomas.

MERRILL
PRENTICE HALL

Teacher Preparation Classroom

See a demo at
www.prenhall.com/teacherprep/demo

Your Class. Their Careers. Our Future. Will your students be prepared?

We invite you to explore our new, innovative and engaging website and all that it has to offer you, your course, and tomorrow's educators! Organized around the major courses pre-service teachers take, the Teacher Preparation site provides media, student/teacher artifacts, strategies, research articles, and other resources to equip your students with the quality tools needed to excel in their courses and prepare them for their first classroom.

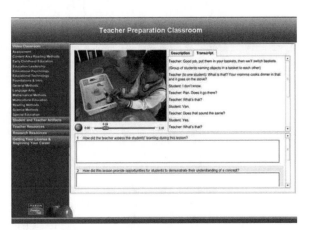

This ultimate on-line education resource is available at no cost, when packaged with a Merrill text, and will provide you and your students access to:

Online Video Library. More than 150 video clips—each tied to a course topic and framed by learning goals and Praxis-type questions—capture real teachers and students working in real classrooms, as well as in-depth interviews with both students and educators.

Student and Teacher Artifacts. More than 200 student and teacher classroom artifacts—each tied to a course topic and framed by learning goals and application questions—provide a wealth of materials and experiences to help make your study to become a professional teacher more concrete and hands-on.

Research Articles. Over 500 articles from ASCD's renowned journal *Educational Leadership*. The site also includes Research Navigator, a searchable database of additional educational journals.

Teaching Strategies. Over 500 strategies and lesson plans for you to use when you become a practicing professional.

Licensure and Career Tools. Resources devoted to helping you pass your licensure exam; learn standards, law, and public policies; plan a teaching portfolio; and succeed in your first year of teaching.

How to ORDER *Teacher Prep* for you and your students:
For students to receive a *Teacher Prep* Access Code with this text, instructors **must** provide a special value pack ISBN number on their textbook order form. To receive this special ISBN, please email: **Merrill.marketing@pearsoned.com** and provide the following information:

- Name and Affiliation
- Author/Title/Edition of Merrill text

Upon ordering *Teacher Prep* for their students, instructors will be given a lifetime *Teacher Prep* Access Code.

AN INTRODUCTION TO CLASSROOM MANAGEMENT AND DISCIPLINE

How students act in school is so bound up with what they are being asked to learn as to raise serious questions about whether classroom management can reasonably be treated as a separate field.

(Kohn, 1996, p. xv)

Classroom management incorporates much more than a classroom discipline system. In this text we look at classroom management as all the structures, routines, and expectations built into the ongoing management of a classroom, whether it be in kindergarten or high school. To be effective, classroom management is woven into the entire instructional process. Students are taught to make good decisions throughout the day. With this approach, the focus moves from simply making students behave to supporting students in the learning process.

When students are off task, or misbehaving, the teacher needs to look beyond the symptom (mistaken behavior) to possible causes, such as students' being asked to do something that is a waste of their time or doesn't match their individual learning styles.

> To focus on discipline is to ignore the real problem: We will never be able to get students (or anyone else) to be in good order if, day after day, we try to force them to do what they do not find satisfying. (Glasser, 1986, p. 32)

Teachers construct the climate in their classrooms, sometimes haphazardly, without much thought or planning. Expectations may not be explicit, and students may not understand them. In his book *Schools Without Failure* (1969), William Glasser makes it clear that when students are fully supported in learning to make good decisions and use their time effectively, they can make the most of their learning and social potential.

Choice Theory in the Classroom (Glasser & Dotson, 1998) introduces ways in which students learn to make decisions. Understanding what is involved in making decisions means that parents and teachers can then model major concepts in both making good decisions and living with the results of the decisions we make. Both of these concepts are inherent in this text.

Classroom talk is another way in which students learn what is expected of them. Open discussions provide them with opportunities to understand what they need to do to be successful in the classroom community. Such discussions also give them ownership of the process and require them to assume some responsibility for the success of the classroom environment. Modeling effective communication is an important factor in a collaborative classroom community.

THE THEORY BASE

This text is based on the research of a number of educational theorists. Having surveyed the hallmark theories of Jean Piaget (1957), Leo Vygotsky (1962), Abraham Maslow (1954), and Erik Erikson (1950), we believe that all teachers should be familiar with the work of these great educational minds. From Piaget's theory we realize that children learn through exploration. As educators, this leads us to provide opportunities for students to manipulate educational materials, solve problems actively, and learn from their mistakes. Piaget's research also teaches us the concept of schema theory—the idea that students have a "filing cabinet" in their minds. Experiences are stored in files in this cabinet, and new concepts and experiences are judged and understood in relation to the stored experiences. For students to properly comprehend and store new knowledge, it must be presented in a way that relates it to their past experiences. Therefore, the activities and lessons in a classroom must always build on students' past experiences. If the teacher determines that students lack the prior experiences necessary to understand new concepts, then he or she must build background before moving forward.

Vygotsky's (1962) theory helps us to understand how a child's language develops. It also provides two other important concepts for teachers. First, the concept of language scaffolding tells us that children learn language from an older, more knowledgeable mentor. Older siblings, more experienced peers, parents, and teachers provide the scaffolding that helps children learn the labels for things, ideas, and concepts. In the classroom, we must also provide this active language scaffolding. As Piaget tells us, students learn through active exploration, but they must have language scaffolding to recognize the names of things they are learning and be able to explain what they understand.

Second, children learn best in their "zone of proximal development" (ZPD): the area of learning located just above the knowledge and skills that they have already mastered. To learn and succeed, they must be gently led into new concepts and skills based on their present levels of understanding. This ZPD is different for each child and even for different curricular areas for the same child. Thus, educators must recognize exactly what each child knows and can do. We can gain this information through assessment ranging from observation, verbal interaction, and informal testing, all the way through more formal testing situations.

Maslow's (1954) theory helps us to understand the hierarchy of human needs. He identifies basic human needs such as food and sleep and recognizes that students cannot concentrate on higher needs, such as achievement and recognition, until their more basic needs are met. For a more complete summary of Maslow's theory, see Figure I.1.

Glasser (2001) builds heavily on Maslow's theory but takes it into the classroom setting, telling us that students need to feel safe in the classroom before they become willing to put forth the effort to become truly successful learners. Glasser maintains that teachers must help students feel connected to them and to the classroom community for learning to be maximized.

Erikson's (1950) theory looks at the stages of development in children and youth and relates those stages to the structure and interactions they experience at each level. For example, in the stage of trust versus mistrust, children learn whether they can trust their caregivers. Although each situation is different, all children's interactions with parents, teachers, and/or caregivers help them understand if they can trust adults. If children enter your classroom with a background of having been constantly disappointed by the adults in their life, you have to start rebuilding their ability to trust before they can become successful participants in the classroom community. See Figure I.2 for a more complete summary of Erikson's theory.

We have also looked at more recent research, such as that of Brian Cambourne (1990) and Elizabeth Cohen (1997). Both have observed and guided preservice students in complex public-school classrooms. We are very interested in what can be done

Figure 1.1   Important Theory

Abraham Maslow 1902–1970

Abraham Maslow is best known for his theory of the hierarchy of human needs. He believed that people are motivated by unsatisfied needs. He grouped human needs into a hierarchy, believing that the lower, more basic, needs must be satisfied before a person can think about satisfying higher needs. Following is his hierarchy of needs:

Self-actualization   The need to become everything one is capable of being (search for knowledge, peace, self-fulfillment, oneness with God)

Esteem   The need to feel competent and recognized

Love   The need to be loved and to belong and be accepted

Safety   The need to feel secure and unthreatened

Physiological   The need for air, food, water, sex; these are the most basic needs and must be satisfied before others can be sought

Maslow believed that people are basically trustworthy, self-protecting, and self-governing. He believed that violence and other evils occur when basic human needs are thwarted. He also believed that there are certain prepotent needs that will overshadow all others, such as the need for heroin in an addict.

Maslow's theory of needs is widely accepted in educational circles, and teachers are advised to make sure that students' basic needs are satisfied by free lunch, antibullying programs, and so on. Then students will be free to apply themselves to intellectual matters.

References

To read more about Maslow's theories, see the following:

Maslow, A. (1971). *The farther reaches of human nature.* New York: Viking.
Maslow, A. (1987). *Motivation and personality* (3rd ed.). New York: Addison-Wesley.
Maslow, A. (1998). *Toward a psychology of being* (3rd ed.). New York: Wiley.
Tribe, C. (1982). *Profile of three theories: Erikson, Maslow, and Piaget.* New York: Kendall/Hunt.

Source: Adapted from Maslow (1987).

Figure 1.2   Important Theory

Erik Erikson, 1902–1994

Erik Erikson is best known for his psychosocial theory on social development. His theory builds on and expands Sigmund Freud's psychosexual theory, looking at critical periods and events in the growth of an individual. He divides psychosocial development into eight stages. Each contains a basic conflict that the individual must progress through and that builds an important element of his or her personality. Erikson believed that an individual must resolve each conflict to be ready to move into the next stage of development successfully. If a conflict remains unresolved, the person will confront and struggle with it later in life.

His theory is not universally accepted. Many other theorists believe that other factors are important in the formation of personality.

Understanding Erikson's theory is important for teachers who are creating physical environments for learning. Teachers who look for the causes of misbehavior, set up the classroom to support the students' feelings of safety, and create a trusting and dependable structure are more likely to support students' feelings of autonomy, success, initiative, and industry.

Erikson's stages are explained in the following chart.

(continued)

Figure 1.2   Continued

Erikson's Eight Stages of Personality Development

Stage	Ages	Basic Conflict	Important Event	Impact on Personality
Oral-sensory	Birth to 12 or 18 months	Trust vs. mistrust	Feeding	If an infant does not form a warm, trusting relationship with the caregiver, a sense of mistrust is developed.
Muscular-anal	18 months to 3 years	Autonomy vs. shame and doubt	Toilet training	The child is developing physical skills such as walking, grasping, and rectal-sphincter control. Through these skills the child learns control but can develop shame and doubt if not handled well.
Locomotor	3 to 6 years	Initiative vs. guilt	Independence	The child continues to take more initiative and may become too forceful, leading to guilt feelings.
Latency	6 to 12 years	Industry vs. inferiority	School	The child must deal with demands to learn new skills or risk a sense of inferiority, failure, and incompetence.
Adolescence	12 to 18 years	Identity vs. role confusion	Peer relationships	The teenager must achieve a sense of identity in occupation, sex roles, politics, and religion.
Young adulthood	19 to 40 years	Intimacy vs. isolation	Love relationships	The young adult must develop intimate relationships or suffer feelings of isolation.
Middle adulthood	40 to 65 years	Generativity vs. stagnation	Parenting	Each generation must find some way to satisfy and support the next generation.
Late adulthood	65 years to death	Integrity vs. despair	Reflecting on life	The person who feels life has been fulfilling faces death unafraid.

in today's classrooms to help our young people become better students and citizens, as this book demonstrates.

Putting It All Together

A community of learners is not created in a day. Building responsibility and good decision-making skills in teachers and students takes time, organization, and a plan. Maintaining discipline and supporting students as they learn to make good choices is especially challenging. You will be introduced to 35 strategies in the next six sections of this text. Each section introduces strategies in a sequential manner, helping the reader to discover ways to help students understand and participate in a classroom community. Not all classroom communities are alike, however. The ages of your students, your tolerance for movement and activity in the classroom, and even your state standards affect the decisions you make. These strategies map out some of your choices.

Keep in mind that you are building a community with your students. Resist the impulse to make all the decisions ahead of time. In a community, everyone owns the rules, routines, and responsibilities. Therefore, students must be included in decisions.

 STEP BY STEP

The steps for creating a classroom community:

• **Keep it simple** Look over the first strategies in each section of the text. Plan ways to include your students in making decisions about setting up the classroom, storing materials, assigning duties, and all the other elements that create the feeling of community. Resist anything that seems too complex. Brainstorm with your students to find simple ways to accomplish the organization you need.

• **Adjust routines and procedures that aren't working** This is a necessary step, and you must always include the students in these types of decisions. Review your decisions often, and remember that one of the goals of a classroom community is teaching students how to make decisions and take responsibility. They will learn these skills only through experiences, both positive and negative.

• **Learn to be responsive instead of reactive** Both you and your students must *respond* to situations rather then *react* to them. As the teacher, you have the opportunity to model this behavior. It is helpful to talk to students about the differences between responding and reacting and help them recognize that their responses are choices over which they have deliberate control.

• **Celebrate things that are working** Stop and celebrate procedures and student responses that support the general community. Focus on specific behaviors that support the good of the whole class. Once you start recognizing these events, the students will begin to notice them also. This strengthens their understanding of good citizenship in a community.

• **Add new elements slowly** Make sure that new elements are carefully explained and modeled. Give students guided practice in any new routines or activities. Stop and evaluate new elements before adding more. Remember that this entire project is a process. Include students in making decisions, evaluating activities, and brainstorming ways to improve them.

• **Keep administrators and parents informed** The support of administrators and parents is vital to a community of learners. They need to understand what you are doing and why. They can help clear barriers such as inappropriate furniture, time-consuming paperwork, and disruptive bells and announcements. However, to be supportive, they must know what you are doing. Verbalize your goals and the research that supports this classroom approach and communicate them clearly and efficiently. Always keep administrators and parents informed when you make changes or add new elements. Also include them in problem solving when you need help.

Applications and Examples

Mrs. Kennedy teaches third grade in a school where the parents are extremely involved. Most parents have a college education and high expectations for their children. The teachers and principal are working together to maximize the amount of teaching time available each day. The principal has eliminated all bells except for the beginning bell in the morning and dismissal bell at the end of the day. No announcements are made over the intercom during the day. Teachers are reminded to check their email messages before school and at lunch each day to get any information they need to pass on to their students. Parents are enlisted so that all fund-raisers and PTA activities are handled outside the instructional day to avoid interrupting teaching time.

Mrs. Kennedy blocks out two large time slots each day for collaboration and integrated learning. The morning is spent in an integrated study, combining language arts and social studies. The students research topics that address the social studies standards. Mrs. Kennedy and her third-grade colleagues collect "text sets" of books on the social studies topics they are required to teach. They make sure that they have books on a variety of reading levels that meet the needs of all their students.

Whenever possible, Mrs. Kennedy integrates the teaching of math and science into the social studies/language arts block. If content needed to meet the standards is not amenable to her integrated format, she sets aside time in the afternoon for cooperative projects in these areas, focusing on the needs of the school or the community. These projects are designed collaboratively, with the students contributing significantly to the planning.

In the beginning of the year, Mrs. Kennedy had some students who found this environment challenging. They were used to a more teacher-directed classroom and had trouble making choices. She used individual contracts with these students, helping them make productive decisions, but limited their choices until they were more self-confident. She gradually increased their choices until they were full participants in the community of learners.

Mrs. Kennedy makes a point of never doing things for the students that they can do for themselves. They distribute materials, maintain the classroom environment, and complete the attendance and lunch reports each day. They feel very competent because they have assumed so much classroom responsibility.

Mrs. Spelling teaches language arts in an urban high school. Her school has not adopted a block schedule, so she has a different group of students each hour. Because she believes that her students need to learn to make decisions and take responsibility she has begun to build a community of learners within the constraints of hourly class sessions. She and her students are gradually incorporating more student decision-making as the school year progresses. Classroom rules and routines are added slowly as needed.

Expectations are posted in the classroom for behavior, positive talk, and academics. Mrs. Spelling actively involves her students in creating rubrics (quality standards) for scoring major assignments. The rubrics are posted in the classroom to help students make decisions about how best to complete their work. Students also post infractions of classroom rules and procedures and confer with Mrs. Spelling on goals for improving their levels of responsibility.

Mrs. Spelling's students file their own work in the class filing crate each day. They take attendance and check the announcements posted on the television monitor in their classroom. The students are encouraged to work together on their writing projects and publications. The class contains five computers and printers, and the students work cooperatively to word-process their writing and share their drafts in conferences. Mrs. Spelling holds an after-school publishing club so that her students can create writing anthologies to share with their peers.

Mrs. Spelling encourages her students to post pictures on the classroom's bulletin boards. They also write captions for the photos. This creates community feeling, since the students often share their accomplishments in school-related and extracurricular areas.

At the end of each semester, Mrs. Spelling hosts a portfolio day when the students share their best writing with parents. She divides the students into groups of five, and each student reads a piece aloud to a small group of parents. Mrs. Spelling and some of the students provide refreshments, and the day becomes a class celebration.

CONCLUSION

Although Mrs. Kennedy's and Mrs. Spelling's classrooms are extremely different, both teachers are dedicated to actively engaging their students. Both value students' needs to make decisions, take responsibility, and feel that they belong to a community of learners.

Some decisions that support a community of learners must be made at the school level. Principals are often supportive when they are asked to make schoolwide changes that allow more teaching time, and groups of teachers often help facilitate such changes. However, principals and parent groups must be given reasons for change and the outcomes expected so that they can serve as strong advocates.

References

Cambourne, B. (1990). *Whole story: Natural learning and the acquisition of literacy.* New York: Scholastic.

Cohen, E., and Lotan, R. (Eds.). (1997). *Working for equity in heterogeneous classrooms: Sociological theory in practice.* New York: Teachers College Press.

Erikson, E. (1950). *Childhood and society.* New York: Norton.

Glasser, W. (1969). *Schools without failure.* New York: Harper & Row.

Glasser, W. (1986). *Control theory in the classroom.* New York: Harper & Row.

Glasser, W. (1990). *The quality school.* New York: Harper & Row.

Glasser, W., & Dotson, K. (1998). *Choice theory in the classroom.* New York: Perennial.

Glasser, W. (2001). *Every student can succeed.* Los Angeles: William Glasser Institute.

Kohn, A. (1996). *Beyond discipline: From compliance to community.* Alexandria, VA: Association for Supervision and Curriculum Development.

Maslow, A. (1954). *Motivation and personality.* New York: Harper & Row.

Piaget, J. (1957). *Construction of reality in the child.* London: Routledge & Kegan Paul.

Vygotsky, L. (1962). *Thought and language.* Cambridge, MA: MIT Press.

Suggested Reading

Kemple, K. (1995). Discipline, management, and education: Rediscovering the whole child. *Teacher Education Quarterly, 22*(2), 107–115.

SECTION II

SETTING UP AN ENVIRONMENT THAT SUPPORTS ENGAGEMENT IN ACTIVE LEARNING

Creating a community of learners is a gradual, carefully constructed endeavor. Several theories of learning contribute to our understanding of this challenge. The theories in this section all support the premise that effective classroom management is based on the active engagement of students in learning.

According to Brian Cambourne (1990) and other educational researchers, certain classroom conditions support students' acquisition of content and decision-making strategies. These conditions also promote students' active engagement in their own education and require the teacher to serve as a facilitator and orchestrator rather than an imparter of knowledge.

In *Every Student Can Succeed,* William Glasser (2001) suggests that students be involved in making decisions about things such as arranging furniture and maintaining a supportive classroom environment. In *Choice Theory in the Classroom* (Glasser & Dotson, 1998), he argues that, to learn to make good choices, students need authentic decision-making experiences.

As active members of a learning community, students build self-confidence and absorb strategies for solving problems, making decisions, working collaboratively, and expressing ideas. Employers list all these attributes as extremely important for employees (SCANS, 2000). Thus, an active student-involvement approach to education not only helps learners acquire traditional content knowledge but also gives them extended practice in skills that are valued in mainstream American society and industry.

Section II focuses on setting up the classroom environment to support active student engagement. The strategies listed help the teacher involve students in arranging furniture and space. The section also suggests accessible resources and materials that will promote opportunities for authentic decision making. We also consider how the teacher might plan and implement time to work, explore, and interact with students while setting up structures for in-depth study and student-driven research. These approaches give students many opportunities to pursue personal interests and become lovers of learning.

Cambourne (1990) found that teachers who actively engage their students are very successful in helping them attain high academic standards. In today's standards-based schools, this is an important reason to focus on student engagement. For more information about Cambourne's theory see Figure II.1.

Figure II.1   Important Theory

Brian Cambourne

Brian Cambourne is an educational anthropologist and professor at the University of Wollongong, Australia. Since the early 1970s, he has been researching literacy learning. He prefers a naturalistic setting for his research and has spent hundreds of hours observing in classrooms.

Cambourne believes that a well-developed learning environment takes advantage of a learner's social nature. He has identified eight conditions or prerequisites that promote literacy learning:

- Immersion   Learners are saturated with literacy experiences.
- Demonstration   Literate behaviors are modeled, formally and informally.
- Expectation   Learners get the message that they can and will learn.
- Responsibility   Learners choose what they will try out or explore intellectually as they are repeatedly immersed in demonstrations of literate behaviors.
- Approximations   Learners approximate literacy behaviors at their own level of development. They are not required to understand and use all aspects of literacy appropriately before attempting to use what they do know.
- Employment   Learners are given opportunities to use and practice what they are learning, alone and with others.
- Response   Learners receive formal and informal feedback.
- Engagement   Learners must actively participate in literacy experiences. They are more likely to engage in literacy activities when the other conditions are present.

These conditions do not exist in isolation but are interdependent. They provide a foundation for learning that should be woven into all aspects of the classroom environment:

- The physical environment, including materials
- Interactions between teacher, learners, and materials
- Routines and events (Cambourne, 2000)

References

Cambourne's works include the following:

Cambourne, B. (1990). *Whole story: Learning and acquisition of literacy and responsive evaluation.* Portsmouth, NH: Heinemann.
Cambourne, B. (1991). *Coping with chaos.* Portsmouth, NH: Heinemann.
Cambourne, B. (1994). *Responsive evaluation: Making valid judgments about student literacy.* Portsmouth, NH: Heinemann.
Cambourne, B. (1995). Towards an educationally relevant theory of literacy learning: Twenty years of inquiry. *Reading Teacher, 49*(3), 182–192.
Cambourne, B. (1999). Explicit and systematic teaching of reading—a new slogan? *Reading Teacher, 53*(2), 126–127.
Cambourne, B. (1999). Turning learning theory into classroom instruction: A minicase study. *Reading Teacher, 54*(4), 414–429.
Cambourne, B. (2000). Observing literacy learning in elementary classrooms: Nine years of classroom anthropology. *Reading Teacher, 53*(6), 512–515.
Cambourne, B. (2002). The conditions of learning: Is learning natural? *Reading Teacher, 55*(8), 758–762.

References

Cambourne, B. (1990). *Whole story: Natural learning and the acquisition of literacy.* New York: Scholastic.
Glasser, W. (2001). *Every student can succeed.* Los Angeles: William Glasser Institute.
Glasser, W., & Dotson, K. (1988). *Choice theory in the classroom.* New York: HarperCollins.
Secretary's Commission on Achieving Necessary Skills (SCANS). (2000). *SCANS report for America, 2000.* Washington, DC: U.S. Department of Education.

ARRANGING THE FURNITURE AND SPACE TO ENCOURAGE COLLABORATION

Classroom arrangement has a powerful effect on the room's climate. By arranging furniture and work spaces to encourage collaboration and movement the teacher sends an important message to the students (Eby, Herrell, & Jordan, 2006.) Grouping desks makes it possible for students to work together on projects. Providing a water supply and a washable floor makes it possible for students to be creative with materials without fear of ruining the carpet. Keeping materials and resources easily accessible to students encourages them to make appropriate choices and become more involved in their own education.

 STEP BY STEP

The steps for arranging furniture and space in the classroom:

- **Make decisions about how you want students to work** Although it isn't usually practical to leave the furniture piled in the classroom until students arrive, you do want to involve them in making choices about changes in classroom arrangements. If teaching students to collaborate is important to your educational goals, then make it clear to them why you have chosen to arrange the furniture in a particular way and how changes might happen if students see the need.

- **Involve students in discussions and decisions** At the beginning of the school year, discuss furniture and space arrangements and enlist student input in deciding if things should be kept in place or relocated. This discussion provides a perfect opportunity for a lesson in mapping. Sketch the classroom arrangement and involve students in an analysis of how the present arrangement is working. Identify any problem areas. During this discussion, explain that you want them to be able to work together, so it is important to have grouped desks rather than desks in rows. Also explain the need for clear routes of movement, accessible storage for materials, and areas for quiet and active learning. See Figure 1.1 for an example of a classroom map with clear traffic patterns and desk groupings.

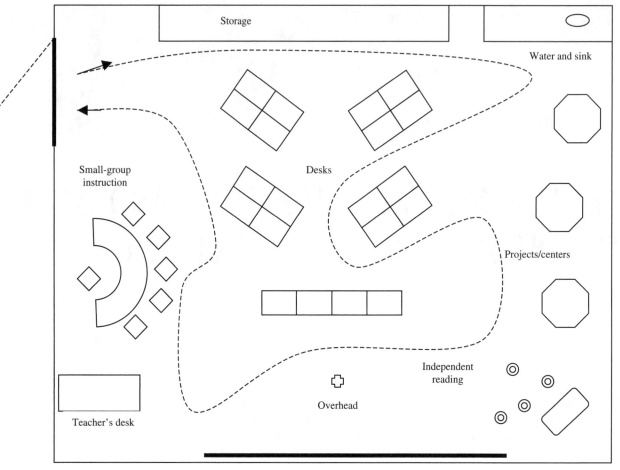

Figure 1.1   Classroom Map Showing Traffic Patterns and Desk Groups

• **Find or create accessible storage**   You may have to be creative in building accessible storage areas. Books should be stored so that they are attractive and easy to recognize; this means using shelves or racks so that spines or covers are visible. Paper and art materials need to be accessible but protected from being spilled or wrinkled. Students must understand the rules, procedures, and responsibilities for using those materials. This will be discussed in more depth in Chapter 2.

• **Teach students to be responsible for materials**   Model how spaces are to be used and materials to be stored, accessed, and used, emphasizing the importance of taking care of community resources. Have students practice taking materials from storage areas and putting them back correctly. Create a routine signal so that students know they will have only a few minutes in which to clean up, and let them know your expectations for how materials should be returned to storage.

FOCUS ON ENGLISH LEARNERS

Modeling procedures and using consistent signals helps English learners understand what is expected of them.

• **Celebrate the creation of a user-friendly classroom**   Once routines and procedures are established and working well, celebrate the effectiveness of the classroom system. Occasionally stop after cleanup time and compliment students who have been especially helpful. Point out areas that look well maintained, and ask for suggestions on ways to improve areas or procedures that might not be working so well. Validate student efforts often.

• **Reestablish routines when necessary**   When new students are introduced to the classroom or current students become lax about maintaining materials and resources, take a few minutes to review expectations. If an area is especially problematic, ask for suggestions about how it could be better maintained. This discussion may result in a change in how materials are stored or the creation of new guidelines for use of materials.

• **Rearrange groups and work areas when needed** Some teachers occasionally rearrange desk groupings to develop feelings of community among students. They may move students into new groups or rearrange furniture and space using student suggestions

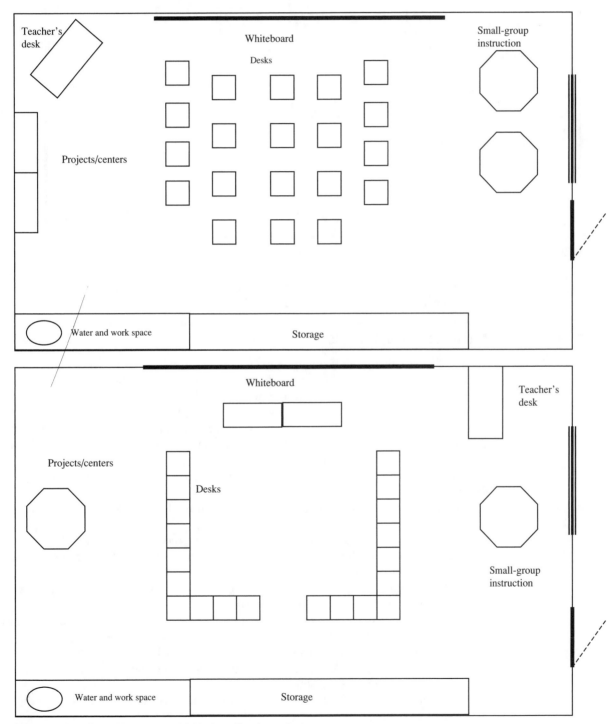

Figure 1.2 One Classroom with Various Furniture Arrangements

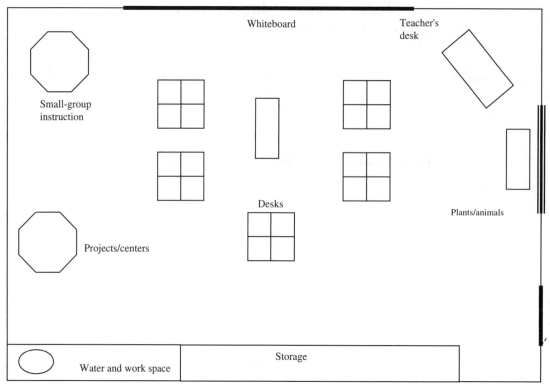

Figure 1.2   Continued

and encouraging problem solving or collaborative planning. See Figure 1.2 for a series of classroom arrangements suggested and tried in one classroom.

Applications and Examples

Ms. McCloskey's first-graders enter their classroom on the first day of school and see their desks in straight rows. Books are piled on the countertop, and the book racks and bulletin boards are empty. Ms. McCloskey begins the day by gathering her students onto a brightly colored carpet.

"This is our classroom," she says. "We want it to look nice, and I want you to help me decide how we should arrange the furniture so that you can work together and be able to move around without disturbing each other."

Kathi raises her hand. "In kindergarten we sat at round tables. Can we sit together this year?"

"How do you think we can do that with desks instead of tables?" asks Ms. McCloskey. "Can you show me how?"

Kathi gets up slowly and walks over to a desk. She moves it next to another desk and then pulls a third desk close to the first two. "We can move the desks together," she says. "Then we'll have more room to walk."

"I think Kathi has a good idea," comments Ms. McCloskey. "I want everyone to go stand by a desk, and we can move them closer together."

As students move desks, they talk about the need for space to walk. Soon they have arranged the desks into groups of six with wide walkways in between.

"How do you think this looks now?" Ms. McCloskey asks.

"I think we need to make the desks straighter," suggests Juan. "We have wiggly rows. My mom always wants the furniture straight."

"Good idea, Juan," says Ms. McCloskey with a smile. "How can we make sure the furniture stays straight?"

"Our rug has lines," says Bernice. "We can use the lines to make our desks straight." She begins to line up her desk with the carpet pattern.

"Now our desks look good, and we can work together, since we're sitting closer," says Ms. McCloskey. "What do you think we should do with all those books?"

The children decide to arrange the books on the racks by categories. Ms. McCloskey picks up each book, and the class helps her decide into which group the book should be placed. Soon they have arranged the books, placed the art paper on wide shelves so they can reach it, and dumped the crayons into baskets in the middle of their desk groups so they can all use them. Ms. McCloskey gets students busily engaged in drawing pictures of the room arrangement as decorations for the bulletin boards, a first step in their study of maps and mapping.

"This is really fun," says Nicki. "I never got to help fix up the room before. Maybe I can rearrange my bedroom when I get home. I'm going to tell my mom what good room arrangers we were today."

Midyear, Mr. Bateman's middle school has decided to move from an hourly period change schedule to a block schedule that engages students in more integrated curriculum over a 3-hour period. He will be responsible for teaching his eighth-graders history, language arts, and technology. The schedule change means that he will teach a familiar group of students in a new context.

"Since we will be spending the morning together now," Mr. Bateman explains, "I want us to talk about some of our activities and decide how we can rearrange our room to make group work, computer research, and video production possible."

"Can we move some of the desks out of the room and bring in more tables?" asks Maria. "I think we'll need more tables so groups can work on the computers and the video-editing machine."

"I'm sure that can be arranged," answers Mr. Bateman. "Let's get into groups of three and see if we can come up with some ideas. But first, let's brainstorm some of our needs."

As students talk, Mr. Bateman writes their suggestions on an overhead transparency. After the discussion, their list looks like this:

Large tables for four computers and video-editing equipment

A lockable storage space for video cameras

Groups of desks or tables for group work

Space between study areas and the group-work areas

Shelf space for books, materials, software

Flat storage for large paper

Containers and storage space for art materials

Work areas near the sink for art projects

Paths that allow for movement

"I think we're ready to draft some room arrangements now," says Mr. Bateman. "Let's work in groups of three and use graph paper to draw some arrangements. I have measured out the room on paper for you. Each square represents 1 foot of space, and the door and windows and unmovable furniture are drawn in."

Students work busily for about 40 minutes; then Mr. Bateman calls them back together to share their room designs. Several groups have focused on storage areas. "My dad is really good at building shelves and cabinets," says Julio. "Maybe we can get him to help us build our own if the school will buy the wood."

"I think that can be arranged," says Mr. Bateman with a smile. "I've already mentioned a work day to Mr. Gilbert, the shop teacher. He says he can open the shop on a Saturday for us."

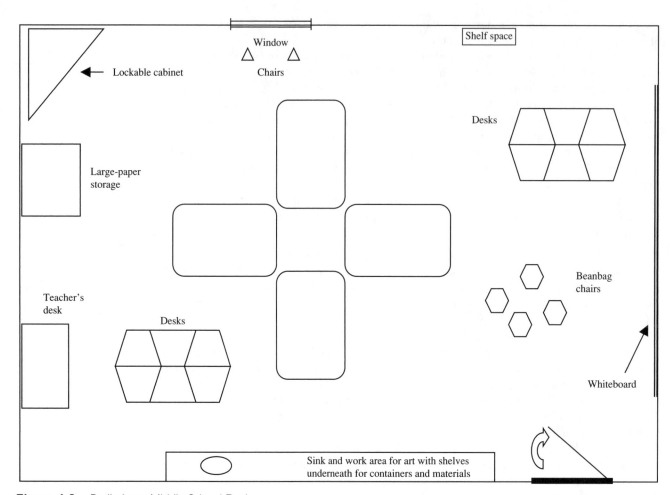

Figure 1.3 Preliminary Middle School Design

Let's have a look at your designs," suggests Mr. Bateman. "Some of you have come up with some interesting approaches." An example of a preliminary student design is shown in Figure 1.3.

After much discussion, the class decides to combine features from several drafts, and a group of students draws their chosen design. The finished drawing is shown in Figure 1.4.

"This really looks good. I'm going to share this with the rest of the faculty. I'm sure some of them will want to do similar things in their classrooms," says Mr. Bateman. "Mr. Gilbert may have to open the shop for a couple of Saturdays."

▶ CONCLUSION

Ms. McCloskey and Mr. Bateman demonstrate alternative approaches to getting students involved in arranging furniture and classroom resources. Group planning builds a feeling of collaboration and community, and setting guidelines to show the value of group work and problem solving is a positive outcome of this approach. As Ms. McCloskey demonstrates, even very young students can be actively involved in making classroom decisions.

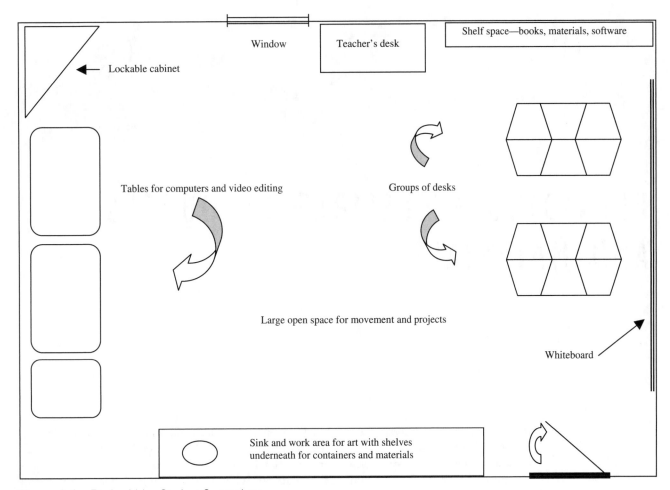

Figure 1.4   Design Using Student Suggestions

References

Eby, J., Herrell, A., & Jordan, M. (2006). *Teaching in K–12 schools: A reflective action approach* (4th ed.). Upper Saddle River, NJ: Pearson.

Suggested Reading

Dunne, D. (2001, April 4). Do seating arrangements and assignments = classroom management? *Education World*. www.educationworld.com

PROVIDING ACCESSIBLE RESOURCES AND MATERIALS

The accessibility of resources and materials plays a crucial role in the level of activity necessary to manage the classroom. Deciding what materials you need for the coming year and making them available in an organized and consistent manner should minimize unplanned student movement and interaction. When students know where resources are located and when they are allowed to access them, the classroom runs much more smoothly with fewer interruptions. Remember, however, that students need good modeling and instruction if the teacher's preparations are to become an integral part of the classroom management system. Giving students responsibility to care for and put away materials after use contributes to their feeling of community and engagement in the learning situation (Cambourne, 1990).

 ## STEP BY STEP

The steps for making resources and materials accessible in the classroom:

• **Choose appropriate materials**   After reviewing state and district curriculum standards and frameworks, begin gathering materials and resources for instruction. Many will probably be provided by the school or district, but you may want to augment them based on your instructional style or your students' backgrounds. It's important to choose a variety of resources at a variety of levels so that the curriculum is accessible to all your students, no matter what their reading or English development levels. Ask your colleagues and administrators what additional resources might be available and how you might obtain them.

• **Prepare student materials**   Prepare student materials, textbooks, and so on for distribution on the first day of school. Materials that students will use often might be placed on desks so that you can review them with students before they put them away. Encourage students to care for books by teaching them how to make protective book covers.

• **Create a library in your classroom**   Set up a classroom library for reading and resource materials. Involve students in categorizing and labeling these resources as a way of building their understanding of reading and resource genres. Assign a student or students the job of class librarian and rotate this duty over the course of the year to include all students. Make the library comfortable and inviting, but be sure you can see it clearly from anywhere in the classroom.

• **Create related collections** Small collections of materials can be grouped in large 2-gallon plastic reclosable bags. These might include related resources: a book, a video, a tape recording, realia, or other support materials. The bag can be hung from a skirt hanger and placed on a standing rolling rack for efficient storage. See Figure 2.1 for ideas for accessible storage.

• **Organize text sets** Magazine files, obtainable at local office-products stores, may be used to store books on similar topics. Create text sets of several books and resources on a single curricular area or unit under study.

Figure 2.1 Storing Supplies and Resources for Student Access

Materials to Be Stored	Storage Ideas	Access Concerns
Textbooks	• Bookshelves • Student desks • Storage room	• Must be low enough for students to reach • Books used daily can be stored in desks • Books used together should be stored together
Library and trade books	• Open shelving • Plastic milk crates	• Display with covers in view • Group books on same topic together • Group books written on the same level together • Keep in students' reach
Big books	• Hang on skirt hangers on racks • Stand up in wire LP record holders	• Keep in students' reach • Group like books together
Construction paper	• Create flat storage on wide shelves or in storage boxes • Create standing storage with stiff dividers for smaller paper • Create a scrap box for small scraps that are still usable	• Separate colors so students can get their own supplies without wrinkling paper • Hold students responsible for maintaining storage • Set up criteria for the size of scraps to be stored in the scrap box
Art supplies	• Store in containers that are easily moved to the work spaces • Store refill supplies nearby • Group supplies for easy use (scissors and glue together)	• Hold students responsible for replacing and refilling supplies • Use color-coding to help students become more responsible (blue group has blue scissors)

Figure 2.2 Labeling Storage Areas to Make Expectations Clear

Storage Areas	Labeling
Bookshelves	• Sticky label on front of shelf with label or picture • Color-coded shelves, materials containers to indicate which container should be placed on which shelf • Space saver (cardboard strip) to be placed where a book has been removed so that students can easily return books to proper places • Small poster with expectations for student use of materials
Toys and manipulatives	• Outlined shape of material on shelf so it can be returned to the proper places • A picture of the storage area with materials properly placed displayed in the storage area so students can put things back in the same places as in the picture • Color-coded storage boxes and materials

• **Place materials in appropriate areas** When teaching younger children, make sure that student materials are stored at a height they can reach.

• **Collect a variety of storage containers** Boxes, baskets, hanging shoe racks, and the like are all good ideas for storage. Transparent plastic boxes are durable and provide quick visual access to the contents. Be sure to make large, clear labels for containers so that both you and the students can find things easily. See Figure 2.2 for ideas on labeling storage to make it more accessible.

• **Involve the students** Involving students in preparing classroom environments increases their understanding of the materials and resources being used for study and makes them feel responsible for the smooth running of the class. As outlined in Chapter 1, students should have a role in establishing rules and procedures for using space and materials. Model how spaces are used and materials stored, accessed, and used, emphasizing the importance of taking care of community resources.

Applications and Examples

Mrs. Everett and her third-graders are excited about their project-based classroom. They have designed a project that will help them meet their reading, language arts, social studies, and mathematics standards by gathering reading materials about the Native American tribes in their state of Alabama. They will be interviewing tribal members and writing stories about Native American names, tribal life and history, and other interesting things they will learn through research and interviews. They have also decided to use the information they gain to create a reader's theater production in which they will wear simple costumes.

Mrs. Everett and the students discuss the materials they will need to complete their projects and how to store those materials to make them accessible. They work together to create a chart that lists the responsibilities and rules for using and caring for materials. Because students will be using tape recorders (which need batteries), art materials of many types, and writing and publishing supplies, they have many decisions to make about storage and care. They also discuss how to make and store the reader's theater costumes so they can be used often and kept in good condition.

FOCUS ON ENGLISH LEARNERS

Working with a small group of students helps English learners make friends and feel more confident about practicing oral English.

The students decide that each table will have a supplies captain, who will be responsible for getting the day's materials and returning them to their designated spots. They also choose a librarian for each group, who will be responsible for getting books from the class library center and returning them. Finally, each group chooses a cleanup committee, who will make sure that the group's area is kept clean and trash is put into the trash can as they work.

The costumes prove to be a problem-solving opportunity. There is no room to hang costumes in the classroom closet, so students must brainstorm ways of storing them. After making a list of possibilities, students decide that they will need to build a storage rack. Mrs. Everett loans them the money to purchase PVC pipe to make their rack.

At the end of their project, the students present their reader's theater production for the other third- and fourth-grade classes. They also invite their parents and the Native Americans they interviewed to the performance. To pay back Mrs. Everett's loan, the students pop popcorn and sell it at their performances in cups for 10¢ each.

Mrs. Speidel's high school literature classes are investigating how people in their central Florida community happened to move to the area. They are exploring the ethnic groups represented by the local residents and collecting personal stories. They plan to create an anthology of local stories and recipes and have an end-of-the-year tasting party where they will serve the foods from their cookbook.

Because Mrs. Speidel teaches five different groups of students each day, she wants to create an organized system for students to store their writing drafts, interview notes, and word-processed stories. She leads a brainstorming session with each class. As a result, students decide that they need a color-coded system of filing boxes. Mrs. Speidel purchases five plastic milk crates and matching colored file folders. The crates can be stacked three high, so they don't take up much room. For each period, a file person is designated to make sure that the class's crate is placed on top of the stack so students can find their files. The five computers in the classroom are assigned on a rotating basis, but students must complete a handwritten draft before they can use the computers to process their writing.

A sign-up sheet is placed beside each computer, and students are responsible for signing up for computer time when they have completed their drafts. They also sign up for conference groups to share their writing, once they have finished a draft and printed it out. This word-processed draft gives them the ability to revise more easily, using suggestions from their conference group.

One person from each writing group is assigned to police the classroom before students leave so that all materials are returned to their proper places and the classroom is neat for the next class. If a file folder is left out of the milk crate, it is easy to see which crate it belongs in, since the folder colors match the crate colors.

 # CONCLUSION

Both Mrs. Everett and Mrs. Speidel have involved their students in making decisions and taking responsibility for the maintenance of their classrooms. Because needs are different between high school and elementary settings, room-storage solutions are also different. But students of all ages can be actively involved in decision making, solutions, and maintenance. Such responsibility helps them learn to make decisions, problem-solve solutions, and take pride in their classroom and their accomplishments.

STRATEGY ON VIDEO
Arranging Furniture and Materials

Strategies for arranging furniture and making materials accessible to students are demonstrated on segment 1 of the DVD that accompanies this text. Focus on the decisions that need to be made as you set up your classroom at the beginning of the year. As you watch this segment think about the following:

- How would this planning process change if you were teaching a different grade?
- How do decisions about furniture arrangement and materials storage reflect a philosophy of teaching?

References

Cambourne, B. (1990). *Whole story: Natural learning and the acquisition of literacy*. New York: Scholastic.

Suggested Reading

Ostrow, J. (1995). *A room with a different view*. York, ME: Stenhouse.

3

PROVIDING TIME TO WORK, EXPLORE, INTERACT

Appropriate use of time during the school day plays a major role in classroom management and success for all students. Teachers must eliminate tasks and distractions that steal instructional time (Allington & Walmsley, 1995). Some schools have found that eliminating such things as bells and intercom announcements supports effective use of time. Teachers have also found ways to collect lunch money and take attendance in ways that free up more time. Figure 3.1 suggests efficient ways to accomplish such housekeeping tasks.

Many secondary schools are moving to a block schedule that combines classes such as social studies and language arts or math and science. By scheduling two-period blocks and integrating subjects, schools have simplified students' days and added teaching and learning time that would have been spent moving students between classes. The schedule also gives students more time to explore topics in depth.

Once the school day is free of time-stealing routines, teachers can use larger blocks of time to involve students in relevant, meaningful curriculum that flows across content areas and leads students on journeys of learning and exploration. Teachers have a chance to show students that learning occurs in an integrated fashion, that subject areas overlap and converge rather than stand alone.

A theme-based curriculum allows a teacher to think in new ways about the organization and delivery of content. Teachers who integrate multiple topics tend to organize content more fluidly and holistically (Powell, McLaughlin, Savage, & Zehm, 2001).

Students are more apt to see connections between content areas and recognize the relevance of contextual learning. They appreciate the opportunity to explore integrated areas in depth, solve real-life problems, and work cooperatively in groups.

 STEP BY STEP

The steps for allocating time in the classroom:

- **Make decisions about how you want to approach your classroom curriculum** A theme-centered rather than subject-centered curriculum lends itself to utilizing

Figure 3.1 Time-Saving Suggestions for Housekeeping Tasks

Task	Time-Saving Suggestions
Calling roll and lunch count	Teacher creates attendance and lunch-count bulletin board just inside the door of the classroom. Students move their attendance stick (a craft stick with student's name written on it) from a pocket labeled "absent" into a pocket labeled "present" as they enter the classroom. Students move a second lunch-count stick into similar pockets labeled "buying lunch" or "brought lunch." One student fills out the attendance and lunch-count sheets for the day and places them on a clip outside the classroom door (or takes them to the office). Kindergarten and first-grade classes have an upper-grade student who stops by to fill out the required paperwork using the information on the bulletin board.
Daily announcements	Intercom announcements are reserved for emergencies only. Teachers receive emails of daily announcements and announce only those that are relevant to their students. Teachers in classrooms with older students print and post the announcements on the front door, holding their students responsible for reading them.
Special assemblies and activities	Teachers decide at faculty meetings which of these activities are worthy of taking away teaching time, judiciously limiting the number.
Fund-raising activities	Parent volunteers distribute information and collect money before and after school or during lunch. Teaching time is never used for these activities.

larger blocks of time and requires innovative teaching activities and arrangements. However, a teacher must be able to consolidate a variety of content areas into a single cogent whole, which may require extensive exploration of a variety of resources beyond the textbook or program provided in the schools. Conventional textbooks may not be appropriate, as they tend to be subject-centered. If textbooks are used as resources rather than the core of the curriculum, teachers must gather library books, websites, periodicals, guest speakers, and so on to support students' more in-depth studies.

• **Think and plan in an integrated manner** Teachers who use an integrated approach to curriculum pay more attention to the diverse backgrounds of their students; they consider their developmental and academic needs and make adaptations where necessary. They attempt to provide a curriculum that directly connects to student interests and needs. Students are often included in the planning, brainstorming topics to be studied, examining their existing knowledge of the subjects, and identifying areas of personal interest. By combining two or more subject areas, teachers have more time to allot to integrated studies.

• **Become familiar with subject-area standards** When choosing theme-based or integrated instruction, teachers must be thoroughly familiar with subject-area standards. They can then plan ways to meet those standards, using a variety of materials and teaching approaches.

- **Organize time and resources**   Teachers who use a theme-based curriculum have many choices among materials, activities, and resources. They are also responsible for organizing instructional time. Many states mandate the amount of daily time allotted to specific subjects. Integrating subjects allows the teacher to combine time allocations for those subjects. Larger time blocks are needed to provide access to resources and explore areas of particular student interest. Appropriate arrangement and use of learning centers, resource areas, groups, and interactive materials becomes the joint responsibility of teachers and students. See Chapter 2 for suggestions about accessibility.

- **Collaborate with colleagues and the community**   One of the most exciting elements of this style of instruction is the teacher's need for ongoing collaboration with colleagues. Teachers may come together as grade-level teams in elementary school or as collaborative-content teams in middle and high schools. Planning an integrated curriculum means that individuals need to come together to make decisions and share ideas and resources. It also broadens teachers' knowledge of content and teaching practices. When teachers work with other teachers and administrators and use community resources, they can build a highly engaging experience for their students.

    In some schools, teachers meet in grade-level or subject-area teams to divide the work involved in locating materials and resources and identifying guest speakers. They also find places to store materials to make them available to all involved teachers.

- **Act as guide and facilitator for the learning process**   In a theme-based classroom, the teacher becomes a learning facilitator rather than just a knowledge dispenser. By presenting a variety of learning resources and activities, teachers offer students opportunities to explore a real-life learning process as well as acquire new and exciting content. The responsibility of teaching students how to learn is very evident in the theme-based classroom. Students are challenged to integrate knowledge and learning in new and meaningful ways, not just memorize facts and figures for tests. A teacher may assist and encourage students in their exploration while keeping close track of the knowledge that students will need to accomplish their goals.

FOCUS ON ENGLISH LEARNERS

Integrating subjects supports English learners in vocabulary development by giving them multiple exposures to new words in many contexts.

- **Accept students as collaborators**   Students take on new roles in this environment, and the teacher must be ready and willing to accept their input and collaboration as proactive learners. Teachers carefully plan and establish complex instruction groups (Cohen, 1994). Students must be taught how to use other students as resources and how to collaborate to accomplish sophisticated tasks requiring a variety of intellectual abilities. The use of cooperative learning groups is a promising answer to the challenge of multilevel heterogeneous classrooms, but students need to be trained in their role as collaborative learners to accomplish their goals. (Collaborative learning will be explored in more depth in a later chapter.) Teachers willing to work with their students as facilitators and collaborators travel an exciting road to discovery and learning.

Applications and Examples

Mr. Chambers's second-grade class is beginning a study of their local community. Mr. Chambers starts the discussion by asking students to share the jobs their parents perform. As they talk, he lists the occupations on the whiteboard. After students share what their parents do for a living, Mr. Chambers asks them where their parents work. He uses a large community map to locate the different businesses as students identify them. He plans to integrate a study of language arts, social studies, and economics with mapping skills and math by creating activities that allow students to investigate the resources and occupations in their community. They will look at things such as population, ethnic variety, health and cultural facilities, and recreation.

    Mr. Chambers plans to develop the concept of community so that the students understand that their town is one community and their classroom is another. He also plans to support students as they begin to explore collaboration. He develops a plan by brainstorming with the students. He opens the session with a question: "How do people in our community earn the money they need to pay their bills and buy groceries?"

The students suggest answers such as selling things in stores, taking care of children and animals, and cleaning houses. The list gets lengthy, but Mr. Chambers writes everything down on the whiteboard. After the brainstorming session, he explains that they will be reading and writing about their community and all the things people do to make money. They will also be writing about jobs in the community and will invite people into the classroom to talk about their occupations.

The students are then given an opportunity to think of relevant questions that they would like to study. They wonder how money gets into the ATM machine, how much money the grocery store makes on each item sold, which jobs pay the most money, and which jobs require a college education. These questions help Mr. Chambers plan a series of explorations and guest speakers to begin the study.

Mr. Chambers introduces a community map, and he and the students locate businesses on the map. They identify places where their parents work and restaurants and stores they visit. He then reads the book *Boom Town* (Levitin, 1998), which introduces the basic concept of businesses that meet the needs of community citizens.

For their first reading and writing project, the students choose an occupation to explore either individually or in pairs. They read some of the books Mr. Chambers has gathered for the study and fill out a data chart showing what they have learned. See Figure 3.2 for an example of the data chart they use for this activity. After completing their research and chart, they will learn how to use the data they have gathered to write a simple report.

Since Mr. Chambers has blocked out the entire morning for this project, his students get a good start on reading their resource books and filling out their data charts during the first two mornings and are ready to begin their research reports.

Ms. David's eighth-grade class is working in a new block schedule. Instead of six 50-minute periods each day, the students are now enrolled in three classes of 2 hours each. Ms. David is responsible for teaching both algebra and life science during her 2-hour block. As she looks over the standards for the two disciplines, she decides to integrate the

Figure 3.2   Data Chart for Exploring Occupations

Occupation _____   Student Names _____

Sources (book and author)	How do you prepare for this job? (education, training)	What skills are needed?	What is difficult about the job?	Other interesting information

study of statistics, graphing, exponential curves, and genetics using fruit flies. To begin the unit of study, she brings in a container of fruit fly larvae and introduces students to the life cycle of the fruit fly. She divides the class into six groups of students and gives each group a medicine bottle with 30 to 40 fruit fly larvae inside. She begins the unit of study with an explanation:

"We will be doing a project in which you must work together. Each group should select a grapher, a note-taker, a materials person, a timekeeper, and two cleanup people. These jobs will rotate every 2 days, so you'll all get a chance to do all the different jobs. The first thing we will do is to put fruit into the bottles so that the larvae will have food as they develop. Two groups will use bananas, two groups will use apples, and two will use pears. One of the things we will be examining is the effect of the different foods on the population growth of the flies. We will be watching several generations of fruit flies, since they live only 10 to 14 days."

As the study progresses and the adult flies emerge, the students put them to sleep with carbon dioxide so they can examine them under a microscope. They sort them by attributes such as eye color, wing shape, body size, and the number of hairs on their backs. The students carefully chart all this information. The flies are not harmed during this step. They wake up and soon lay eggs.

Ms. David introduces the study of genetics using a Punnett square and demonstrates how students can predict the probability that these attributes will appear in the second-generation flies based on the cross-linked information plotted on the Punnett squares for the first generation.

Once the first generation dies and the next generation of adult flies is counted, a comparison of populations and genetic characteristics is made and cross-referenced based on food type available to the larvae. The whole process is repeated for three generations, giving the groups several opportunities to practice genetic probability problems, exponential population curves, statistical analysis of scientific data, several different graphing approaches, and careful scientific journaling.

The students seem eager to complete each step of the project. They are thoroughly engaged in their exploration for the entire 2-hour period and reluctant to leave for their next classes. Ms. David is convinced that integrated learning is a powerful approach.

 ## CONCLUSION

Both Mr. Chambers and Ms. David are finding ways to integrate learning and make academic studies more meaningful to their students. They began by examining the academic standards and finding ways to explore their topics through hands-on learning. Even though they find the planning and organization of integrated teaching challenging, both feel the effort is worthwhile. Their students seem enthusiastic about the approach.

References

Allington, R., & Walmsley, S. (1995). *No quick fix*. New York: Teachers College Press.

Cohen, E. (1994). *Designing groupwork* (2nd ed.). New York: Teachers College Press.

Levitin, S. (1998). *Boom town*. New York: Orchard Books.

Powell, R. R., McLaughlin, H. J., Savage, T. V., & Zehm, S. (2001). *Classroom management: Perspectives on the social curriculum*. Upper Saddle River, NJ: Merrill/Prentice Hall.

Suggested Reading

Baloche, L. (1998). *The cooperative classroom*. Upper Saddle River, NJ: Merrill/Prentice Hall.

Tomlinson, C. A. (1999). *The differentiated classroom*. Alexandria, VA: Association for Supervision and Curriculum Development.

SETTING UP THE STRUCTURE FOR IN-DEPTH STUDIES AND ONGOING RESEARCH

In *The Quality School,* William Glasser (1998) stresses the need to teach students to recognize quality work, arguing that student ownership of assignments provides the most motivation. Students must see their work as important and personally relevant, and important work cannot be done in short periods of time. However, it can be broken into small pieces that fit together into a larger whole.

To engage students in deep study of a topic, teachers must provide several things:

- Blocks of time to look more deeply into a topic
- Resources for research: Internet, books, people
- Space to store and manage work over time
- Instruction in how to break big projects into small parts

When students know that they will have time to explore knowledge in depth and are taught how to break a project into doable pieces, they can take the first steps toward doing quality work. If obstacles such as brief 50-minute periods have already been removed, the teacher's job is easier. However, long-term projects are possible even in traditional time allotments, as long as the steps necessary to complete the projects are clearly delineated.

STEP BY STEP

The steps in setting up classroom structures for in-depth studies:

- **Identify projects that will meet standards in several academic areas**   This is not difficult; any in-depth study will involve reading, writing, and an academic area such as science, math, or social studies. Standards in speaking and listening are often easily integrated, as are those for visual and performing arts and physical education.

Be specific about the standards you are working toward, and share that information with your students. The most engaging projects allow students some choice. Knowing which standards they must meet will enable them to choose appropriate project elements.

- **Block out regular time**   Students need to know exactly how much time they will have to work on the projects each week. They don't need time every day, but they should have at least two blocks set aside for project work each week. This allows them to gather information or complete steps.

- **Brainstorm and locate needed resources**   Some resources are basic, such as computers, construction paper, markers, and books on the topic. Others will have to be located and made available. Involve the students in compiling a list of needed resources. Always remember that you are teaching organizational and planning skills along with content when you design long-term projects.

- **Provide storage for ongoing projects**   Once students have begun work on their projects, they will need space to store work and resources. Students who are sharing books can use color-coded sticky notes to mark their areas of interest. Shelves for ongoing projects are helpful, as are cardboard boxes, accordion folders, large reclosable plastic bags, clear plastic containers, and even book bags.

- **Teach the steps**   Never assume that your students know how to approach long-term research. Even in high school many students have never completed a long-term assignment in an organized manner. Break the project into small steps, teach each step, and then give students time to complete the step. Steps might include note-taking, using note cards and other organizational approaches, citing sources, searching the Internet, using data charts, writing the first draft, planning visuals, creating a presentation format, and finding visuals and graphics on the Internet.

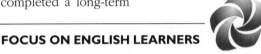

FOCUS ON ENGLISH LEARNERS

Explicitly teaching study and research skills helps English learners learn to support their own academic progress.

- **Monitor student progress**   Each completed step should be monitored. Students should know that you are available for support, explanation, or consultation. They should also know exactly what needs to be done at each stage of the project.

- **Find innovative ways for students to share their projects**   This step should involve more than simply showing and telling. Students should be expected to share the expertise they have gained. See Figure 4.1 for suggestions on ways to share projects.

- **Collaboratively design scoring rubrics**   Involve the students in creating a scoring rubric for the projects. Discuss the elements that need to be part of a quality project. Identify indicators of quality for each aspect of the rubric. See Figure 4.2 for an example.

- **Document student efforts**   To do quality work, students must believe it is important. While they are working, take digital pictures or videos. Display the visuals they create, and videotape their presentations. Use the videos to help them critique their own work and set goals for future long-term projects.

Applications and Examples

Mrs. Bridges's kindergartners are learning to work and share. She wants to give them some time each week to explore the characters in the fairy tales that they are studying. She sets aside a 2-hour block on Tuesday and Thursday afternoons for students to work on their projects.

To introduce the project time, Mrs. Bridges talks to her students about the fairy tales they are reading. "I think it's time for us to act out some of these fairy tales," she begins. "How do you think we could act out the stories in the books we are reading?"

Some children want to do a play about Hansel and Gretel by dressing up and acting out the parts. Others decide they want to do *Goldilocks and the Three Bears* using sock puppets. Another group wants to use paper-plate puppets as they have done in the past. Mrs. Bridges helps the children organize themselves into story groups and divide up the character roles in their books. She then she asks them to think about the materials they

Figure 4.1 Sharing Long-Term Projects

Strategy	Description
PowerPoint presentation	Student must be taught how to use the computer for the presentation. Slides can be prepared one at a time as research is done. During the presentation, the student provides commentary as the slides are shown on the computer or projected on the screen. The same approach can be used for overhead transparencies, which are then shown using an overhead projector.
Group conferences	Four students present at a time, in different parts of the room. Other students move from group to group until they've seen all four presentations. These can be scheduled over time so that everyone gets to share. The strength of this approach is that students do the presentation multiple times.
Project-celebration conferences	A conference is scheduled on a Saturday or a nonstudent day. It is set up like a formal conference with parents, siblings, and other students attending sessions of their choice. Lunch is served, and a guest speaker such as a local professor gives a brief luncheon presentation about the value of research.
Evening events	One group of parents is invited to bring their families, and a small group of students presents their projects. Other students are encouraged to attend.
Videotaped presentations	Students stay after school or come early to have their presentations videotaped. Videos are reviewed and critiqued by the student presenter and the teacher. Videos are available for viewing at free-choice time in the classroom. Students prepare a one-page handout for other students, summarizing the main points of the presentations.

will need for their plays. "You will each be making a costume or puppet for your character," she says. "Think about what you need to make your character."

The students help Mrs. Bridges make a list of materials. After she gathers the materials, she stores them in plastic buckets. On Tuesday she carefully explains the first step in their project: making costumes or puppets. She asks the groups to get together, look at all the different versions of the story they have chosen, and pick the one they want to act out. She asks her students to retell the story to each other, taking turns in their group. While they are telling each other the story, Mrs. Bridges goes around to each group to get them started on their project. After she has everyone working, she continues to circulate around the room, monitoring behavior and giving support.

By Thursday some of the students are ready to begin writing their skits. Mrs. Bridges explains and models exactly what she wants students to do. Each student is responsible for writing the script for the character he or she will play. The students must retell the story and practice their lines orally. They have to go through the story several times. Since they can't write well yet, they depend on oral practice to learn their lines.

The class fairy tale project lasts for 2 weeks. The students practice their plays, and when they are ready, parents are invited to view the productions.

Before the students present their plays, Mrs. Bridges tells parents, "This project has been our first long-term assignment. In doing this we have been addressing language arts

Figure 4.2 Long-Term Project Scoring Rubric

Name _____		Project title _____		
Quality of research				
1	2	3	4	5
Incomplete	Minimal	Adequate	Strong	Outstanding
Quality of visuals				
1	2	3	4	5
Missing	Minimal	Adequate but doesn't represent all components well	Strong	Outstanding
Standards met				
1	2	3	4	5
A few	Most in one area, others missing	Most met in all areas	All met	Went beyond what was required

standards such as speaking in complete sentences, retelling a story in proper sequence, identifying a storybook character, and using graphic materials to represent a character."

The students are proud of their productions, and parents begin to see that kindergarten play can also address the academic standards for the grade.

Mrs. Salazar teaches a 10th-grade block in which she is responsible for both language arts and social studies. She wants to introduce her students to the concept of integrating primary-source information into research assignments.

She begins this study by reading aloud *Zebra,* a short story by Chaim Potak. The story introduces a character who is a Vietnam veteran. Before she reads the story, she asks the students what they know about the Vietnam war. She is surprised to find that they've seen some recent television news stories about Jane Fonda and the war and seem to understand some basics, such as how veterans were treated when they returned from the war. She has the students locate Vietnam on a map and talk about the climate there. Then she reads the story.

After the reading, she introduces a special guest, a teacher in their school who served in Vietnam. "I want you to learn different ways of doing research," she says. "Mr. Johnson was in Vietnam. If we get information from him about his experiences there, that's called using a primary source." The students enjoy asking Mr. Johnson questions and hearing about his views on the war, his personal experiences, and how he was treated when he returned to the United States.

The next day, Mrs. Salazar explains that the class will be working on long-term research assignments for the next few weeks. Their assignment is to identify a real-life hero. The hero does not have to be a war hero, but part of their assignment is to explain why they consider the person to be a hero. They can use the Internet, books, magazines, newspapers,

Figure 4.3 Timeline for Mrs. Salazar's Class Hero Project

Week	Assignment	Due
1	Research hero Complete note cards	Topic and draft plan
2	Research hero Complete note cards Identify websites	Note cards to be checked for progress
3	Research hero Complete note cards Work on presentation	Conference with teacher about progress and method to be used for presentation
4	Work on draft of presentation	Completed note cards to be checked Presentation draft, if complete, submitted for approval
5	Work on visuals for presentation	Presentation scheduled

and primary sources. The primary source doesn't have to be the actual hero they are researching but can be someone personally familiar with the hero, the time in history, or the location of the event.

Mrs. Salazar explains the procedure that will be used and the timeline they will follow. Since the class will have to continue other studies during this project, students will have project time only on Fridays. She will introduce each step of the project, model it, and give them the entire 2-hour period each Friday to work. They also may have to spend time outside of class to meet the deadlines. See Figure 4.3 for the timeline Mrs. Salazar presents to the class.

Mrs. Salazar displays a "Resources Needed" list at the front of the room. Students add anything they need to the list, although they are encouraged to locate their own materials, if possible. They can store their note cards and research materials in accordion files labeled with their class and individual names. They can even post a list of helpful Internet sites on the whiteboard to support one another. Several students have already located primary sources needed by other students. The group is working as a community.

The students are innovative in their approach to the hero topic. Their choices include a local firefighter, a national hero killed on 9-11, war veterans whose stories they find on the Internet, and even their own parents and grandparents.

 ## CONCLUSION

Students of all ages benefit from being taught the organizational skills needed to produce long-term projects. When time, space, and resources are allotted during the school day for students to work on projects, they begin to understand the concept of working together to produce quality results that cannot be accomplished in a short period of time.

References

Glasser, W. (1998). *The quality school: Managing students without coercion*. New York: Harper-Perennial.

Potak, C. (2000). Zebra. In *The language of literature*. Evanston, IL: McDougal Littell.

Suggested Reading

Chard, S., & Katz, L. (2000). *Engaging children's minds: The project approach* (2nd ed.). New York: Ablex.

Helm, J. H. (2003). *The power of projects*. New York: Teachers College Press.

5

PROVIDING OPPORTUNITIES FOR PURSUING PERSONAL INTERESTS

One strength of a community is its diversity of people, interests, and abilities. To build on the diversity of a classroom community, the teacher must enable students to pursue and share special interests.

An exciting way to begin is for teachers to share their own special interests, relating them to topics under study whenever possible. Once students know that a teacher is passionate about quilting, for example, they will understand why she relates their math lessons to quilting squares. They will also begin to appreciate the beauty of quilts when their classwork is displayed in a quilt pattern.

By encouraging students to talk about their special interests, the teacher learns important facts about them that can enliven the curriculum and be incorporated into long-term projects.

 STEP BY STEP

The steps for encouraging students to integrate special interests into the curriculum:

• **Share your interests and passions**   Allow students to get to know you better by sharing your hobbies, interests, and even the books you like to read. Integrate this information into the curriculum whenever appropriate but also use small sections of time to share. If you have a few minutes before lunchtime, share an interest with the students.

• **Discuss and write about personal interests**   Encourage students to share their personal interests and relate them to curriculum whenever possible. Give students time to write in personal journals or develop a system of interaction through dialogue journals, where students gain writing practice by "talking" to you.

• **Provide a format for pursuing personal interests in connection with class projects**   Once you are familiar with the students' interests, you can help them make connections between classwork and their personal passions. This raises their motivation in class projects (Schiefele, 1991).

- **Encourage students to appreciate the strengths and interests of others**
When students share their personal interests, teachers must help others accept and appreciate them. Sharing makes students vulnerable to others' opinions, and this risk-taking should be celebrated and discussed and expectations for behavior and comments made clear. Because you, as the teacher, have shared your interests, you can relate your own concerns that others may not understand how a person can be interested in quilting or folk dancing, for example.

FOCUS ON ENGLISH LEARNERS

Celebrating diverse interests and backgrounds helps English learners become active members of the learning community.

- **Celebrate student contributions** When students share their special interests, recognize their efforts and abilities. Recognition is a factor in motivation (Turner & Paris, 1995). If possible, ask students to explain exactly how an activity is done and why they are fascinated by this pursuit, whether it's dancing, music, baseball, or gymnastics. Help other students see the student's attraction to this endeavor.

Applications and Examples

Miss Link has recently begun long-term projects in literature with her third-graders. Her students have the entire morning each day to read and write. She relates their reading and writing to science or social studies projects on an alternate schedule, which allows students to focus on their literacy skills.

Miss Link often shares her passion for reading with her students. She tells them about books that she enjoyed when she was in elementary school and what she is reading now. The students know she enjoys historical novels and mysteries, which has encouraged them to begin to read and write mysteries as well.

To encourage her students to relate reading and writing to their personal interests, Miss Link has them complete a once-a-month project related to a book they've read. The class has brainstormed possible literature projects and created a list:

- Create a diorama showing the setting for your book.
- Design a board game that relates to your book.
- Cook and share a recipe that the characters in your book might have enjoyed. To be authentic, be sure to research the time and place in which the story took place.
- Write a skit or puppet play about your book.
- Research the games children might have played during the time of the book.
- Create and model a costume that shows how people in your book dressed.
- Create a story box containing props and realia that might be used to retell the story.

The students enjoy sharing their projects. One student plays the guitar, and he frequently writes and sings a song about his book. After the first time he did this, he shared how scared he had been that the students would laugh at him. Miss Link helped by talking about how hard she had tried to learn to play the guitar—unsuccessfully.

Miss Link knew that her class was truly becoming a community the day Anita shared a modern dance depicting the events in her favorite book. At first, the boys held their hands over their mouths to keep from laughing. Miss Link gave them a "teacher look," and they calmed down. By the time Anita had finished her dance, everyone stood and applauded. Miss Link then asked Anita questions about how long she had studied dance and asked her to teach them all a step. The boys found out that dancing is really quite strenuous.

Mr. Rowell's seventh-grade history class is studying the Middle Ages and the feudal system. Mr. Rowell has brought a number of resources into the classroom, including books, magazines, and graphic representations of a feudal manor and a diagram of the levels of society in the system.

Figure 5.1 Feudal Websites

www.learner.org/exhibits/middleages/feudal.html

http://argos.evansville.edu

http://www.fordham.edu/halsall/sbook.html

http://www.georgetown.edu/labyrinth

http://www.the-orb.net/index.html

To support his students' explorations, Mr. Rowell proposes that they work in groups to research different aspects of feudal life. As a part of their assignment, the groups are to prepare an exhibit for a "museum day" when they will talk about the aspect of feudal life they have chosen to explore, show illustrations or graphics, and briefly assess how much the other students have learned about their section of the museum tour.

The students work together to plan their displays and do their research, but it soon becomes evident that Joseph is serving as a resource person for all the groups. The other students often call him over to the computer when they're working, and Joseph seems to be a big help in surfing the Internet.

After observing these interactions, Mr. Rowell asks Joseph to prepare a short presentation for the whole class on finding topics on the Internet. He makes this request on Friday but has no idea how seriously Joseph will take his assignment. On Monday, Joseph makes a PowerPoint presentation to the entire class, walking them through the process of researching topics on the Internet. He shows websites that will support the feudal study, and the other students busily take notes. To look at Joseph's list of websites, see Figure 5.1.

Mr. Rowell shakes Joseph's hand after the presentation and congratulates him in front of the class. "That was amazing, Joseph. I knew you were interested in the Internet and technology, but I had no idea how well informed you were."

In the process of the feudal study, Mr. Rowell and his students learn a lot about each other's interests and strengths. The students learn that Mr. Rowell likes to draw detailed graphic representations and once studied to become a graphic artist. He helps the groups create their diagrams and shows them how to draw them to scale.

The biggest surprise outcome of the study, though, is a shy Pakistani girl, Amini, an avid reader who rarely talks aloud in class. She brings a book to share with the class at the conclusion of the study, saying, "I want everyone to know that the feudal system wasn't always in the far distant past. It existed until quite recently in my home country. The United States has helped to cause big changes since 9-11, though." She talks about the book *My Feudal Lord* by Tehmani Durrani (1992) and tells the story so compellingly that several of the other students sign up to borrow the book from her.

Mr. Rowell has learned so much about his students during this study that he determines to find ways to learn more about their special interests and incorporate them into future studies. He has never seen students so engaged as these became when they were allowed to pursue their passions.

 CONCLUSION

Because a community of learners is, by definition, a group of diverse people working together for the good of the group, it is important to encourage students to share their interests. Using those unique interests in the pursuit of academic excellence is a perfect way to fire student motivation, as both Miss Link and Mr. Rowell have discovered.

References

Durrani, T. (1996). *My feudal lord*. Neutral Bay, Australia: Transworld Publications.

Schiefele, U. (1991). Interest, learning, and motivation. *Educational Psychologist, 26*(3/4), 299–321.

Turner, J., & Paris, S. (1995). How literacy tasks influence children's motivation for literacy. *Reading Teacher, 48*(8), 662–673.

Suggested Reading

Wang, S., & Han, S. (2001). Six c's of motivation. In M. Orez (Ed.), *Emerging perspectives on learning, teaching, and technology*. Available as an e-book at http:www.coe.edu/epltt/6csmotivation.htm.

ESTABLISHING A CLASSROOM MANAGEMENT SYSTEM BUILT ON MUTUAL RESPECT AND CARING

This section focuses on establishing discipline and management systems that foster mutual respect and a smooth working environment. For a community to function well, all members must understand their responsibilities and the benefits of classroom routines and procedures. Participating in a well-functioning community is sometimes a new experience for students. They need explicit instruction and support from both adults and other students before they can understand the rewards of collaboration and positive communication.

Effective teaching strategies play an important part in establishing and maintaining a positive classroom atmosphere. As Susan Ohanian (1982) writes, "There's only one true technique for good discipline and that's good curriculum" (p. 17). When teachers plan an exciting curriculum and actively engage students in learning activities, the students are much less likely to spend time off task or distracting others. Major studies on classroom management have found that teachers who are able to maximize instructional time and clarify their expectations for students spend much less time on classroom discipline (Evertson & Harris, 2002). Effective teachers explain and illustrate rules and expectations so that the students clearly understand them. Such teachers also help students rehearse new activities so that they will learn by experience. Throughout lessons, these teachers use good pacing, sequencing, and monitoring to keep students engaged. They let students know that they are aware of off-task behavior but don't waste valuable learning time berating students. They set up rules, expectations, and consequences in advance, and they follow through. Applying rules and consequences fairly and consistently helps students remember and follow classroom procedures.

FOCUS ON ENGLISH LEARNERS

English learners benefit from simultaneously seeing and hearing what is expected of them.

Glasser (2001) stresses the importance of teaching students to make wise choices. A positive learning community also depends on actively involving students in setting up rules, consequences, and classroom maintenance. (For more information about Glasser's theory see Figure III.1.) By taking responsibility for classroom chores, maintaining materials, and feeling the resulting pride of accomplishment, students become active community members (Charles, 2002).

This section introduces strategies gradually so that both teachers and students can learn procedures and expectations and work collaboratively to solve problems. This approach recognizes that students come to school with varying levels of self-discipline and impulse control, which can make the classroom challenging and interesting for both students and

FIGURE III.1 Important Theory

William Glasser 1925–present

William Glasser is a psychiatrist who became interested in creating schools where all students could achieve success. His choice theory states that people are driven by six basic needs that influence their choices: survival, power, love, belonging, freedom, and fun. Glasser believes that parents and teachers must be aware of these needs as they support children in learning to make wise choices. Understanding these drives helps us become aware of the importance of making choices that improve the quality of our world.

Glasser advises parents and teachers to remember the following axioms of choice theory:

- The only behavior we can control is our own.
- All we can give another person is information.
- All long-lasting psychological problems are relationship problems.
- What happened in the past has everything to do with what we are today, but we can only satisfy our basic needs right now and plan to continue satisfying them in the future.
- We can only satisfy our needs by picturing what we want to see in our quality world.
- All we do is behave.
- All behaviors are Total Behaviors and are made up of four components: acting, thinking, feeling, and physiology. All Total Behaviors are chosen but we have direct control over the acting and thinking components.
- We can only control our feeling and physiology indirectly through how we choose to act and think.
- All Total Behavior is designated by verbs and named by the behavior that is the most recognizable (e.g., "I am choosing to depress," instead of "I am suffering from depression").

Glasser maintains that 95% of discipline problems are due to a child's struggle for power. He believes that children must learn to make good choices; parents and teachers should not attempt to control behavior. He has established an institute in California for the support and training of teachers and works actively with schools that adopt his methods (which are known as Glasser Quality Schools).

References

Glasser's works include the following:

Glasser, W. (1969). *Schools without failure.* New York: Harper & Row.
Glasser, W. (1990). *The quality school.* New York: Harper & Row.
Glasser, W. (2001). *Every student can succeed.* Los Angeles: William Glasser Institute.
Glasser, W., & Dotson, K. (1998). *Choice theory in the classroom.* New York: Perennial.

Source: "The Ten Axioms of Choice Theory" from *Choice Theory* by William Glasser. Copyright © 1998 by William Glasser, Joseph Paul Glasser, Jana Dolores Glasser, Nathaniel Alan Thompson, Jullianna Kay Thompson, and Martin Howard Glasser. Reprinted by permission of HarperCollins Publishers. Please note that this list presents the opening sentences of paragraphs that expand on the axioms in Glasser's work.

teacher. These strategies will support all community members in solving problems in mutually rewarding ways.

References

Charles, C. (2002). *Elementary classroom management* (3rd ed.). Boston: Allyn & Bacon.
Evertson, C., & Harris, A. (2002). *Classroom management for elementary teachers* (6th ed.). Boston: Allyn & Bacon.
Glasser, W. (2001). *Every student can succeed.* Los Angeles: William Glasser Institute.
Ohanian, S. (1982, April). There's only one true technique for good discipline. *Learning, 82,* 17–20.

MODELING AND BUILDING MUTUAL RESPECT: TEACHER/STUDENT, STUDENT/STUDENT INTERACTIONS

Modeling, practice, and rehearsal are the cornerstones for establishing a warm and caring learning environment. Because students in public school classrooms come from many social and ethnic backgrounds, the teacher must establish expectations for acceptable verbal interactions. This is done primarily through modeling but must also include explicit teaching of socially acceptable conventions and procedures.

Students often need to be taught strategies for acceptably resolving conflicts and differences of opinion. The basic rule for any classroom is "Always be respectful of others." Respect includes honoring other people's personal space, belongings, opinions, and efforts to be recognized and accepted in the classroom.

 ## STEP BY STEP

The steps for modeling and building mutual respect in the classroom:

• **Establish classroom expectations**   Begin the school year by talking to students about the meaning of respect as well as respectful attention and verbal interactions. In this way, you set a tone and commit to modeling respect in all interactions with students. The students can then be expected to uphold classroom expectations and procedures once they are established.

• **Practice respectful interactions**   Prepare a series of situations that are likely to occur in the classroom. (See Figure 6.1 for some suggestions.) Ask the students to think about how they might react to each situation, and both you and the students act out a scenario using students' suggestions. They then analyze the responses for signs of respectfulness, always allowing others to state their thoughts and opinions. The class establishes a series of actions to be followed in case agreement cannot be reached. Ask students to act out the scenario using the respectful interactions they discussed. The discussion should also include talking about words that are not respectful or that do not help solve problems.

Figure 6.1   Classroom Scenarios

Michael wants to walk next to his friend in the line going to the cafeteria. When his group is called to line up, he moves to the front and pushes in next to his friend, displacing several students who are already in line.
Justine is trying to work on a project with her cooperative group partners, but they tend to chat and goof off instead of doing the work necessary to complete the task. She's very frustrated by the fact that the group is not making progress on the task.
Cha has a favorite book in the classroom book collection. When the teacher allows the children to "free read," he races to the reading area and grabs the book. He will not share with the others, even when they ask politely.

Figure 6.2   "Respect" Word Collections

What Respect Is ...	What Respect Is Not ...
Listening to the other person's point of view	Interrupting while another person is talking
Being willing to compromise	Thinking, "It's my way or nothing"
Being honest	Coloring the facts to sway opinion in your favor
Being open to a solution	Closing your mind to constructive discussion

Figure 6.3   Walking the Peace Bridge

Steps

1. Agree to be honest, not call names, not interrupt, and work hard to solve the problem.
2. Listen to the other person's story, restate what he or she said, and ask how that person feels about the problem. Then, tell your side.
3. Each person tells what he or she wants and is willing to do to solve the problem.
4. Gather all the *wants* and *willings* from both sides of the dispute and try to find a solution.
5. Summarize the solution and say what you will do if something like this happens again.

Source: Adapted from Lane-Garon, 1998.

• **Chart nonrespectful words and possible substitutions**   Ask the students to think about words that do not show respect and to identify other words that can be substituted to solve problems and show respect. These words can be charted on a large piece of paper. See Figure 6.2 for an example.

FOCUS ON ENGLISH LEARNERS

English learners benefit from simultaneously seeing and hearing what is expected of them. This enables them to process visual cues in the context of language without having to rely entirely on language.

• **Create a classroom chart of problem-solving procedures**   Lead a discussion of ways in which problems can be solved, and help students brainstorm approaches they might use to achieve a mutually acceptable solution. See Figure 6.3 for an example of a classroom problem-solving protocol known as Walking the Peace Bridge (Lane-Garon, 1998).

- **Use classroom situations to further the students' understanding** As situations arise in the classroom, model respectful interactions and teach approaches to problem-solving. If additional procedures are needed, they can be taught and added to the classroom chart of problem-solving approaches.

Applications and Examples

Miss Tatsumota's third-graders are lined up outside their new classroom on the first day of school. As they wait for the bell to ring, several discuss what they've heard about their new teacher.

"My brother had Miss T. last year," says Renee. "She's very nice, but she has really strict rules."

"What kind of rules?" asks Tomas.

"She doesn't let anyone argue in her class," answers Renee.

"That's silly!" responds Tomas. "How can she keep you from arguing? Sometimes I don't agree with someone else."

"I don't know, but that's what my brother said," declares Renee.

At this point Miss Tatsumota walks up to the line. "Let's talk about this inside," she says with a smile. "We need to learn how to get along."

Inside the classroom Miss Tatsumota gathers her new students on the carpet at the front of the room. "I understand some of you have heard about the rules in my classroom," she begins. "I think third-graders are old enough to learn how to talk to one another with respect. I will always speak to you with respect, and I expect you to do the same for me and also for your classmates. Do all of you understand what I mean when I say *respect?*"

Tomas raises his hand, and Miss T. calls on him.

"My dad always says we have to show respect to our elders," he answers. "I think it means to be polite."

"That's part of it, Tomas," she responds. "But it's more than that. It's really listening when others talk. It's also trying to understand other people's ideas and thoughts and not always demanding your own way."

"Renee says her brother said you don't allow anyone to argue in your class," says Tomas. "Sometimes I argue when I don't agree with something. Is that OK?"

"You are certainly allowed to tell us what you think, Tomas," says Miss T. with twinkling eyes. "But in this class we're going to learn ways to talk to one another so that we avoid arguments. We're going to learn to discuss things and make decisions that will satisfy us all. For example, when you argue, maybe you say things like 'You're wrong!' and maybe there's a better way to make your point. Let's make a chart of words that cause you to argue. Let's start with 'You're wrong!' Is there another way that you could say that?" She writes "You're wrong!" on the left side of a large sheet of chart paper.

Renee raises her hand. "Maybe you could say, 'I think it might be something else.' "

"That's good," replies Miss T. "You didn't make him feel like you were sure you were right. You just let him know that you had another idea."

The class suggested other words that might cause an argument and brainstormed alternative ways of presenting their views. When they were finished, their chart listed several suggestions for peaceful words. See Figure 6.4 for the suggestions the class made.

Miss T. knows her work in teaching peaceful problem-solving is just beginning. Each time a major conflict arises, she walks the students through the steps to a peaceful solution, making sure they are talking and listening and following the steps. As the year progresses, her third-graders become better able to walk through the steps without her help.

Mr. Diaz teaches inner-city high school students and often feels verbally attacked by them. When he confronts them about their disrespect, the situation seems to escalate rapidly. He decides that he will take a chance and teach some lessons on respectful conversation. He plans to incorporate discussions of words and conflict into his 10th-grade writing lessons on dialogue.

Figure 6.4 Using Words for Peace

Words That Cause Arguments	More Peaceful Words
You're wrong! You can't do it! I'm better at that than you are. I hate you! Shut up!	I think it might be something else. Do you need some help? You can do that very well. Can I try? I don't like it when you do that. Be quiet a minute so I can think.

Mr. Diaz begins by talking to one of his students about using the student's writing as an example during the class. "Greg, you're doing a great job of writing a story about a young man who is having a difficult time in school. I'd like to use what you've written to help everyone in the class to learn a couple of things. First, I want them to see how you develop a character in your writing. Second, I would like to teach the importance of the way people express themselves in developing relationships. Would this be OK with you?"

"My main character is having a lot of problems at home and school. He doesn't express himself very well," responded Greg. "I would love to make my story better, though. Go for it!"

Mr. Diaz made some overhead transparencies of Greg's story and planned a lesson on developing characters that would engage the reader. He began the process the next day.

"When you read a good story, what in the story makes you want to keep reading?" asks Mr. Diaz.

"An exciting plot," answers Jennifer.

"Interesting characters," adds George.

"What makes characters interesting?" asks Mr. Diaz.

"They have distinctive ways of talking and acting," says Greg.

"Exactly!" responds Mr. Diaz. "Authors have several ways of helping the reader get to know the characters."

Mr. Diaz begins to make a list for the overhead. "Authors help us get to know characters by having the characters talk. We learn about them by what they say." Mr. Diaz writes, "What they say" on the transparency. "Authors also help us get to know characters by what they do, what they think, and how they look." He adds to his list as he speaks.

"Now, let's use one of your stories as an example," adds Mr. Diaz. "This is Greg's story." He puts the transparency of Greg's story on the overhead and begins to read orally.

Lenny came into the classroom and slumped down into his seat. He took out his notebook and pencil and began to doodle on the cover of the notebook. When the bell rang, Mr. Brown stepped to the front of the room and began to talk about the story the class had been assigned to read.

"The main character in this story has a problem," Mr. Brown states. "Lenny, what do you think the problem is?"

Lenny doesn't look up but mumbles, "He's afraid of his old man."

"Exactly!" states Mr. Brown. "His father abuses him verbally, and Jonathan is afraid of him."

"So what's the big deal?" asks Lenny under his breath.

"What was that, Lenny?" responds Mr. Brown.

"Nothin'," replies Lenny, slumping farther into his chair.

Mr. Diaz stops reading and looks up at the class. "What picture of this character are you getting in your mind?"

"Greg has done a good job of painting a picture," says Jennifer. "I can see Lenny slumping in his seat and mumbling under his breath. You can tell he has an attitude."

Figure 6.5   Actions That Help Us Understand Character

Action	What It Tells Us about the Person
Slumping in the chair	Person is bored or tired (not too interested)
Foot stomping	Person is angry or annoyed
Crying	Person is sad
Shouting	Person is angry or excited
Waving arms	Person is trying to get someone's attention
Shaking a fist	Person is threatening someone

"Let's do some brainstorming," suggests Mr. Diaz. "What are some of the things you can use to create an image of the character in the reader's mind?"

"Body language is important," says Greg. "The writer needs to describe what the character does, not just what he says."

Mr. Diaz starts a list labeled "action," and he and the students brainstorm some actions that relate to character attributes. See Figure 6.5 for the list the class creates.

After Mr. Diaz and the class finish brainstorming the list of actions, he divides the class into small groups of students to create lists of "thoughts," "dialogue," and "descriptions" that help build characters. This activity produces a lively discussion.

After the class has worked on their lists, Mr. Diaz calls them back together to use some of the suggestions from each list to create characters. The students gain confidence as they combine actions, thoughts, dialogue, and physical descriptions to clarify characters in their stories.

Mr. Diaz closes his lesson by asking students what they learned about the importance of building a character. "I think we found out a lot about how actions, words, and thoughts help other people create impressions of a person," says Jennifer.

"Does that work in real life?" asks Mr. Diaz. "Or is it just in works of fiction?"

"It's important in real life," says Greg. "When you see someone slumped in their seat and mumbling answers in class, you know that's not a good student."

"I never thought of body language as so important," says Jennifer. "And look around the room. We're all sitting up much straighter now."

The whole class laughs, but what Jennifer says is true. The whole class seems to be sitting up straighter. No one is mumbling now.

"Tomorrow, when we come into class, I'd like us to pick some of the items from the lists we created today and see if we can set some standards for our class," says Mr. Diaz. "We need to identify the actions, words, and thoughts that we expect in our class so that we are all showing respect for one another and opening our minds to learn as much as we can in class and from our interactions with one another."

The next day the class selects items from each list to create a chart of student and teacher expectations. They decide to label their chart "Showing Respect." After that day, Mr. Diaz refers students to the charts whenever necessary. However, he finds he needs to use the charts less frequently as the students achieve more success in their writing about characters. They seem to understand the importance of words and body language in communication. They've also made the connection between their work in the classroom and real life.

 CONCLUSION

As both Mr. Diaz and Miss Tatsumota have shown, students must understand the expectations and standards of the class culture before they can function comfortably in a classroom community. Both teachers found ways to involve students in establishing standards and becoming a working community. One of the nation's most successful teachers, Ron Clark, has written a book in which he describes how he establishes his expectations for behavior: "We must establish the expectations and then make sure that our classrooms are engaging, accepting places where students can take risks in learning, enjoy interactions, and know what is expected of them" (Clark, 2003, p. 26).

References

Clark, R. (2003). *The essential fifty-five*. New York: Hyperion.

Lane-Garon, P. (1998). Addressing kindergarten students' conflict behavior: Encouraging social-cognitive development. *Kindergarten Education: Theory, Research, and Practice, 3,* 93–105.

Suggested Reading

Johnson, G., Poliner, R., & Bonaiuto, S. (2005). Learning throughout the day. *Educational Leadership, 63*(1), 59–63.

7

ESTABLISHING ROUTINES AND SMOOTH TRANSITIONS

Classroom routines set the stage for a harmonious environment. They must be established early in the school year and used consistently. Students may be actively involved in choosing routines, but the teacher is responsible for consistency. If a routine is not working, teacher and students should discuss problems and adjust the routine accordingly.

Routines help students understand when things will happen and what is expected of them. The teacher must carefully set expectations as well as the consequences for students who make poor choices (Glasser & Dotson, 1998).

Classroom routines differ depending on student age but should always support smooth transitions. See Figure 7.1 for examples.

 ## STEP BY STEP

The steps for establishing and implementing classroom routines:

- **Involve students in setting classroom routines**   Discuss the purpose of classroom routines and decisions that need to be made about them. Ask students to recall routines in other classrooms and evaluate how well those routines worked. List their suggestions and include your own, after you explain them.

- **Choose a set of routines**   From the list, choose three to five with which to begin. Explain that these routines will be tried and evaluated before they are kept or changed.

- **Discuss natural consequences**   Talk about making choices and what happens when we choose to break a rule or not follow a routine. Give examples, such as "What happens when you come home and drop your book bag in the middle of the floor instead of bringing it to your room, which is the routine your parents expect you to follow?" When the students answer, "We get in trouble," discuss the fact that dropping the bag instead of following the routine was a choice they made. Ask students how their parents

Figure 7.1   Classroom routines

Routine	Expectations
Entering the classroom	Place coats and sweaters in closet, lunchboxes on back shelf, homework in homework file.
Roll and lunch count	Take name sticks and put in proper containers (present—for attendance, and hot or cold lunch).
Classroom duties	Check duty board for your name and perform your duties as needed.
Help needed	Stand up your "help" sign and wait for assistance, going on with other work while you wait.
Changing activities	Listen for the signal, clean up your area, and walk quietly to the gathering spot.
End of the day	Clean up your area, put your chair on your desk, and wait quietly by your desk until you are dismissed.

handle a poor choice like that. After discussing responses, ask what should happen if they drop book bags in middle of the classroom. Stress that the classroom is a different from home because it has many more people. Twenty-five book bags in the middle of the floor would create a huge mess as well as a safety hazard.

• **Chart routines**   Create a chart listing routines and students' names. See Figure 7.2 for an example.

• **Conduct periodic evaluations and reset routines as necessary**   Monitor the effectiveness of routines, and chart infractions as well as students' choices. Every week or so in the beginning of the year and whenever necessary later, discuss routines with the class: how are they are working, and how should we change them? Establish new routines as necessary.

• **Deal with students who regularly ignore routines or make poor choices** Remember that not all students have the same ability to make good choices. Discuss infractions privately with the student. Make it clear that you see the problem as poor choice-making. If the student is not ready to make good choices, tell him or her that you will have to make the choices for a while. Give such students the opportunity to tell you when they are ready to make their own choices.

• **Respond rather that react**   When you discuss infractions or set up new routines, be sure that you respond to the problem instead of react to it. When you respond, you remain calm, discuss problems in terms of poor choices, and support student growth in making better choices. When you react, you may show anger or frustration. Then, the focus is on punishment rather than problem-solving.

Figure 7.2 Routines Chart

	Student Initials													
	TA	**BB**	**RC**	**TD**	**YD**	**HH**	**TJ**	**KJ**	**LK**	**RM**	**IM**	**PN**	**GS**	**BT**
Routine														
Entering the classroom														
Roll and lunch count														
Classroom duties														
Help needed														
Changing activities														
End of the day														

Note: Students can be given plus signs for following routines well and minus signs when they don't meet expectations.

Applications and Examples

Miss Garcia has been working with her first-graders to develop the habit of using words of respect. It is now the third day of school, and she has gathered her class on the carpet to discuss the routines they need to establish in their classroom.

"I want you to think about how you came into the classroom this morning. When you first came in, what things did you have to remember to do?" she asks.

"We have to hang up our jackets," responds Jason, who had forgotten to do that.

"We have to put our pictures on the 'I'm here today' board," adds Charity.

Miss Garcia took pictures of each student with her digital camera on the first day of school. She placed the pictures labeled with each student's name onto a magnet that she uses to take roll and lunch count. The children place their picture magnets on a section of her filing cabinet labeled "I'm here today." They place another picture magnet in another section labeled with a picture of a lunch tray or lunchbox to show what they will be eating that day. A sixth-grade student comes by each morning to fill out the attendance and lunch-count forms and take them to the office. The first-graders will assume these duties under the supervision of the sixth-grader in just a few weeks.

"We have a new routine to learn today," Miss Garcia says. "I've noticed that when I'm working with reading groups, sometimes you need help. Can you think of a way to let me know that you need help without disturbing the reading group?"

Gloria suggests, "We could raise our hands."

Rebecca adds, "We could have a special signal. My mom does that when we have company."

"Good idea, Rebecca," Miss Garcia responds. "Maybe we can use your name tags. We could write 'help' on the back so you can use them to signal that you need help."

FOCUS ON ENGLISH LEARNERS

Demonstrations give English learners visual cues that support their growth in processing language.

Miss Garcia holds up one of the name tags she gave to each child on the first day of school. She holds it vertically and shows students how to write "help" on the back of the tag.

"Whenever you need help, you can stand this sign up on your desk. While you are waiting for me to come to your desk, you need to go on with your work. If you can't finish what you are working on until I get to you, you can go to the next thing on the "To Do" board. If you've finished everything else, you may read your library book. Now I want you to tiptoe back to your seats, and we will make "help" signs and practice how to use them." See Figure 7.3 for directions for making "help" name tags.

After students have written "help" on their name tags, Miss Garcia asks them to take out some paper and write their name and the date at the top.

"Now, Georgette, pretend that you need help. What do you do?" asks Miss Garcia.

Georgette stands her "help" sign on end.

"Very nice!" exclaims Miss Garcia. "You put up your sign, and then you went on working. You didn't raise your hand. You didn't interrupt the reading group. You didn't call out my name. That was exactly right. Now, when am I going to come talk to you?" Miss Garcia asks.

"When you get finished with the reading group," replies Georgette.

"That's right!" says Miss Garcia with a smile.

The students practice several more times before Miss Garcia calls her first reading group. For a while everything seems to be working well, but then she sees Rodney approaching the reading-group table. She continues to work with the group, not making eye contact with Rodney but pointing to his seat as a signal for him to return to it.

"Miss Garcia! Miss Garcia!" Rodney interrupts.

Miss Garcia continues to instruct her group as she rises and gently but firmly leads Rodney back to his seat and stands up his "help" sign, never making eye contact with him. However, she makes sure that she goes to his desk immediately after she finishes with the group. She talks to him softly, reminding him about the routine they have practiced. She then goes to the two other children who have put up their "help" signs and smiles broadly at them, congratulating them on remembering to raise their signs and not interrupt the group.

Miss Garcia will work with her students to gradually choose and establish routines and help them understand that she will consistently expect them to remember and follow those routines.

Mr. Goodson teaches seventh-grade science in a middle school where they change classes every 50 minutes. With the goal of using class time wisely, he and his students have brainstormed ways to take care of classroom tasks to free more time for learning. The class has decided that students can initial a roll sheet as they enter the classroom and place their homework into a designated folder at the front of the room. The students have formed learning teams, and each team has a materials coordinator who collects materials for the group.

In response to a student suggestion, Mr. Goodson has selected several student assistants who arrive at school early each day. The students help him assemble learning packets with materials for each day's lesson. This routine makes it easy for the materials

Figure 7.3   Making Name Tags with "Help" Signs

1. Fold a piece of construction paper into four sections.

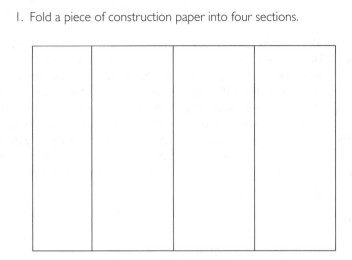

2. Fold the paper so it forms a three-dimensional triangular shape.

3. Write the student's name on the front section of the triangle.

4. Holding the name tag vertically, write the word "help" on one of the other sides.

coordinators to pick up materials and distribute them during class. Mr. Goodson chooses his assistants by observing which of his students are standing outside the school when he arrives. He notices several of his students among the early birds and asks them to come into the classroom to help him.

When Mr. Goodson introduces new procedures in his classroom, he demonstrates exactly how materials are to be handled. Because he has several English learners in his classes, he particularly wants to make sure they understand safety procedures. Therefore, he demonstrates those procedures using Total Physical Response (TPR) (Asher, 1969). This technique involves showing and practicing routines and procedures while repeating the directions until students understand exactly what they need to do. Mr. Goodson consistently monitors safety and classroom routines. Any student who ignores safety routines is required to watch the experiments, not perform them, but must make up the lab in an after-school session with Mr. Goodson. However, he rarely has to conduct after-school experiments.

 ## CONCLUSION

Both Miss Garcia and Mr. Goodson have high expectations for their students, even though their teaching assignments are very different. They know they must consistently help their students follow rules and routines. As a result, their students work productively in an environment that supports their learning. The students in these classes have been taught the necessary routines and how to make appropriate choices in carrying them out. They are learning academics, but they are also learning behaviors that will serve them well throughout their school years.

STRATEGY ON VIDEO
Modeling and Building Mutual Respect, Routines, and Transitions

Modeling and building respectful verbal interactions and establishing routines and procedures in a fourth-grade classroom are demonstrated on segment 2 of the DVD that accompanies this text. Watch carefully for evidence that this teacher responds to his students' needs. As you watch this segment, think about the following:

- How does a teacher use vocal tone and inflection to gain student cooperation?
- What does this teacher do when his expectations for behavior are not met?

References

Asher, J. (1969). *Learning another language through action: The complete teacher's guide.* (2nd ed.). Los Gatos, CA: Sky Oaks Production.

Glasser, W., & Dotson, K. (1998). *Choice theory in the classroom.* New York: Perennial.

Suggested Reading

Kohn, A. (1996). *Beyond discipline: From compliance to community.* Alexandria, VA: Association for Supervision and Curriculum Development.

8

USING INDIVIDUAL CONFERENCES AND GOAL-SETTING

A learning community focuses on collaboration, setting personal goals, and self-reflection. Two important tools for establishing and meeting these outcomes are individual conferences and goal-setting. Students become self-reflective only after they recognize both their strengths and areas for improvement (Bridges, 1995.) They also must begin to take responsibility for their actions and responses.

Teachers must schedule individual conferences in a way that fits into the school day without reducing teaching time. Conferences must take place regularly if they are to be productive (Eby, Herrell, & Jordan, 2006). See Figure 8.1 for scheduling suggestions.

One element of a successful individual conference is personal goal-setting. Personal goals are different for almost every student. They can relate to behavior, cooperation, choices, homework, academic standards, and even positive verbal interactions. Identifying appropriate goals for individual students requires the teacher to closely observe student interactions, behavior, and academic achievement.

 STEP BY STEP

The steps for implementing individual conferences and goal-setting:

- **Explain the purpose of individual conferences and goal-setting** Involve students in a discussion about what conferences are, how often they will occur, and their purpose. Stress that all successful athletes and scholars set goals for themselves and work hard to achieve them.

- **Demonstrate a conference** With the help of a willing student, model the process by conducting a demonstration conference in which you look at a piece of work and set goals together. Also discuss goals for the student's cooperation with others, encouragement of others, or some other factor that will contribute to the learning environment.

Figure 8.1   Scheduling Individual Conferences

When	How
During center time	Schedule 2–3 students per day during center time. Keep conferences short.
At the end of each reading group	Meet with one student per day at the conclusion of the reading group.
Before and after school	Schedule one conference each day before school (10 minutes) and one after school (for students who do not ride buses).
Lunchtime	Invite one student each day to meet with you as you eat lunch together.
During independent work or study time	Schedule 2–3 students each day. Meet with them during independent work time while other students are engaged in class work.

- **Discuss elements of a successful conference**   Talk about the demonstration conference. Point out the student's involvement (make sure you have chosen a student who will contribute and self-evaluate), how strengths are identified, and how goals are set for the next conference.

- **Collaboratively design a conference report sheet**   Work with students to design a conference report sheet that will document the elements discussed, the goals set, and the approximate time for the next conference (2 weeks or a month later). See Figure 8.2 for an example of a conference and goal-setting report sheet.

- **Set up a conference schedule**   Explain how you will set up conferences and when they will take place. Explain that conferences will be short but will take place regularly. Display the schedule so that students will know exactly when they will meet with you.

- **Prepare for the conferences**   At first, it is helpful to ask students to bring a specific piece of work to the conference. Before the conference, use the report sheet to briefly note any strengths or concerns you want to address.

FOCUS ON ENGLISH LEARNERS

Individual conferences enable the teacher to focus on English development, support the student in setting goals, and celebrate the student's growth without embarrassment.

- **Involve the student in the process**   Be sure to give students a chance to talk during the conference. Ask them to identify their strengths, both academically and behaviorally, and to note what areas they need to work on. Have students sign the forms at the end of the conference and provide them with a copy for their work folder or portfolio. (Some schools have two-part copies of conference report forms that yield a copy for the student.)

- **Keep the process going and growing**   For success, conferences must be scheduled regularly. Once a month may be enough for most elementary students, but you may need to meet with others more often. Secondary teachers may schedule most conferences once a quarter or once a semester but meet with students who need extra support more frequently.

Figure 8.2   Conference and Goal-Setting Report Sheet

Student's name _____ Date of conference _____

Academic topics _____

Behavior topics _____

Responsibility topics _____

Academic goals set _____

Behavioral goals set _____

Responsibility goals set _____

Other goals set _____

Student's signature _____

Teacher's signature _____

Approximate date of next conference _____

Comments:

Note: A blank, blackline master of this form is included in the Teacher Resources section of this text.

Applications and Examples

Mr. Lopez's kindergarten class includes a number of English learners whose first language is Spanish and a group of native English speakers, none of whom have had preschool experience. He constantly supports his students as they learn classroom rules and routines. Mr. Lopez selects work samples for each student to help parents and students better understand student growth. He wants to help his students set goals for themselves and feel proud of their progress. Therefore, he decides to conduct individual conferences and begin simple goal-setting.

He starts the process by talking to his students. "Today, while you are working in your centers, I will start to call on you one by one to talk to me. We are going to look at your colors and numbers and see how well you are doing. We will also be talking about how well you are following the classroom rules. I won't get to meet with everyone today, so this is the schedule we will follow."

Mr. Lopez shows his students a chart listing the names of the three students he will meet with that day. He explains that he will talk to all 25 students in the following 2 weeks. He also plans to meet one additional time with three students who seem to be struggling with the class rules.

Once the students begin working in their centers, Mr. Lopez calls one student over to a table. He sits with his back to the wall so that he can keep an eye on the entire class. He begins the conference by showing the student a paper from the day before. The student had been asked to color boxes labeled "red," "green," and "yellow," the three colors they have studied so far. The student had also been asked to label sets of objects with the numbers 1, 2, or 3.

"You did a very nice job on this paper, Jerome," Mr. Lopez begins. "You colored all the boxes with the correct colors. You also counted very well. Do you see anything you need to work on?"

"I guess," answers Jerome. "My dad says my numbers are messy."

"Do you want to work on making your numbers neater?" asks Mr. Lopez.

"Yes," responds Jerome. "I want my dad to say they're nice."

"OK, Jerome. That's what we call a *goal,*" explains Mr. Lopez. "Having a goal means you have something to work on. If you're very careful when you're writing your numbers, it will help you to be neater. I'll give you some practice guides so you can see how to make the numbers easily and neatly. You can also practice writing your numbers on the whiteboard during center time. Sometimes that helps people learn how to write them."

Mr. Lopez shows Jerome the conference report form. He writes, "Jerome will work on writing very neatly," reading the sentence aloud as he writes it.

"OK," continues Mr. Lopez. "Now we need to talk about how well you are following the class rules. How do you think you're doing?"

Jerome looks down at his shoes and shrugs his shoulders. "Not too good," he finally replies.

"How can I help you do better?" asks Mr. Lopez.

"Maybe remind me?" suggests Jerome tentatively.

"OK, we'll try that," says Mr. Lopez. "But let's have a signal. If I see you starting to break a rule, I'm going to pull my ear." He demonstrates by pulling his ear. "If you understand that I'm reminding you to follow the rule, you look at me and pull your ear. Do you think that will help you remember?"

"I think so," answers Jerome.

Mr. Lopez writes, "Jerome will remember to follow the rules. Mr. Lopez will remind him by pulling his own ear." As he writes, he reads the goal aloud.

"Thank you, Jerome," says Mr. Lopez as he shakes Jerome's hand. "I will meet with you again in about 2 weeks. We'll see how well you're doing with your number writing and following the rules. Please ask Jenny to come over to talk to me now."

Mr. Lopez confers with three students each day for 2 weeks. He meets with all his students at least once. When he's met with everyone, he has a second meeting with students who are still struggling with their goals.

Ms. Carruthers teaches ninth-grade social studies. She is introducing her students to group work, and she wants them to start to monitor their interactions as they work. To support student reflections, she decides that they need to discuss behaviors that support group efforts.

She begins the discussion: "Since we've been working in groups, I've noticed that some of you are more involved than others. I want you to think about behaviors that help the group be successful. Tell me some of the things a good group member does. I'll write your suggestions on the overhead."

One by one, the students suggest the following:

Everyone needs to read the assignment.

Someone needs to start the discussion.

Everyone needs to listen to other people's ideas.

People need to volunteer to do what needs to be done.

Everyone needs to do a job, not let one person do it all.

Everyone needs to use polite language.

Everyone needs to take notes and make suggestions.

After the students run out of ideas, Ms. Carruthers tells them, "Tomorrow, when we work in groups, I will ask you to evaluate yourself on your group participation. I will

Figure 8.3   Group-Work Self-Evaluation Sheet

Name _____ Date _____

My role in the group _____

What I contributed to the group _____

I encouraged others in the group by _____

I helped the group achieve its goal by _____

I remember to use respectful words

sometimes   most of the time   always

I do my share of the work

sometimes   most of the time   always

I am cooperative with others

sometimes   most of the time   always

Signed _____

My goal for improvement in group work is to _____

_____

Note: A blank, blackline master of this form is included in the Teacher Resources section of this text.

make a self-evaluation sheet for each of you to use, based on the things you said today. After groups tomorrow I will begin to confer with each of you to help you think about how you can improve your work as a group member."

The next day, Ms. Carruthers passes out the self-evaluation sheets to each student. (See Figure 8.3 to see the sheet.) She tells students that she will be circulating around the room during group time and taking notes. "I want you to think about how well you are participating, but sometimes a teacher sees things that you don't notice about yourself. Starting tomorrow, we will be talking about these things."

Ms. Carruthers observes the groups working together and takes copious notes on index cards so she will be able to make suggestions during student conferences. The groups will be working on their projects for the next 2 weeks, and she plans to confer with all students during that time. She will try to talk to each member of one group, taking approximately 2 days per group. She will also videotape some of the group sessions so students can do another self-evaluation to check for progress.

When Ms. Carruthers begins a conference, she first asks the student to look over the self-evaluation sheet. If students have been truthful and accurate in their self-appraisals, she helps them set goals based on their notes and her observation notes. If they've been less than accurate, she makes suggestions for improvement.

At the end of the study Ms. Carruthers asks students to write evaluations of the conferences and the goal-setting process. She wants them to think about whether the conferences have helped them improve their group participation.

 CONCLUSION

Whether you teach kindergarten or high school, it is important to support students in self-evaluation and goal-setting. This process takes time and organization but is worth the effort. From conferences teachers learn a lot about students' approaches to learning, their current levels of functioning, and their ability to evaluate themselves. This method is also a powerful support for students who are learning socially acceptable behaviors. The strength of the process comes from revisiting the goals and keeping a record of discussions. Then the students get the message that these conferences are important.

References

Bridges, L. (1995). *Creating your classroom community*. York, ME: Stenhouse.

Eby, J., Herrell, A., & Jordan, M. (2006). *Teaching in K–12 schools: A reflective action approach.* (4th ed.). Upper Saddle River, NJ: Merrill/Prentice Hall.

Suggested Reading

Schunk, D. H. (1995). Self-efficacy and education and instruction. In J. E. Maddux (Ed.), *Self-efficacy, adaptation, and adjustment: Theory, research, and application* (pp. 281–302). New York: Plenum.

Zimmerman, B. J. (2000). Attaining self-regulation: A social cognitive perspective. In M. Boekaerts, P. R. Pintrich, & M. Zeidner (Eds.), *Handbook of self-regulation* (pp. 13–39). San Diego: Academic Press.

USING CONTRACTS TO BUILD INTRINSIC MOTIVATION

An individual contract can change student work habits, interactions, or behaviors. It is not appropriate for every student but is usually reserved for those who need extra motivation to accomplish goals (Brophy, 2004).

To be successful, contracts depend on student acceptance. The student must recognize the need for change and be willing to adopt a plan for solution (Marshall, 2002). The contract spells out exactly what the student will do to address the area of concern, and both teacher and student sign and date it. There is space on the contract to schedule an upcoming date to review progress. Once goals have been set, this review can take place at the end of a regularly scheduled individual conference.

 STEP BY STEP

The steps for writing and implementing a student contract:

• **Identify specific behaviors or goals to be addressed**   Being specific is key. The student must understand exactly what is expected, and the teacher must suggest a plan that the student can follow. Complex academic challenges or behavior concerns often must be broken into small steps.

• **Involve the student in the conversation**   Before a teacher ever suggests a contract, he or she must verify that the student is willing to work on the problem. Many teachers begin by asking, "Would you like to work on this?" Once the student agrees to set a goal, a contract can be negotiated. By definition, a contract is an agreement between two parties: one party agrees to do something, and the other party agrees to do something else in return. If a student can set goals and follow through with them, a contract is not necessary. A contract is intended to create extra leverage for teachers working with students who consistently have difficulty changing behaviors.

FOCUS ON ENGLISH LEARNERS

One-to-one conversations allow English learners to hear and respond to standard English and enable the teacher to provide individual feedback.

Figure 9.1 Andrew's Work Contract

I, Andrew Jones, agree to complete my assigned work each day before lunchtime. For each day that I finish before lunch, Ms. Rivers will allow me 5 extra minutes of free-time activity. If, at the end of the week, I have completed my work every day, Ms. Rivers will allow me to do free-time activities with my friends instead of by myself. I understand that my friends and I must work quietly enough so that we don't disturb the other students.

Signed on this 19th day of September, 2006.

_____   _____
Student's signature   Teacher's signature

- **Establish the incentive** To support student accomplishments, contracts usually involve incentives. Incentives must be tailored to each student but be appropriate for a learning environment. Stay away from material rewards. Instead, offer free reading time, work with a self-selected partner, extra computer time, or the chance to listen to music (on headphones) when completing in-class writing assignments.

- **Draw up the contract** The contract is formally written, word-processed, signed, and dated. The elements must be specific and the expectations clear. See Figure 9.1 for an example of an academic contract.

- **Monitor student progress** Check in with the student each day to monitor progress. Acknowledge progress with a thumbs-up signal, verbal encouragement, or any other brief celebration.

- **Follow up on the appointed date** At the next conference, discuss student progress. If the student has accomplished his or her goals, follow up with the incentive. If the student has made progress but has not met the goals, extend or revise the contract. Never award the incentive unless the student fully meets the terms of the contract. This is often difficult for teachers. Keep the conference positive; and if the student is nearing the goal, agree to meet again in a week or two to review progress.

- **Acknowledge the student's accomplishment** When the student has accomplished the goal, celebrate that accomplishment with the rest of the learning community. Keep it simple, but let other students know how hard the student has worked and how important it is for him or her to set goals and accomplish them.

- **Move from the incentive to the intrinsic** The student's feeling of accomplishment after fulfilling a contract becomes the basis of a discussion between student and teacher. Point out that the feeling of doing something well is much more powerful than a simple incentive. Discuss the importance of being a worker who does the best work possible and the feeling of pride that emerges from doing quality work. Help the student realize that he or she has the ability do what is required. If additional contracts are needed to keep the student working well and confidently, begin decreasing incentives and eventually eliminate them, moving the student toward self-motivation and intrinsic rewards.

Applications and Examples

Ms. Rivers's second-graders are quickly becoming a learning community. Most students are taking responsibility for their behavior and moving toward producing quality academic work. But one student, Andrew, is having great difficulty completing assignments. He seems distracted by classroom movement and spends too much time socializing instead of applying himself to his work.

When Ms. Rivers meets with Andrew, she first encourages him by pointing out the things he is doing well. She then asks if there is anything he feels he needs to improve.

"I guess I need to finish my work," he says sheepishly. "You're always reminding me to get back to work."

"Yes," agrees Ms. Rivers, "you do spend a lot of time watching the other students or visiting with your friends. What do you think you can do about that?"

"I don't know," replies Andrew. "It's hard to keep working when your friends are all finished and getting to choose their free-time activities."

"I hear you saying that you would like to finish your work more quickly so you can have more free time," says Ms. Rivers.

"Yes!" responds Andrew with a big smile.

"I think this is the goal we need to address," says Ms. Rivers. "What can we do to make it happen?"

"Maybe I need to do my work in the study carrel," suggests Andrew. "Then my friends wouldn't bother me."

"That's an excellent suggestion, Andrew," answers Ms. Rivers. "That's good thinking. If you aren't distracted by your friends, maybe you can complete your work and get to choose some free-time activities."

"If I start finishing my work," asks Andrew, "can my friends and I do free-time activities together?"

I think that can be arranged," responds Ms. Rivers with a smile. "Let's make this official. I'm going to draw up a contract for us both to sign. For every day that you complete your work on time, you can have 5 extra minutes of free-time activity. If you finish your work every day this week, you and your friends can do free-time activities together on Friday. Does that sound fair?"

"Yes! I can do that," says Andrew. "But I think I need to work in the carrel."

Ms. Rivers types and prints the contract, and she and Andrew sign it. He moves his papers to the study carrel and settles down to work. Ms. Rivers feels sure that Andrew is on the way to becoming a worker. Figure 9.1 shows the contract she and Andrew signed.

In a learning community Ms. Rivers has learned that students have different needs. She wants to help them learn to solve their problems, so she offers them some choice in their studying situations. She has created some portable study carrels by purchasing science-project trifold boards that can be placed on a flat table to create a private sanctuary for students who need less visual stimulation. The study carrel proves to be a great technique to help Andrew work with less time off task.

Mr. Sanders has an interesting student in his 11th-grade calculus class. David is extremely gifted in math but seems less than motivated by Mr. Sanders's class. He has earned an almost perfect score on his PSAT, but he never does his calculus homework, which Mr. Sanders computes as a part of the course grade. As a result, the most promising student in the class never gets an A in calculus.

Mr. Sanders decides to hold a conference with David to try to solve this problem. He begins by asking David what he plans to do after high school.

"I want to be a physicist and work at Cape Kennedy in the space program," responds David. "I plan to go to college, but I haven't decided where to go yet."

"Your PSAT scores should help you get a scholarship," says Mr. Sanders. "The B's in calculus aren't going to help you, though."

"I've wanted to talk to you about that," begins David tentatively. "The homework is such a waste of time. Is there any way I could do something else instead?"

Normally, Mr. Sanders would argue that homework is *not* a waste of time. But he doesn't feel he can make that point with David, who rarely makes any mistakes on his tests.

"I hear you," Mr. Sanders says, "but you need to develop some discipline in your study habits if you are going to do well in challenging college classes. I'm willing to have you do something else for homework. What do you have in mind?"

"How long do you figure everyone else spends on calculus homework every night?" asks David.

"Well . . . not the *hours* they claim to spend," responds Mr. Sanders with a smile. "I think a half hour each night should get it done."

"Well, suppose I spend half an hour each night doing calculus problems that relate to something I'm working on," suggests David.

"I'll agree to that, on one condition," says Mr. Sanders. "Find a practical application for the calculus solutions we study in class each day, do some problems to show how they work, and then share what you've found with the class. Maybe that will help other students see how practical calculus can be."

"Will this substitute for my homework grades?" asks David.

"It sure will. I want to write up a formal contract, though. You agree to spend at least 30 minutes on calculus each evening, finding practical applications to share with the class. You explain what you've found to the class each day, and I'll use those presentations in computing your grade," says Mr. Sanders.

The contract is written, dated, and signed by both Mr. Sanders and David. David begins working on it that evening and makes his first presentation the next day. Because David is an avid bicycle racer, he uses integral calculus to find the power output necessary on his mountain bike to complete the climb on a familiar local hill. He explains that, with front gears of 39 and 53 teeth each, and nine back gears, he has a range of gearing available from 39/23 to 53/11. He demonstrates how he figures his ability to put out a specific amount of power. He does this by evaluating the power output he has been capable of during his most recent training ride, using a power tap. He then calculates the power output required for each gear ratio by working through the calculus equations that are required for the force vectors involved. He shows the students how he sets up the problem and plugs in his weight, the various gear ratios, and the severity of the climb to obtain the power required for each gear ratio. Finally, he determines which gear ratio would best fit the climb, given his weight, the severity of the climb, the gear ratios available, and the amount of power he is capable of producing. The students are very interested, and Mr. Sanders feels as if he and David have arrived at a win-win solution for a troublesome problem.

 CONCLUSION

Although neither Ms. Rivers nor Mr. Sanders uses contracts with all students, they find them to be extremely helpful in motivating students to self-correct academic or behavioral problems. They try to use them to show students that following the rules and completing their work can be positive behaviors. Both teachers have also found that once students experience success, they are more likely to become contributing members of the class-room community (O'Neil & Drillings, 1994).

References

Brophy, J. (2004). *Motivating students to learn*. Mahwah, NJ: Erlbaum.

Marshall, M. (2002). *Discipline without stress, punishments, or rewards*. Los Alamitos, AZ: Piper.

O'Neil, H., & Drillings, M. (1994). *Motivation: Theory and research*. Hillsdale, NJ: Erlbaum.

Suggested Reading

Alderman, M. (1999). *Motivation for achievement: Possibilities for teaching and learning*. Mahwah, NJ: Erlbaum.

Schunk, D., & Zimmerman, B. (1994). *Self-regulation of learning and performance: Issues and educational applications*. Hillsdale, NJ: Erlbaum.

IMPLEMENTING CLASS MEETINGS

Team-building is vital to developing a community of learners. Make time each day for the class to express concerns and celebrate successes. Class meetings provide a perfect forum for this interaction (Glasser, 1969).

Develop procedures and expectations for the smooth, responsible operation of classroom meetings. This gives both teacher and students an opportunity to interact in a responsible, caring environment and opens the door to new voices and ideas.

Class meetings involve students in making decisions, solving problems, and offering suggestions for the good of the group. To ensure that meetings run smoothly and respectfully, class members must establish rules and strictly follow them. Donna Styles, author of *Class Meetings: Building Leadership, Problem-Solving and Decision-Making Skills in the Respectful Classroom* (2001), recommends that teachers do the following:

- Use a formal process and hold meetings weekly.
- Have all students sit in a circle, facing each other.
- Model respectful behavior.
- Do not dominate the process.
- Trust your students to lead meetings, participate in the process, choose solutions, and make decisions.

Class meetings can serve several purposes. They are commonly used to resolve problems arising from student disagreements. They can also be used to decide on changes in class routines such as seating arrangements or homework expectations.

In the beginning the teacher is the group leader, involving students in setting expectations for respectful interactions, time limits, and rules for conducting the meetings. Once the routine is established, the teacher turns management of the meeting over to a student leader and serves as participant and mediator, if necessary (Styles, 2001).

STEP BY STEP

The steps for conducting class meetings:

- **Seat students in a circle** Students should be seated so they can make eye contact with everyone in the group. They can move their desks into a circle, sit in chairs around a circle, or sit in a circle on the floor.

- **Explain the purpose and expectations for the meeting** Students should be involved in setting the purpose and expectations for meetings. In the first few meetings, this may take some time. But after rules are established, they are briefly reviewed, and meetings begin quickly. Students should understand that class meetings are a time for mutual respect. Establish a method to make sure that no one, even the teacher, monopolizes the discussion. For example, when a student holds a small object, that object designates him or her as the speaker. When the object is passed, the next student has the floor. Such signals are helpful in establishing the expectation that only one person at a time may speak.

- **Establish the agenda** The teacher sets up a class-meeting agenda box in the room. The students may submit agenda items using a form that they complete. See Figure 10.1 for an example of a class-meeting item form.

  The teacher looks through the submitted agenda items and works with a committee of three or four students to decide which can best be resolved in a class meeting. If working with a pair of students to solve a particular problem seems best, the teacher has that option. If one student is mentioned on a number of submitted items, the teacher must make a judgment call. The class meeting is a good forum to discuss these problems once students have a firm grasp of the respectfulness rule.

  At the beginning of the meeting, the teacher or student leader briefly shares what has been submitted. The group collectively sets the agenda for the day. A time limit is set on each agenda item, and the discussion can begin.

- **Begin with compliments** To set a positive tone, students are given an opportunity to compliment one another. One student may thank another for help or recognize someone's good behavior or kindness. The meeting leader can ask for volunteers at this stage or pass an object (such as a flag) around the circle. Receiving the object does not obligate anyone to speak. Students may choose to pass it to the next person, saying, "I pass," or "I have nothing to add."

- **Conduct the discussion** Students are allowed to discuss the problem, sharing their views and experiences as long as they stay respectful and take turns. The teacher or a designated timekeeper watches the clock. When discussion time has elapsed, the leader calls for solutions.

- **Brainstorm solutions** Students suggest solutions, which are written on the board or a chart tablet. The teacher may serve as scribe, or a student may be designated. All suggestions are written down without judgment. After the list is complete, the group votes on which solution to try first. An alternative solution may also be chosen in case the first proves unsuccessful. Remember that class meetings are an exercise in learning to

Figure 10.1 Agenda Item Form for Class Meetings

Name _____ Date _____

Class-meeting agenda item _____

_____

If this is a problem with another student, how have you tried to work it out?

cooperate in making good decisions, and students should understand that backup plans are sometimes necessary.

 • **Move through the agenda**   The group leader must keep the agenda moving. Teachers may want to hold class meetings at the end of the day or right before lunch to ensure that they do not exceed 15 to 20 minutes for young children or 30 to 45 minutes for older students (Styles, 2001).

 • **Review the plan**   At the end of the meeting, briefly review the plan and note the next meeting date. Make it clear that an emergency meeting can be called before the next scheduled meeting, if necessary.

Applications and Examples

Mrs. Saunders and her third-graders have been working on using words of respect since the beginning of the year. Now it is almost Halloween, and Mrs. Saunders feels the students are ready to begin class meetings. She starts by explaining to the class, "I have made a box to use for sharing classroom suggestions or problems. Once a week, I will ask some of you to help me decide which of the suggestions should be discussed in a class meeting. We will hold our first class meeting on Wednesday, so if you have anything you would like to discuss at the meeting, you can fill out one of these forms. On the form you must write your name and the date. You also write your suggestion. It can be something you would like us to try out in the classroom or a problem you think we need to solve. However, if your problem involves another student, you need to try to solve that problem with the student before you submit it to the class. Do you have any questions?"

The students have lots of questions about issues that can be submitted for the meeting. They want to know if they can use the meetings to change some of the class rules, ask to have someone punished for bad behavior, or even eliminate homework.

Mrs. Saunders responds by reminding them of their responsibilities as members of a learning community. "We can discuss any of these things," she says. "But we need to make responsible decisions. We don't want to do anything to hurt anyone in our community, but we want to find ways to make things work more efficiently. You will be able to suggest punishments for rule breakers, though."

After all the questions, Mrs. Saunders decides to make some posters spelling out the roles of students, teacher, and group leader during class meetings. She posts and reviews the posters just before the first class meeting. Figure 10.2 shows those posters.

FOCUS ON ENGLISH LEARNERS

Visual cues help English learners process information, which aids in English development.

Figure 10.2   Class Meetings

The teacher	**The group leader**	**The other students**
• Acts as part of the group • Serves as secretary • Serves as mentor to the group leader	• Keeps the meeting running smoothly • Opens and closes the meeting • Follows the agenda • Keeps discussions on topic • Lets students know if they are out of order	• Speak respectfully • Talk one at a time • Participate in solving problems • Support group decisions

Before the first meeting, Mrs. Saunders asks the table captains to help her read through the class-meeting agenda items that have been submitted. There are several suggestions about rotating table assignments and rearranging table groups, so the committee decides it's a good item for the agenda. There are also some complaints about not enough playground balls. Three students have submitted complaints about a boy who has been too rough at recess. All three of the students say they have already asked him not to play roughly. The committee decides to put all three items on the agenda. Mrs. Saunders asks the table captains if any of them would like to serve as group leader for the meeting. Since no one is willing to serve, Mrs. Saunders says she will conduct the first meeting. But she tells them she wants one of them to try acting as group leader with her support. One student agrees to serve as leader as long as Mrs. Saunders agrees to help her.

At the beginning of the first meeting, Mrs. Saunders announces that Ginny has agreed to serve as group leader. Ginny explains that the committee has set the agenda to include the following:

1. Plans for rotating seat assignments
2. Need for more playground balls
3. Playground behavior

Ginny asks if anyone has any emergency issues to add to the list. Since no one has any more items, Ginny shows the class the Peace Bear she has brought from home. "This is a Care Bear who works for peace. Since we want our class to work peacefully, we will use him to help us remember to take turns talking. When you are holding Peaceful you are allowed to speak. If you want to speak, ask for Peaceful by raising your hand. We're going to start our meeting by sharing good things we've noticed happening in our classroom or school this week. We'll pass Peaceful around. When he comes to you, you may share something good or give a compliment. If you don't have anything you want to share, just pass Peaceful to the next person."

The first class meeting is off to a good start. The class decides to keep the discussions to 5 minutes for each item, and they come up with lots of suggestions for solutions to the agenda ideas. They decide to draw names for table assignments once a month, petition the principal for additional playground balls, and adopt a "no touching each other rule" on the playground, since some of the students have trouble deciding when a touch is friendly and when it's too hard. There is a long conversation about "accidental touching," and it is decided that an apology would solve that problem. They agree to try this new rule for a week to see if it's working. If anyone breaks the rule on a regular basis, the agreed-on punishment is to lose recess for a day.

Mrs. Saunders is pleased with the results of the first meeting. She intervenes minimally, and Ginny does a good job as group leader. Peaceful the bear is a good symbol to pass, and that was Ginny's idea. The community seems to be growing nicely.

Miss Lyons's eighth-grade students meet in a 2-hour block for language arts and history. She is encouraging them to maintain classroom materials and file their own work in portfolios but notices that some students are not contributing to the classroom duties. She decides to hold a class meeting. Since her students have not participated in class meetings before, she sets up the expectations in advance. She has students move their chairs into a circle and begins the meeting with a brief explanation of the meeting's purpose. She asks students to share any positive comments they have about the way other students are working to keep class materials in order.

Several students note that Kelly and Amanda are both working hard to make sure the class is cleaned up and everything put away before the end of the period. One of the students says he thinks Kelly and Amanda do too much, since everyone is supposed to be helping. Miss Lyons writes, "How can we make sure everyone contributes to keeping the room neat?" on the chalkboard.

"I would like to make this our first agenda item," she says. "If you want to continue to have class meetings, we can use this process to help us solve other problems as well."

Since the students work in table groups, six students to a table, the class decides that each group should be responsible for its area. They agree that everyone should help and no one should be responsible for the entire room.

"What should we do if we have someone at our table who is not helping?" asks Jeremy.

"Vote him off the island," responds David. "If he's not doing his share, have him sit by himself for a while."

Several other students have suggestions, but the class thinks that David's suggestion makes sense. They decide to try the new approach for a week and then meet to see if they need to come up with another solution.

Miss Lyons asks students to make suggestions about anything that needs to be addressed at future meetings. She convenes a committee to prepare a suggestion box and agenda item forms for suggestions. She also asks students to think about volunteering as group leader for class meetings. David immediately volunteers, and the class votes to accept his offer. He agrees to work with the suggestion box committee to review suggested agenda items before the next meeting, which is set for the following Friday.

Miss Lyons thinks the students have arrived at some good solutions. She plans to meet with the suggestion committee when it goes through the suggestion box and begin to develop an agenda and rules for class meetings, which they will later present to the whole class.

CONCLUSION

According to Glasser (1969), class meetings are a forum in which the teacher and students can jointly discuss and solve problems of behavior and other class matters. Class meetings allow teachers to help students develop communication skills, learn to look at situations from other points of view, and begin to understand the process of solving problems in groups. All these skills will be highly valued by future employers and will improve students' future personal relationships.

STRATEGY ON VIDEO
Implementing Class Meetings

Class meetings are demonstrated in first grade and middle school on segment 3 of the DVD that accompanies this text. Watch carefully to see the sequence that each teacher uses to involve students in the discussion. As you watch this segment think about the following:

- How does a class meeting change as students get older?
- In what ways do both teachers demonstrate their belief in the abilities of their students?

References

Glasser, W. (1969). *Schools without failure.* New York: Harper & Row.

Styles, D. (2001). *Class meetings: Building leadership, problem-solving and decision-making skills in the respectful classroom.* Toronto: Pembroke.

Suggested Reading

Child Development Project. (1996). *Ways we want our class to be: Class meetings that build commitment to kindness and learning.* Oakland, CA: Developmental Studies Center.

BUILDING RESPONSIBILITY FOR THEIR OWN ACTIONS AND WORDS IN THE MEMBERS OF THE LEARNING COMMUNITY

This group of strategies provides a sequence of concepts and techniques necessary to build responsibility for their own actions and words in students involved in a community of learners. Participation in a learning community goes far beyond the normal student responsibilities of keeping on task and completing work. Members of a learning community are responsible to one another, responsible for helping to maintain the community as a whole, and responsible for making sure their words and actions are supportive of one another and the good of the learning atmosphere. One model for teaching responsibility that has been successful in several educational settings is the Teaching Personal and Social Responsibility Model (TPSR) designed by Don Hellison (1995). This model was developed to help students learn to be responsible by giving them increasing amounts of responsibility and gradually giving them more responsibility for making decisions in the classroom. See Figure IV.1 for a summary of Hellison's model.

Strategies in this section are used for many purposes. Teachers model the power of positive verbal interactions and hold the students accountable for using positive words in their interactions with other students and adults in the classroom and school. Teachers set up classroom structures that support students as they learn to resolve conflicts.

In a collaborative learning community the students become very actively involved in all aspects of the community. They learn to resolve conflicts and to serve as peer mentors when their colleagues are in need of support. They also learn to think from the other person's point of view and to make compromises for the good of the group. None of this occurs naturally but must be modeled and taught.

All of this requires careful planning and modeling on the part of the teacher but pays off handsomely in student involvement and responsibility. Brian Cambourne (1990) in his study of effective teachers found that modeling, responsibility, and active student engagement are three very important conditions for learning in the classroom. This section of the text focuses first on the importance of choosing words that facilitate communication rather than conflict. Strategies for the teacher confronted with disrespectful or angry students are explored. Strategies for conflict management and moving students into solving their own conflicts, eliminating bullying, and using outside resources when necessary are also addressed in this section.

Figure IV.1   Important Theory

Don Hellison

Don Hellison is a professor of kinesiology at the University of Illinois at Chicago. His research focuses on the development, implementation, and evaluation of alternative physical education programs and teaching students to take more responsibility for their own well-being and the well-being of others. His Teaching Personal and Social Responsibility Model (TPSR) promotes self and social responsibility by empowering students to take responsibility for their own lives and to be concerned about the rights, feelings, and needs of others.

Hellison places the achievement of responsibility outcomes into a progression of levels that teachers and students can use to become aware of their behaviors and more sensitive to the needs of others. His levels describe the movement from irresponsibility to responsibility, from respect for oneself to respect and concern for others.

The levels in the TPSR model are

1. Respect (self-control)   Students at this level are able to control their behaviors (with very little teacher direction) to avoid interfering with other students' right to learn.
2. Participation (involvement)   Students at this level show respect for others and participate willingly in classroom activities. They should have an understanding of the role of effort and persistence in improving their learning and skill levels.
3. Self-direction (self-responsibility)   Students at this level work without direct supervision and take on more responsibility for their own well-being. They are able to work independently on personally-set goals.
4. Caring   Students at this level respect others, participate, are self-directed, and extend their responsibility to cooperation with others, giving support, showing concern, and helping others.
5. Concern outside of school   Students at this level apply the behaviors described above at home and in the community.
6. Work and leisure   Students at this level are able to make connections between the levels of responsibility and the adult world of work and leisure.

References

Hellison's published works include the following:

Hellison, D. (1995). *Teaching responsibility through physical activity.* Champaign, IL: Human Kinetics.

Hellison, D. (1999). Promoting character development through sport: Rhetoric or reality? *New Designs for Youth Development, 15*(1), 23–27.

Hellison, D., & Templin, T. (1991). *A reflective approach to teaching physical education.* Champaign, IL: Human Kinetics.

References

Cambourne, B. (1990). *Whole story: Natural learning and the acquisition of literacy.* New York: Scholastic.

Hellison, D. (1995). *Teaching responsibility through physical activity.* Champaign, IL: Human Kinetics.

USING WORDS POSITIVELY: MODELING AND PRACTICING

The teacher serves as a powerful model in providing examples of ways for students to support one another with words of encouragement, questions for clarification, and entry to collaboration. Just modeling is not enough, however. Students must become fully aware of the ways in which their words help to support an environment for collaboration and communication. The teacher must constantly be observing in order to recognize and bring attention to students' use of powerful, positive verbal interactions (Bridges, 1995.)

Many students have little or no experience in the use of positive, supportive words in communicating with other students. Because of the highly competitive atmosphere in many classrooms in the United States, the concept of using communication skills to support another student or build a collaborative task must be explained, modeled, and reinforced consistently.

 STEP BY STEP

The steps in modeling and practicing the use of positive words:

• **Model and make positive interactions visible**   Introduce the power of positive words by modeling ways to encourage others, ask questions for clarification, or gain entry into a group. As these different situations are introduced, present good and poor examples of verbal interactions.

• **Discuss the impact of word choices**   Provide examples, encouraging a discussion of how the words, both negative and positive, make a listener feel.

• **Provide daily feedback**   During the day collect examples of positive verbal interactions and use these actual classroom examples to help students begin to self-monitor their choice of words in verbal interactions.

• **Monitor and hold students accountable**   Monitor verbal interactions and encourage students to give each other feedback if and when positive words are not being used. The expectation that positive verbal interactions in the classroom are always expected should be clearly stated and reinforced daily.

- **Discuss and celebrate student progress**   In the beginning of the school year hold daily discussions using examples of positive and negative word choices heard in the classroom and celebrating progress. As the year moves along, this type of discussion should not be necessary daily, but positive examples should be recognized and reinforced on a regular basis.

Applications and Examples

To introduce the power of positive words in his fourth-grade classroom Mr. Jordan divides his class into four groups. Each group selects one student who is asked to wait in the hallway. Once the four students are out of the classroom, Mr. Jordan explains the task to be accomplished when they come back into the classroom: "When the four students come back in, I will give each of them this simple puzzle to put together. I want the two groups in the front of the room to use positive words to encourage your team members as they work on the puzzle. You can say that they're doing great, they're really good at this, they look like they're good puzzle builders, they're doing well . . . things like that.

"The two groups in the back of the room are going to do just exactly the opposite. No matter what your students do, use negative words like 'Oh no!' Tell them they're doing it wrong, that's the wrong piece, that won't fit, or they're not too good at this . . . things like that."

The students enjoy the activity and get into the swing of it easily. The two students who receive encouragement quickly finish their puzzles, while the other two students seem frustrated and are angry with their peers. Once the two students in the front of the room have finished their puzzles, Mr. Jordan stops the others and asks the puzzle builders how they feel.

"I can't believe how mean my group was to me," says Jennifer. "They were saying awful things to me, and it made me so mad I couldn't think. I'm usually good at puzzle building."

Mr. Jordan explains the purpose of the activity and leads a discussion of the importance of providing support and encouragement to one another in the classroom.

"I'm sure going to think before I say anything discouraging," says Jennifer. "That made me feel awful."

"I never realized how much help it is to have people cheering for me," adds Ramon.

"That's going to be our class project this year," says Mr. Jordan. "We are going to be cheering for one another, and we'll all learn more that way."

Mrs. Burdette and her seventh-graders are working on narrative stories about a time when they had to solve a problem. The students have already done a prewriting activity in which they identified the characters in the story they will write, the problem that needs to be solved, two steps in the problem-solving process, and the solution they will employ. Using this brief outline for each of their stories, each student takes a turn in the author's chair.

"As you sit in the author's chair, you should briefly explain the outline you have made for your story," she explains. "The rest of the class will be listening carefully to your outline and then will ask questions. The class should be thinking of questions to ask that cannot be answered with a yes or no response. The idea of this activity is to help the author understand the types of things the readers are interested in knowing about as they read the story. It will also help the author get ideas for expanding the outline. The class should be listening to the questions and thinking about how they could answer the same types of questions about their own story when it is their turn in the author's chair. Each of you will have a turn to share your outline in the author's chair. This will help you begin to write your story and include enough detail to make it interesting to the reader."

Figure 11.1   Clarifying Questions

About the Characters	About the Sequence of Events
What did this character look like? Why did this character do that? How did the main character feel about this character? What might he be thinking while this is taking place?	What took place first? What was the last thing you did? How can you make the middle part more exciting?

"Can you give us an example of the type of questions we should ask?" queries Carlos.

"Yes, Carlos," responds Mrs. Burdette. "And by the way, that question was a wonderful example of a clarifying question. You needed more information, and you worded the question well. Now I know exactly what type of information you need. You might ask questions about many different elements of the story. You could ask about the sequence of events, such as what happens first or exactly when certain events take place. Anything in the story that needs clarification as you listen to the outline may be the source for a question. The purpose of your questions is to identify areas where the author has not made the story clear or areas that are interesting to you and warrant more detail or description."

She continues: "Let's make a chart together. Suppose you want to know more about the main characters in the story. What questions might you ask the author?" Mrs. Burdette leads the class through an exercise in which they think of possible clarifying questions, and they create a chart together. See Figure 11.1 for the chart they created.

FOCUS ON ENGLISH LEARNERS

English learners benefit from visual cues that they can use to become more active participants.

After Mrs. Burdette and the class complete the chart with examples of clarifying questions, she draws a student's name from a box containing all the names of students in the class and asks the student chosen to take a seat in the author's chair. The other students listen attentively as the student explains the elements to be included in his story and then they begin to ask clarifying questions. When confusion arises about the exact information the questioner requires, Mrs. Burdette intervenes to help the student reword the question more clearly.

After the first question-and-answer session, the students are given time to work on their stories using some of the information gained from the activity. Each day for the next few weeks one student begins the writing period by answering questions from the author's chair. As the days pass, each author has fewer questions to answer. The questions asked and answered by previous students have already helped them incorporate more ideas and descriptions into their stories based on their clarifying questions.

CONCLUSION

Both Mr. Jordan and Mrs. Burdette know that students need practice in becoming encouragers. Because of this, they plan activities that help their students understand how powerful words can be in classroom interactions. They don't expect perfection from their students, but they practice what they preach by encouraging the students as they begin to practice this new verbal skill.

References

Bridges, L. (1995). *Creating your classroom community*. York, ME: Stenhouse.

Suggested Reading

Heller, P. G. (1995). *Drama as a way of knowing*. York, ME: Stenhouse.

Short, K., Harste, J., & Burke, C. (1995). *Creating classrooms for authors and inquirers* (2nd ed.). Portsmouth, NH: Heinemann.

AVOIDING POWER STRUGGLES IN THE CLASSROOM

Personal empowerment and a feeling of self-worth are important to everyone. Unfortunately, in every classroom, we have students who suffer from deficits in these areas. It is these students who are most likely to engage in power struggles (Glasser, 1988).

Every teacher has experienced a confrontation with a student in which the student is asked to do something and simply refuses or lashes out in anger. When the teacher reacts angrily, the situation becomes a power struggle. It is vital to avoid these types of interactions and to respond to the student in a calm and controlled manner. The teacher should realize that these challenges are generally not personal in nature and should react

FOCUS ON ENGLISH LEARNERS

When working with English learners, be extremely careful not to interpret misunderstanding as misbehavior.

appropriately and professionally. Once we recognize and accept that these confrontations are not personal attacks, it's easier to approach their resolution in a controlled manner. There are several proven approaches to defusing volatile situations, but all require teachers to remain calm and in control (Braithwaite, 2001).

As with any confrontational situation in the classroom, the message to a defiant student should always be "Your behavior is unacceptable, and we need to find a solution." Solutions cannot be found when people are shouting at one another, so the sequence of interactions must be controlled, at least on the teacher's part.

STEP BY STEP

The steps in avoiding power struggles:

• **Disengage from the struggle** The most important thing to remember when confronted with a defiant or noncompliant student is to remain outwardly calm. If you have a student with whom conflicts are common, practice responding in a calm manner in front of a mirror. No matter what else you do, respond to the situation rather than react to it. Disengaging from the struggle means you remain calm and professional and don't react to the student's anger or disrespect. See Figure 12.1 for disengaging tactics.

Figure 12.1 Disengaging Tactics

Response	Explanation
Maintain self-control	Take a deep breath and release it slowly. This gives you time to plan an appropriate response (Braithwaite, 2001)
Speak calmly	Respond to the student in a neutral tone. Keep your response calm and businesslike (Mayer, 2000).
Be brief	Short teacher responses give the student less chance to escalate the confrontation or obtain negative attention from the interaction (Sprick, Borgmeier, & Nolet, 2002).
Don't overreact	If a student comment is merely annoying, ignore it. If it contains an insult or challenge to authority, briefly state in a neutral tone that the remark was inappropriate, impose a preselected consequence, and move on (Walker, 1997).

• **Interrupt the escalation** Whenever you observe that a situation is developing, you can interrupt the interaction before it gets out of hand. Occasionally, a student becomes unable to control his own anger, and the situation erupts quickly. Nevertheless, you must remain calm and respond in a neutral tone while using a tactic to interrupt the escalating anger. See Figure 12.2 for interrupting tactics.

• **De-escalate the conflict** When a student is very angry or upset, he often uses poor judgment and acts impulsively. You must have at your disposal several techniques for supporting the student in de-escalating his anger. These tactics reduce the student's sense of threat or defensiveness and lower emotional tension. After the de-escalation occurs, you and the student can begin to talk about the causes and consequences relative to the action. The student does not avoid punishment for confrontational behavior, but you maintain control by defusing the student's anger, giving him time to cool down, and then discussing the problem, finding a solution, and assigning appropriate consequences. Tactics for defusing the student's anger and helping him to calm down are suggested in Figure 12.3.

• **Identify the problem and find solutions** Once the volatile situation is defused, you and the student need to meet and discuss the problem and devise some possible solutions. You can then assign consequences if the student has been disrespectful to her or to another student. A contract may be negotiated to make your expectations for future behavior clear and obtain the student's commitment to improving future interactions. (See Chapter 9 for information on student contracts.) As throughout the sequence of events leading to this conference, you must remain calm and professional. The student must come away from the meeting feeling that the teacher is concerned about him, is committed to supporting him in solving the problem, and expects behavioral changes.

• **Recognize effort and progress** Once a course of action is agreed upon, you should provide recognition to the student for his efforts in working toward improvement. Be very specific about noting progress. Use words such as "I noticed today that you walked away from a confrontation with Gina. I saw you use the cool-down space to get yourself under control. That was very mature behavior."

Figure 12.2   Interrupting an Escalating Confrontation

Tactic	Explanation
Diversion	If the student is showing only low-level defiant or noncompliant behavior, you may be able to redirect the student's attention to another topic.
Time away	If the student is becomes argumentative with other students or acting defiant toward adults, you may want to send him on an errand to get him out of the classroom and give him time to regain composure.
Cool down	Every classroom should contain a calming spot. Any place in the classroom where students can sit and regain their composure will work. It should be discussed in advance of any confrontations and be available for students who recognize their own need for cooling-down time. You may use study carrels, confined spaces such as teepees, large cardboard boxes, or simply a desk set away from classroom traffic for this purpose. Be sure the area is clearly visible so you can monitor the student at all times. Use calming words to send the student to cool down. ("Jerry, I want to talk to you about this, but first I need you to calm down.")
Paraphrasing	Sometimes the student's anger escalates because he feels no one is listening to him. Paraphrase the student's concern, using words such as "It sounds as if you are concerned about...." With active listening you demonstrate respect for the student's point of view. It also may help clarify the problem (Lanceley, 1999).
Open-ended questions	Ask *who, what, where,* and *how* questions to clarify the problem and look for solutions. Avoid asking *why?* This can imply that you are blaming the student (Lanceley, 1999). The point of questioning is to make sure you understand the problem and are looking for possible solutions along with the student.

Applications and Examples

Ms. Irons teaches kindergarten in an urban school. Her students often come to her without preschool experiences and so she works hard at helping them learn to be members of a classroom community. She spends a lot of time at the beginning of the school year modeling acceptable behavior and making the students aware of the classroom expectations.

Ms. Irons has set up a cool-down corner in her classroom. She brought in a cardboard refrigerator box, and the students helped her paint it to look like a house. The box is nice and roomy and has a window in the side so that the teacher can see the student at all times. She explains to them that the house is a place for them to go and calm down if they're feeling angry or upset.

One day during free-play time, Ms. Irons notices that Bruce is having trouble. She watches for a minute and then realizes that he is getting angry at Peter, because Peter is

Figure 12.3 Strategies for Reducing Student Anger

Approach	Explanation
Use positive words	When your request is stated positively, you are more likely to inspire responsiveness. Replace "Get back to your seat; you're interrupting the reading group" with "Wait at your desk, and I can help you as soon as I finish with this reading group."
Use nonverbal strategies	Confrontations can escalate because of nonverbal signals such as finger wagging, arm crossing, or even negative facial expressions. Watch your body language and use deliberate calming strategies. Sit down next to the student, and lengthen your pauses between responses to slow down the interchanges. Lean toward the student to show interest, and be aware of your facial expression. Keep it neutral.
Acknowledge the student's choice	Make the student responsible for the choice. "You may choose to sit with your head down, not completing your work, and stay in during recess to finish up. Or you may choose to finish now so that you don't miss recess." Just make sure you acknowledge the student's choice in a neutral, calm voice, and then walk away.
Offer a face-saving route	Ask a question such as "Is there any way we can resolve this so you will feel comfortable about cooperating?" Be prepared for a sarcastic remark in return and simply ignore it. Then repeat the question. Often the second question produces a more positive response (Thompson & Jenkins, 1993).
Use humor	By responding with humor to a defiant student, you give her an opportunity to save face. Be sure you don't use sarcasm, which makes things worse. After the situation is defused and the student has calmed down, meet with her and discuss the situation so that she understands the inappropriateness of her behavior (Braithwaite, 2001).
Label the emotion	When you observe a student slamming his books down on the desk as he enters the room, go over to the student and quietly ask, "Ken, you seem angry. Can you tell me what's wrong?" This often gives the student a chance to vent without continuing the acting-out behavior and averts a confrontation.
Examine the cause	Be sensitive to confrontations that may arise because the student feels threatened or exposed. Asking a student to perform a task for which she is unprepared may cause an angry reaction.

banging blocks on the table as Bruce, who is sitting next to Peter, is trying to draw. She goes over to the table and calmly moves Peter and his blocks to the next table, saying calmly, "I think the block banging is bothering Bruce. Let's move you over here where you won't bother anyone."

Once Peter is moved, she goes back to Bruce and says, "I see that you are angry, Bruce. Is there anything I can do?"

Bruce answers her with anger in his voice, "I hate Peter. He made me mess up."

"Do you need a new piece of paper?" Ms. Irons asks calmly.

"NO! I want Peter to not sit by me anymore!" shouts Bruce.

"Well, I hear you," responds Ms. Irons, "but before I move you, I want you to think about how you could have solved this problem without getting upset. Go sit in the cool-down house for a while, and once you've calmed down, we'll talk about it."

Bruce stomps off to sit in the cool-down house, and Ms. Irons goes to Peter and asks him what he could have done differently.

"I could have moved, but I wanted to sit by Bruce. He's my friend," Peter replies. "Only now he's not." He begins to cry.

"Why don't you tell him that you're sorry and you want to be his friend. But wait 'til he calms down first. We'll talk about it together then," says Ms. Irons.

Peter stops crying, and Ms. Irons goes back to monitoring the class activities. A little while later Bruce comes to her and tells her that he's ready to talk. She talks to him for a while and then calls Peter over to apologize. Bruce decides that he still wants to sit by Peter and will move to another table if the situation should arise again. Ms. Irons is pleased with the progress her five-year-olds are making in learning to solve problems.

Mr. Stanton teaches 11th-grade chemistry, and a number of his students find the subject challenging. He has one student in particular, Marvin, who comes to class late every day. Marvin manages to manipulate his lab partner into doing most of the work whenever they have lab assignments, and his own work is slipshod, to say the least.

Mr. Stanton has decided that he has to put a stop to Marvin's late arrivals, which disrupt the class and necessitate his repeating instructions almost every day. He plans to talk to Marvin about the problem but wants to avoid a power struggle, so he thinks about possible approaches. The next day, when Marvin comes in late again, slams down his books, and plops into his chair, Mr. Stanton goes over to Marvin's desk and quietly says, "You seem upset, Marvin. Is there something I can do to help you?"

"Like you're really interested in my problems," Marvin replies.

"Well, believe it or not, I asked because I am interested," Mr. Stanton replies. "But let's not get into that now. The students have already begun on today's lab. Rachel probably needs your help. Stay for a minute after class and let's talk about this."

"Are you giving me a detention?" asks Marvin angrily. "I didn't do anything."

Mr. Stanton takes a deep breath and answers calmly, "No, Marvin, I am *not* giving you a detention, but we do need to talk. I think outside of class is the place to do that, or we can talk now and you can do the lab by yourself later, or you can work with Rachel and we'll talk after class. It's your choice."

"Oh, OK! I'd rather work with my partner," Marvin responds and moves off to his lab station.

After class Mr. Stanton begins the conversation by saying, "Marvin, you are a smart guy. You have no problems with the chemistry work, but I want to see you getting the full benefit from the class. I need you to come to class on time so I don't have to disrupt class in order to repeat instructions for you. You need to begin to take responsibility for that. What can I do to help you?"

"Nothing, that's the problem," Marvin replies. "My dad wants me to work in his carpet stores when I graduate. He doesn't see any reason for me to go to college, so none of this high school stuff is important. I just need to get out and go to work for him."

"I hear you saying that you want to go to college," replies Mr. Stanton.

"Well, that's right. But my dad is not going to change his mind. He says he never went to college and he owns 16 carpet stores. He says he wants me to learn the business the way he did," Marvin says.

"Well, it seems to me that you would be more help to him if you learned something about the carpet business that he can't do himself," Mr. Stanton suggests. "Think about that. What does he need in the business that he has to pay for?"

"Well, OK, I see where you're going with this. He hires a lawyer, and an accountant, and an advertising company. And he's always complaining about how much those guys charge him," Marvin replies, obviously thinking about the situation. "OK, I get it. I'll research this. I could do one of those jobs for the company and still get to go to college. I'd even go to State, here in town, so I could work for him part-time while I'm finishing my degree. This is a good idea, Mr. Stanton. Thanks! And I'm sorry I said you weren't interested. And," he adds sheepishly, "I'll be on time to class tomorrow."

"Well, see that you do that," Mr. Stanton replies with a smile. "You need a good grade in chemistry if you're going to college."

 # CONCLUSION

Teachers who plan ahead and prepare a sequence of tactics for dealing with disruptive students and power struggles find that they can be handled with a professional approach. The first tactic may not result in positive responses, however. Teachers must be willing to commit to improving their interactions with students and must convince them that they truly care about them and their success in the classroom. Building a level of trust with these students is paramount to succeeding in changing not only behavior but also their own perceptions of self-worth and self-esteem. Teachers must have an entire repertoire of approaches for these types of interactions. They must also be observant and recognize that the reasons for negative behaviors may be different for each student. The important thing to remember is to stay calm and let the student know that you care about him and that you're willing to work with him. He needs to know that you're *not* going to give up on him.

References

Braithwaite, R. (2001). *Managing aggression*. New York: Routledge.

Glasser, W. (1988). *Choice theory in the classroom*. New York: HarperCollins.

Lanceley, F. (1999). *On-scene guide for crisis negotiators*. Boca Raton, FL: CRC Press.

Mayer, G. (2000). *Classroom management: A California resource guide*. Los Angeles: Los Angeles County Office of Education. Retrieved May 3, 2005, from http://www.cde.ca.gov/spbranch/safety/resourceguides/classroommgmt.pdf

Sprick, R., Borgmeier, C., & Nolet, V. (2002). Prevention and management of behavior problems in secondary schools. In M. R. Shinn, H. M. Walker, & G. Stoner (Eds.), *Interventions for academic and behavioral problems II: Preventive and remedial approaches* pp. 373–4. Bethesda, MD: National Association of School Psychologists.

Thompson, G., & Jenkins, J. (1993). *Verbal judo: The gentle art of persuasion*. New York: Morrow.

Walker, H. (1997). *The acting-out child: Coping with classroom disruption*. Longmont, CO: SoprisWest.

Suggested Reading

Mendler, A. (1997). *Power struggles: Successful techniques for educators*. Rochester, NY: Discipline Associates.

13

EMPOWERING STUDENTS TO RESOLVE CONFLICTS

With an emerging nationwide focus on teaching students to resolve conflicts without the use of violence; teachers, parents, and school personnel are looking for ways to educate students in conflict resolution. Many schools are approaching the problem with widespread training for both teachers and students.

In 1996 the American Medical Association issued a report on a longitudinal study focused on protecting children from harm (AMA, 1996). The report linked students' "connectedness to school" as important protection against risk behaviors such as violence. According to James Garbarino (1999), "connectedness to school" means, in part, "perceived peer acceptance."

Several promising practices are emerging in schools today. Teachers and students are being taught strategies for active listening in an effort to improve communication and understanding. See Figure 13.1 for active listening techniques commonly taught and practiced in some of these programs.

Other schools have expanded training beyond the teaching of active listening and are now training students in the use of peer mediation. The "tool skills" of mediation are taught through exercises in communication and self-regulation, and practiced in real-life situations, usually on the school playground, where conflicts are often common. This process allows students to practice their active listening and mediation skills and supports other students in seeing a process that works in real life. Students who have been helped by a peer mediator report an appreciation for the mediator and the process (Johnson & Johnson, 1999; Lane-Garon, 2000).

Early research on peer mediation programs in which only a few students are trained as mediators indicates that they do not prevent violence or support optimum positive outcomes (Johnson & Johnson, 1998). However, there is evidence that more global training across campuses provides effective results (Lane-Garon, 1998). These promising outcomes suggest that training in active listening and peer mediating should be a practice in all classrooms. Whether or not the conflict-resolution training progresses to create peer mediators or simply empowers students toward better communication skills, the steps and lessons in the process are valuable.

Figure 13.1   Active Listening Techniques

Statement	Purpose	To Do This ...	Examples
Encouraging	1. To convey interest 2. To encourage the other person to keep talking	... don't agree or disagree ... use neutral words ... use varying voice intonations	"Can you tell me more?"
Clarifying	1. To help you clarify what was said 2. To get more information 3. To help the speaker see other points of view	... ask questions ... restate wrong interpretation to force the speaker to explain further	"When did this happen?"
Restating	1. To show you are listening and understanding what is said 2. To check your meaning and interpretation	... restate basic ideas and facts	"So you would like your parents to trust you more. Is that right?"
Reflecting	1. To show that you understand how the person feels 2. To help the person evaluate his or her own feelings after hearing them expressed by someone else	... reflect the speaker's basic feelings	"You seem very upset."
Summarizing	1. To review progress 2. To pull together important facts and ideas 3. To establish a basis for further discussion	... restate major ideas expressed including feelings	"These seem to be the key ideas you've been expressing...."
Validating	1. To acknowledge the worthiness of the other person	... acknowledge the value of the person's issues and feelings ... show appreciation for the person's efforts and actions	"I appreciate your willingness to resolve this matter."

Source: Adapted from Community Boards of San Francisco, *School Initiatives Program,* p. 181.

STEP BY STEP

The steps for teaching and practicing conflict resolution strategies:

- **Teach active listening**   Begin by modeling active listening when students and parents talk to you. Respond with encouraging words such as "I'd like to hear more about that." Clarify, restate, reflect, summarize, and finally validate. Once you are using active listening consistently, introduce the topic to your students. Explain and model each of the techniques and encourage students to practice when they speak to each other. Some teachers have even held evening meetings where they explain and teach active listening to parents. This way, students hear consistent messages at home and at school.

> **FOCUS ON ENGLISH LEARNERS**
>
> English learners benefit from the clarifying and restating used in active listening. These steps give them multiple opportunities to make themselves understood.

To remind students to use the active listening techniques, create a poster for the classroom. When you notice that students are not listening to each other, remind them to consult the poster.

- **Demonstrate a sequence of interactions**   Once your students are familiar with active listening and are practicing it, introduce them to the mediation sequence. Use a teachable moment to demonstrate the steps with a pair of students who have an actual conflict. Explain that, for this process to work and a solution to be found, students must agree to follow the mediation rules. Once you have students' agreement, proceed by explaining each step in the process and then walking the students through each step. See Figure 13.2 for an explanation of the mediation steps.

In this demonstration, you, the teacher, serve as the mediator. Explain to students that you want them all to serve as mediators if they see a conflict arising. Also explain that once they know the steps in finding a solution, they can use them to solve their own conflicts. Remind them that the piece that is missing when they solve problems without a mediator is the paraphrasing. Point out that when they have to do that for themselves, it's hard because they may be upset.

- **Practice in mock situations**   Encourage the students to practice helping each other walk through the steps. Group the students in threes and give them a mock situation. Post the steps of the process and walk them through each of the steps, with one of the students posing as the mediator. Give them a second situation and have a different student act as mediator. Using a third situation, give the third student a chance to serve as mediator. Circulate around the room, observing and encouraging as this takes place. Note students who are good at paraphrasing and use their words as examples after the exercise. For examples of scenarios you can use for this exercise, see Figure 13.3.

Be sure to debrief the students at the end of this exercise. Ask which steps they found difficult and compliment them on their efforts. Explain that when real conflicts come up in the classroom, they can use the mediation steps by asking one of their colleagues to serve as mediator. Post a chart showing the steps so they can refer to it whenever they serve as mediators.

- **Practice with real situations**   As conflicts arise in the classroom or on the playground, encourage the students to serve as mediators and find solutions. If students comes to you with a complaint, ask if they've tried to mediate the dispute. If they haven't, ask if they'd like you to choose a mediator for them. In the beginning, you will have to supervise.

- **Debrief the participants**   Ask the students to file a brief report on any mediations they conduct. See Figure 13.4 for an example of a mediation report. When you receive a mediation report, be sure to debrief the participants and congratulate them on their conflict-resolution skills.

Figure 13.2 Mediation Steps

Stage	Explanation
Introduction	Remind the students that the process is designed to solve a problem. Tell the students that you are serving as a neutral person to help them through the process. Review the rules and get the students' agreement to follow the rules. The rules are: 1. Let each person tell his story without interrupting. 2. Use no inappropriate language or physical fighting. 3. Be as honest as you can be. 4. Work hard to solve the problem
Listening	Ask one student what she thinks the problem is and how she feels about it. Paraphrase what the person said. Thank the other person for listening patiently. Then repeat the process for the other participant.
Wants and willings	Ask the first person two questions: 1. "What do you want to happen?" Then paraphrase the response. 2. "What are you willing to do?" Then paraphrase the response. Repeat the two questions and paraphrases with the second participant.
Solution	Say: "It sounds like you have a solution. I hear that, *first name,* you are willing to _____ and you, *second name,* are willing to _____. Is that right?"
Debrief	"You have agreed to _____. Are you willing to come back and talk some more if this doesn't work? Congratulations! You have solved the problem."

Source: Dr. Pamela Lane-Garon (personal e-mail communication, May 4, 2005)

• **Continue the training** Observe as students conduct mediations and examine the report forms to see what problems are being encountered. Do periodic retraining to keep the rules and sequence fresh in everyone's minds. Be sure to compliment the students' efforts and congratulate them when solutions are followed. Remind them that some situations may take more than one mediation session.

• **Celebrate the results** Use the class newsletter to celebrate the progress of the mediation project. Keep parents informed of the project and share successes with them. Be sincere but provide positive feedback as frequently as possible.

Applications and Examples

Dr. Pamela Lane-Garon of California State University, Fresno, developed Mediator Mentors—a school-university collaboration in which she trains her credential students in mediation and they, in turn, along with school staff, train students at the school. Over the past 5 years more than 300 student mediators have been trained. Herndon-Barstow School is one of the 10 sites in which the program has been nurtured.

Figure 13.3   Scenarios for Mock Mediation Practice

Peter always leaves his bookbag on the floor next to his desk. Janie has tripped over it several times and has asked him to put it into the closet. Peter is ignoring her requests. One day, Janie trips over the bookbag and hits her knee on the desk as she falls. She is very upset with Peter and says he is not a responsible citizen. Peter says he wants his bookbag close to him because he has some CDs in it that he doesn't want to lose.

Becky never remembers to bring a pencil to school. She borrows pencils from Maria almost every day and never remembers to return them. One day Maria asks Becky for her pencils back. Becky gets angry and says that Maria is not a good friend or she wouldn't mind loaning her pencils.

Nathan never does his homework, and he's always wanting to copy Francine's homework. She tells him no almost every day, but she's getting impatient with these interactions and tells him she's going to report him to the teacher if he asks for her homework one more time. Nathan calls her a "narc" and storms away angrily.

The program at Herndon-Barstow began with volunteer university students working with upper-grade students who were mentoring younger students. The university students commit to one lunch period a week on the school campus. Students at the school are trained in mediation, and the university students serve as supervisors. Student mediators and university student supervisors are rewarded with field trips at the end of the school year.

The program at Herndon-Barstow has been so successful that 10 schools have now implemented similar programs, with four more on the waiting list. These schools

Figure 13.4   Sample Mediation Report

Mediator's name _____   Date _____

Participants _____

_____

What was the problem? (be brief)

Did both participants follow the mediation rules? If not, what was the problem?

What solution was agreed on?

---

are elementary and middle schools (Lane-Garon, personal communication, 2005). The participants in this program feel that the students are learning important communication skills as well as building confidence in their peace-building abilities. Mediator Mentors now provides university mentors with an opportunity to assist in conflict-resolution program development over an entire academic year. Eleven future teachers and counselors have taken advantage of this opportunity. Summer Avila, Mediator Mentor in 2003–2004, is now an elementary vice principal. She credits the program with helping her build networks of support among school staff. Within these relationships she developed the necessary organizational and communication skills to lead—both children and adults.

Mrs. Richardson teaches eighth-grade language arts in an urban middle school. She is becoming more and more concerned about her students' personal interactions. She often overhears verbal conflict when her students are moving around the room. They also have problems using respectful language to one another, and put-downs are becoming more frequent. She decides that a review of respectful language and a conflict-resolution intervention is needed. At first she worries about taking time away from the language arts curriculum, but then she takes another look at the standards. Listed under the language arts standards she rediscovers a standard that reads: "Uses listening and speaking strategies for different purposes." Under this standard are listed the following indicators for grades 6–8:

- Plays a variety of roles in group discussion (e.g., active listener, discussion leader, facilitator)
- Asks questions to seek elaboration and clarification of ideas
- Uses strategies to enhance listening comprehension (e.g., takes notes, organizes, summarizes, and paraphrases spoken ideas and details)
- Conveys a clear main point when speaking to others and stays on the topic being discussed

With the standards in mind, Mrs. Richardson prepares a lesson on conflict resolution using mediation steps. She prepares several scenarios based on interactions she has heard in her classroom and in the hallway. After modeling and explaining active listening she places her students in small groups and gives them a topic to discuss using active listening. She deliberately chooses controversial passages from a piece of literature the class has just read and asks the students to discuss the author's motivation for writing this passage. She reminds the students to use active listening and circulates to monitor the exercise. During debriefing she compliments students who have used the active listening strategies and gives examples of how they were able to contribute to a valuable conversation using this method.

The following day, Mrs. Richardson introduces them to mediation and the use of language in paraphrasing. Again they practice, in groups of three this time, using scenarios that sound very familiar to them. The postmediation discussion is very lively, and the students seem to be understanding the power of clarifying, paraphrasing, and summarizing. As an extension activity on the following day, Mrs. Richardson describes a situation involving conflict between two friends and asks the students to write a dialogue in which the friends utilize a third person as mediator to settle their dispute. The results demonstrate to Mrs. Richardson that the students understand the conflict-resolution process. Her challenge to them is to utilize it in everyday life. "Anyone can pass a test on a topic," she reminds them. "The real question is whether or not you really learned anything. If you did, you can use these skills in real life."

CONCLUSION

Skills in active listening and mediation are valuable to students of all ages. They have even been taught successfully, though simply, at kindergarten level. To stem the tide of violence in our schools and society, teachers must expand their efforts in teaching these needed skills. They are not outside of the curriculum; language arts standards clearly expect teachers to teach speaking and listening skills. Students can serve as mediators for one another and gain vital connectedness to school in this capacity.

STRATEGY ON VIDEO

Empowering Students to Resolve Conflicts

Conflict-resolution strategies are demonstrated in a fourth-grade classroom on segment 4 of the DVD that accompanies this text. Think about the types of readiness training these students have had to prepare them to participate successfully in this interaction. As you watch this segment, also think about the following:

- How does the teacher establish the ground rules?
- What expectations does the teacher make clear to the students?

References

American Medical Association. (1996). *Protecting adolescents from harm: National longitudinal study,* Washington, DC: Author.

Garbarino, J. (1999). *Lost boys: Why our sons turn violent and how we can save them.* New York: Simon & Schuster.

Johnson, W., & Johnson, R. (1998). Why violence prevention programs don't work and what does. In A. Woolfolk (Ed.), *Readings in educational psychology* (pp. 201–205). Boston: Allyn & Bacon.

Lane-Garon, P. (1998). Developmental considerations: Encouraging perspective taking in student mediators. *Mediation Quarterly, 16*(2), 201–215.

Suggested Reading

Begun, R. (2002). *Ready-to-use social skills lessons for grades 7–12.* San Francisco: Jossey-Bass.

Hollenbeck, K. (2001). *Conflict resolution activities that work!* New York: Scholastic.

Kreidler, W. (1999). *Teaching conflict resolution through children's literature (grades K–2).* New York: Scholastic.

Lane-Garon, P. (1998). Addressing kindergarten students' conflict behavior: Encouraging social-cognitive development. *Kindergarten Education: Theory, Research, and Practice, 3,* 93–105.

Lane-Garon, P., Nelsen, E., & McWhirter, J. (1997). *Building a peaceful community: A handbook for implementing a comprehensive, school-based conflict resolution program.* Tempe: Arizona Educational Information System.

Lane-Garon, P., & Richardson, T. (2003). Mediator mentors: Improving school climate—nurturing student disposition. *Conflict Resolution Quarterly, 21*(1), 47–69.

Leber, N., & Leber, N. J. (2002). *Easy activities for building social skills.* New York: Scholastic.

Teolis, B. (2002). *Ready-to-use conflict resolution activities for elementary school.* San Francisco: Jossey-Bass.

Helpful Websites

www.ericdigests.org/1992-5/conflict.htm

www.ericdigests.org/1996-2/conflict.html

www.esrnational.org/about-rccp.html

www.responsiveclassroom.org/articlelibrary/feature_44.asp

www.teachernet.gov.uk/teachingandlearning/socialandpastoral/peermentoring/foreword

ELIMINATING BULLYING IN SCHOOLS

Historically, adults have not given a lot of attention to bullying among children and youth. Bullying was often thought of as a rite of passage, and parents and teachers often encouraged children to work it out for themselves. In recent years, however, research has shown bullying to be increasingly prevalent among schoolchildren, with approximately 30% of children being directly involved (Nansel et al., 2001). As of 2003, at least 15 states had passed laws designed to eliminate this problem and provide resources for support. Although bullying is described in slightly different ways in various state laws, it is commonly defined as

- Punching, shoving, and other acts that hurt people physically
- Spreading bad rumors about people
- Keeping certain people out of a group
- Teasing people in a mean way
- Getting certain people to gang up on others

In March 2004 Federal Health and Human Services Secretary Tommy G. Thompson announced a national campaign to educate Americans about bullying and youth violence, both of which have an extremely negative impact on children's success in school and their overall well-being.

"Bullying is something we cannot ignore," Secretary Thompson said. "From the schoolrooms to the schoolyards we must nurture a healthy environment for our children. By engaging the entire community in preventing bullying we can promote a more peaceful and safe place for children to grow."

According to the U.S. Department of Education, one in four children who act as bullies will have a criminal record by the age of 30. These same students are much more likely to smoke, drink alcohol, and have lower grades in school. While we tend to think of the impact of bullying on the victims, we must not ignore the bully. These students are also our responsibility.

The U.S. Health and Human Services campaign against bullying is called "Take a Stand, Lend a Hand. Stop Bullying Now!" The campaign includes a web-based, animated story, among many other resources for teachers, administrators, and parents. See its website at www.stopbullyingnow.hrsa.gov.

 ## STEP BY STEP

The steps for eliminating bullying in your school:

• **Do your homework**   Learn as much as you can about the dynamics of bullying and begin to collect resources for teaching your students about this problem. Learn how to intervene directly if you see any bullying in progress. See Figure 14.1 for direct intervention steps.

When you identify a student who is being bullied, let him or her know that you are available to help. However, be careful about how you lend support. See Figure 14.2 for guidelines and suggestions.

• **Increase students' understanding of bullying**   Involve the students in an exploration of bullying. You can use the animated cartoon from the "Stop Bullying Now" website or an appropriate children's book to start the conversation. Be sure to let the students know exactly what bullying is. Some students think bullying always involves physical assaults. Have students write about incidents of bullying they have observed and then talk about how it made them feel to watch something like this. Talk about what they can do in the future if they see something like this happening. Keep the conversation open for future interactions by letting the students know that they must all be active in eliminating this type of behavior from the school. Make sure that they understand that this is a topic of great importance. Tell them about the state laws that are being passed to make sure bullying is eliminated in all schools.

• **Explore the effects of bullying**   With older students you may want to explore current news events about bullying. You can obtain a video of a special show that Dr. Phil aired in April 2005 about bullying by visiting www.DrPhil.com. On this show he had several students who had been bullied and one set of parents whose child committed suicide because of extreme bullying. If you order the tape, be sure to preview it before you show it. Allow enough time to stop the tape and discuss it as well. Other available videos are listed in Figure 14.3.

• **Teach strategies for students to avoid bullying**   Review the steps students can take to avoid being bullied. As you discuss the points, make a list and keep it on display in the classroom. Bullies like to attack students who are by themselves. Warn students to try to stay in a group. They should also try to stand up to a bully whenever a reasonable response is possible. Bullies prefer to pick on people who won't defend themselves. If students observe bullying, they should try to stand up for the person being bullied, as well. In all cases, the bullying should be reported to a responsible adult. Students should always understand that help is available in a school setting, and that bullying will not be tolerated. Bullying isn't going to go away unless everyone begins to stand up to bullies. Remind students to make sure they remain calm and try to make a joke, if they can. Sometimes humor can defuse the situation, and it can also serve to distract the bully. See Figure 14.4 for additional strategies for students.

FOCUS ON ENGLISH LEARNERS

Since English learners can often be the targets of bullies, giving them avoidance strategies and a script to follow when confronted is vital.

Make sure students know that they must always tell an adult about the situation. Reassure them that the teachers and other adults at the school are all working to eliminate this problem and they need help in identifying students who are bullying. Assure them that telling a teacher is vital, even if they need to have someone go with them to report the incident.

• **Increase students' understanding of bullies**   Help students understand that bullies are *not* powerful people. Help them see that bullies are dominating others with

Figure 14.1 What to Do, as an Adult, If You See Bullying

Step	Explanation
Immediately stop the bullying.	Step between the students. Block eye contact between them Don't send bystanders away.
Refer to the behavior and the school rules.	Use a matter-of-fact tone to state the behaviors you observed or heard. Let the students know that bullying is unacceptable and against the school rules.
Support the bullied student in a way to help him save face.	Make a point to see the student later, in private. Do not ask him what happened at the time of the incident. Let his teacher know what happened and watch for future incidents.
Include the bystanders in the conversation.	Don't put bystanders on the spot. Do use a calm voice to let them know that you noticed their inactivity or that you are pleased that they tried to intervene. You might want to say, "Maybe you didn't know what to do. Next time, please tell the bully to stop or get an adult if you feel you can't handle it."
If appropriate, immediately impose consequences on the bully.	Do not require students to apologize in the heat of the moment. The consequences should be logical (loss of recess time, detention during lunch period). Let students who bully know that you will be watching their future behavior very closely. Take the bully under your control, if necessary. Have her stay with you for a while, talking with her about what transpired, before you release her back into the student population.
Do not require students to meet and work things out.	Conflict-resolution strategies are not appropriate here. Bullying is an unbalanced situation, not a conflict between equals.
Provide individual follow-up.	Meet privately with both parties. Bullied students need to process the situation and vent their feelings, and may need help in building self-esteem or practicing assertive behavior. Students who bully may need help in recognizing their behavior, developing empathy and perspective-taking, and learning to focus on socially acceptable interactions.
Talk with bystanders privately.	Review their responsibilities if and when they should observe bullying behavior again.

Source: Adapted from www.StopBullyingNow.hrsa.gov

physical force or name-calling because they are not powerful and they want to be. They feel powerful only when they are picking on someone who won't stand up to them or is smaller than they are. See Figure 14.5 for characteristics of bullies.

• **Increase skills of bystanders to help stop bullying** As you are discussing bullying, be sure to make it clear that it is a problem shared by everyone. If they observe bullying, they need to support the person who is the target of the bullying. Bullies often leave the scene when they feel they are outnumbered or being singled out.

Figure 14.2   Helping a Student Who Has Been Bullied

Suggestion	Explanation
Offer help privately.	Because kids are concerned about their peers, don't put them on the spot. Offer your support and gestures in private.
Spend time with the student.	Learn what's been going on. Practice active listening. Tell the student that you are sorry for what happened and that it is not her fault.
Praise the student for courage in talking about this subject.	Explain that he is being brave and helpful by having this conversation. Explain that other students may be suffering from bullying also. Help him see that this problem can be corrected if everyone works together.
Ask the student what he needs to feel safe.	Give the student a voice and respond to his needs, if possible. Be sure to talk to a number of students about bullying to help protect the student's identity if consequences are imposed against the bully. Assure the bullied student that anything he says to you will be kept in confidence.
Communicate with colleagues.	Ask for help in supervising to make sure the student is protected.
Do not force a meeting between the bully and the bullied student.	This is *not* a situation that is helped by "talking it out." This is a very unequal balance of power.
Plan for next steps and share your plans with the student.	Use an intervention plan to help the student feel safe. Encourage and support the bullied student to make friends. Encourage the student to stay close to friends and other students.
Explore involving parents.	Explain that telling parents may provide additional support for the student. Talk with parents and the bullied student together, if it seems appropriate.

Source: Adapted from www.StopBullyingNow.hrsa.gov

Figure 14.3   Videotapes about Bullying

For grades 3–5:
Bullying. (1996). South Carolina Educational Television.
Bullying and how to handle it: A video for 3rd & 4th graders. (2003). Hazelton Publishing & Educational Services.
Bullying: Not just a guy thing. (2003). AIMS Multimedia.
McGruff's bully alert. (1999). AIMS Multimedia.
Using your wits: Strategies to stop bullying. (2002). Laurie Rae Baxter.

For grades 6–9:
Bully dance. (2000). Bullfrog Films.
Bully no more: Stopping the abuse. (2000). AIMS Multimedia.
Teasing: It's no joke. (1999). AIMS Multimedia.

For school administrators, teachers, and staff:
Bullying: What every adult needs to known. (2003). Paraclete Press.
So you want to be a mentor. (2004). Cheryl Dellasega.

Source: Adapted from www.bullyingresources.org

Figure 14.4 Avoiding Bullying

Strategy	Example	
Turning insults into compliments	*Bully:* You're a real dweeb.	*You:* Why, thank you. What a kind thing to say.
	Don't show emotion. Pretend the words were a compliment. Smile when you reply.	
Asking questions	*Bully:* You're such a dweeb.	*You:* Well, you're entitled to your opinion, but why are you talking to a dweeb? Are you trying to be my friend?
Agreeing	*Bully:* You're such a dweeb.	*You:* You mean I've been spending all my time thinking I was a Californian? Stupid me.
Golden nuggets	*Bully:* You're so fat!	*You:* I'm glad you noticed. Why don't you like fat people?
	Bully: Cause you're disgusting.	*You:* I'm glad to hear you're trying to rid the world of disgusting people. That's nice of you.
Tone twisters	*Bully:* You're so stupid!	*You:* (look puzzled) Stupid? What does that mean?

Source: Adapted from Cohen-Posey, 1995.

Help the students practice using calm, authoritative voices to tell the bully such things as "Stop being a bully. You know it's against the rules!" This works much better if all the bystanders show disdain for the bully. Remind students that name-calling is also a form of bullying and should not be tolerated.

• **Build a feeling of cohesion among students** Some schools have designed an antibullying pledge that all students sign as a part of the antibullying campaign. Other classes have made posters to display around the school urging students to stop bullying or report any bullying. Once the students feel that they are a part of a united front against bullying, it will serve to give them more courage to stand up to bullies and report them.

• **Build schoolwide programs** If your school has not adopted an antibullying campaign, approach your principal and tell him or her about the "Stop Bullying Now" campaign and ask if your school can get involved. There are a number of steps available for administrators on the website to provide support in researching the prevalence of bullying at their schools and setting up a program schoolwide. These types of programs are proving to be very successful (Rigby, 2002).

Applications and Examples

Mr. Stevens has been working on using respectful language with his fifth-graders all year. He has noticed lately that they sometimes forget the rules when they are on the playground.

Figure 14.5 Characteristics of Bullies

A student may be a bully if he shows

- Excessive feelings of rejection
- Low interest in school and poor academic performance
- Violence in drawing and writing
- Uncontrolled anger
- Patterns of impulsive and chronic intimidating
- History of discipline problems
- History of violent or aggressive behavior
- Intolerance for differences

What we know about bullies from their behavior:

- Bullies expect insulting replies to their comments. They don't know what to do when they hear a compliment.
- When you disagree with them, they insult you more. If you agree, they don't know what to do.
- They enjoy negative attention. Don't give it to them. Keep it light.

Source: Adapted from Cohen-Posey, 1995, and Beane, 1999.

He has noticed certain students becoming almost verbally abusive in the heat of their softball games. One day, Albert, a small boy with glasses, asks if he can stay in during recess. "Why would you want to do that?" asks Mr. Stevens.

"The other kids say I'm no good at softball," Albert replies. "The other day they called me a dweeb and said I mess up their game."

"OK, I see we have a problem," Mr. Stevens replies. "I think we have to review our rules about respectful language."

"Is there something else you like to do on the playground?" Mr. Stevens asks.

"I'm really good at footbag," replies Albert with a smile. "But everyone else is playing softball."

"Well," replies Mr. Stevens, "I've always wanted to learn to do that. Why don't we go outside and you can teach me to play footbag."

They went outside and Mr. Stevens was soon delighting the students with his ill-fated efforts in trying to keep the footbag going with his feet. Soon there was a group of students gathered around watching Mr. Stevens and asking to have a turn. "Well, it's Albert's footbag, so you'll have to ask him. He can teach you to do it. He's really good."

Mr. Stevens watched the students playing footbag for a while and then went inside. He decided to have a lesson on bullying after recess. He began by reviewing their rules about respectful language and then told the students about a show he watched on television the other afternoon. It was all about bullying.

The class discussed bullying and what it was. Many of them thought bullying was hitting and pushing. They were very surprised to find that name-calling was a form of bullying. Mr. Stevens made a poster as they talked about bullying. It listed forms of bullying and then said, "Bullying is against school rules!"

Mr. Stevens had the students write in their writing journals about any bullying that they had observed. After they finished writing, the class discussed how they felt when they observed bullying. They then talked about what they should do if they ever witness bullying again. They created another poster listing what to do. Mr. Stevens said, "No matter what you do, remember that bullying is not something a strong person does. It is something that a person without power does to make himself or herself feel strong."

Students in high schools surrounding Charlotte, North Carolina, are on a mission. The teens approached their principals in September 2004 with an idea for eliminating bullying in their schools. With the approval of the administration, they began their campaign using materials from the national "Stop Bullying Now!" campaign. Partnering with school clubs, leadership classes, and student governments, the Healthy Teen Task Force introduced a student pledge of zero tolerance for bullying. They created banners on which they placed and signed their handprints, pledging to watch for bullies and learn more about ways to confront them and eliminate bullying behaviors. They wear ribbons to create interest and awareness and recruit other students to sign the antibullying pledge. (See the "Teacher Resources" section of this text for an example of an antibullying pledge form.)

This schoolwide approach, which began in one county high school, has quickly spread to all high schools in the county. The teens are becoming aware of the seriousness of bullying and are committed to eliminating it in their schools (*Charlotte Examiner*, February 6, 2005).

CONCLUSION

Students of all ages are in need of information about bullying: what it is and how to stop it. Programs have begun in individual classes around the country and are expanding to schoolwide and districtwide efforts. Bullying is an enormous problem in some urban areas, and students need support in learning how to deal with it. Thanks to the U.S. Department of Health and Human Services, there are resources available for teachers and administrators to aid in the elimination of this problem. The students must understand their responsibilities in the effort, however. This takes careful instruction, support, and knowledge to effectively deal with the problem.

STRATEGY ON VIDEO
Eliminating Bullying in Schools

Strategies for eliminating bullying in schools are demonstrated in a middle school classroom on segment 5 of the DVD that accompanies this text. You will see a middle school class discussion and a school leadership team meeting to plan strategies to eliminate bullying. As you watch this segment think about the following:

> In what ways do the students describe bullying?
> What assumptions do the members of the leadership team seem to be operating under?
> Do you think the school leadership team's approach might have been different if they had witnessed the class discussion?

References

Cohen-Posey, K. (1995). *How to handle bullies, teasers, and other meanies*. Highland City, FL: Rainbow Books.

Nansel, T., Overpeck, M., Pilla, R., Ruan, R., Simons-Morton, B., & Scheidt, P. (2001). Bullying behaviors among U.S. youth: Prevalence and association with pychosocial adjustment. *Journal of the American Medical Association, 285,* 2094–2100.

Rigby, K. (2002). *Stop the bullying: A handbook for schools*. New York: ACER Press.

Suggested Reading

Beane, A. (1999). *The bully free classroom: Over 100 tips and strategies for teachers K–8*. Minneapolis: Free Spirit Press.

Coles, R. (1990). *The call of stories: Teaching and the moral imagination*. New York: Mariner Books.

Education Development Center. (2004). *MetLife Foundation read for health program (Taking action to stop bullying: A literacy-based module)*. New York.

Mullin-Rinder, N. (2003). *Relational aggression and bullying: It's more than just a girl thing*. New York: Wellesley Centers for Women.

Mullin-Rinder, N. (2003). *Selected bibliography about teasing and bullying for grades K–8*. New York: Wellesley Centers for Women.

Olweus, D. (1993). *Bullying at school: What we know and what we can do*. Malden, MA: Blackwell.

Rubenstein, F., & Chorney, A. (2002). *Block the bully cycle*. Westport, CT: Franklin Learning Systems.

Salas, J. (2005). Using theater to address bullying. *Educational Leadership, 63*(1), 78–82.

Schniedewind, N., & Davidson, E. (1997). *Open minds to diversity: A sourcebook of learning activities to affirm diversity and promote equality* (2nd ed.). Needham Heights, MA: Allyn & Bacon.

TROUBLESHOOTING PROBLEM AREAS: IDENTIFYING AND RESPONDING TO STUDENT NEEDS

One of the most important skills for success in teaching is the ability to identify and rectify problem areas in the classroom. The identification of possible problem areas before they emerge is an important responsibility in creating a classroom community. This involves planning, testing management procedures, and being open to making changes. Identifying problems that are unique to individual students is somewhat more complex. Sometimes classroom arrangements and/or expectations are only problematic for a few students. An effective teacher is observant and notices when a student is experiencing difficulties. The appropriate action then becomes responding to the individual needs of the student before the student resorts to misbehavior, or, as we prefer to call it, mistaken behavior (Stein, 2001.) The key here is that the teacher is supporting the student by adjusting the situation to the student's needs.

The important sequence for an effective teacher to remember is

1. Plan—be proactive in anticipating problems
2. Observe for symptoms of problems
3. Analyze the cause of the problem
4. Respond to the problem
5. Adjust the situation to support the student
6. Observe again to make sure the adjustments are working

In order to be truly responsive to the needs of students, teachers cannot adopt a "one size fits all" approach to teaching or management (Powell, McLaughlin, Savage, & Zehm, 2001.) Plan with the needs of the group in mind, but always keep the individuality of your students uppermost

FOCUS ON ENGLISH LEARNERS

Cultural and/or language factors must be carefully examined and explored to ensure that students can successfully participate in class and school activities.

in your mind. For instance, some students need more guided instruction before they're ready to work independently. Some students work best in a very quiet, secluded environment and will need a study carrel or a quiet corner of the room to do their best work. Others can work well in a group situation or in an area with movement around them.

Effective teachers remain alert to signs that students are not meeting classroom expectations, respond to the situation, and make adaptations so that all students can be successful participants.

 # STEP BY STEP

The steps for troubleshooting problem areas:

- **Plan for smooth distribution of materials**   Before you start a lesson, plan the way in which materials will be distributed and at what point in the lesson they will be needed. Do not distribute materials before the students actually need to use them. If they need the materials to understand the directions for the activity, distribute them immediately and keep the students focused on them step by step. Otherwise, distribute them after the students have heard the directions, been given modeling, and are ready to use them.

- **Observe closely as students work**   Watch carefully to make sure that students are working with the materials and seem to know what to do. If they're talking to one another or seem to have a lot of questions, respond by walking them through the directions again or creating a visual that they can follow.

- **Identify any students who seem to be having difficulty**   Difficulty with an assignment can appear as mistaken behavior or refusal to do the work.

- **Research the cause of the problem**   Instead of "taking it personally" and reacting to the behavior, you should consider the causes and look for possible solutions that will benefit the individual, the class, and you.

- **Formulate a plan**   Once you decide on some possible solutions, examine them for ease of implementation, support you will need, and likelihood of success. Plan to implement the one that seems more likely to succeed without disrupting your class routines. Always keep an alternative plan in mind in case you encounter difficulty with your first approach.

- **Implement the plan**   After choosing possible solutions, begin the process of implementation. A very important initial step is the discussion with all parties involved of any changes in procedures and expectations. Be aware that the first plan you try might not be the ideal one. It may be necessary to alter the plan or try another solution. Be sure and give each trial an appropriate amount of time and do not discard it just because it doesn't work immediately.

- For examples of additional behaviors to watch for and possible responses, see Figure 15.1.

- **Celebrate progress**   It is very important to celebrate successful approximations as you implement changes. Don't immediately expect students who have been doing no homework to turn in homework every day. Celebrate with them on the days they successfully fulfill the new expectations. Think of troubleshooting as an ongoing process rather than an instant fix for deeply rooted behaviors.

Figure 15.1   Troubleshooting Guidelines

Student Behavior	Possible Causes	Possible Remedies
Not doing the assigned work	Not understanding the directions	Guided practice—creating a visual for support.
	The work is too difficult	Provide additional guided practice before asking the student to work independently.
	The work is too easy	Add a challenge to the assignment, preferably a practical application.
	The student is distracted by other students	Move the student to a study carrel or quiet area of the room, facing away from the others.
	Poor work habits	Create a contract with the student (see Chapter 9).
The student gets into conflicts with the teacher or other students	The student may be avoiding work in certain curriculum areas	Use active listening to see how confident the student is in the curriculum in question (see Chapter 13).
	Conflict involves the same students regularly	Use conflict-resolution strategies (see Chapter 13). If necessary, separate the students to ease the tension between them.
	The student may have had negative experiences with former teachers or other adults.	Monitor your reactions to the student to detect any negative body language on your part. Use active listening and try to reserve judgment until you hear all the facts (see Chapters 12 and 13).
Calling out/ interjecting answers or information at inappropriate times	Family pattern of communication. Need for recognition. Lack of understanding of established classroom procedures.	One-on-one discussion to establish that the student understands the need for respectful classroom interaction. Establish an acceptable signal to show the student that you recognize he knows the answer and you need to hear from others in the group as well. The key to the success of this strategy is *consistency*. Do not permit the student to gain the floor by "calling out."
Students getting up and wandering around the classroom	Student needs (physically) to move around.	Build activity breaks into or between your lessons. Provide planned movement to help address the student's need to move about.
	Student may be avoiding the work because it's inappropriate	See "not doing the assigned work," above
	A change in expectations from previous year's class	One-on-one conference reviewing this year's expectations and possible creation of a behavior contract if necessary (see Chapter 9).

Figure 15.1 (Continued)

Student Behavior	Possible Causes	Possible Remedies
Student takes a long time to complete written work	Poor fine-motor skills	To begin with, shorten the task. As skills improve, begin to lengthen the task. Allow the student to use the word processor for lengthy writing tasks.
	The task is too difficult	See "not doing the assigned work," above.
	The student is distracted	See "not doing the assigned work," above.
Student doesn't turn in homework	No materials or space to work at home	Send a homework packet (pencils, paper, etc.) home with the student containing all the necessary materials to complete the assignment. Communicate with parents about homework expectations through newsletters, notes home, parent meetings, etc.
	Assignment is inappropriate for individual students.	Adjust assignments to individual student needs (see Chapter 23).
	Overscheduled after-school time	Communicate with parents relative to limiting after-school involvement to allow time for homework and study. In specialized situations (religious activities, holidays, etc.) allow for flexible submission schedules. For example, it might be turned in a day early, or a day late).

Applications and Examples

Ms. McCloskey is a first-grade teacher in a very diverse city in California. Many of her students are originally from Laos and speak a language called Hmong at home. Because her students' families are very poor and can't afford to buy books, Ms. McCloskey sends home small duplicated books for them to use in practicing their reading skills. She is frustrated, however, because her students tell her they couldn't practice their reading "because my mother threw my book away."

After hearing this excuse several times, Ms. McCloskey talks to a Hmong paraprofessional at her school about the problem. "My students tell me that their mothers throw their books away when they bring them home," she complains to Miss Vang. "What can I do to help the parents understand the importance of having reading materials at home for their children to practice their reading?"

Miss Vang laughs. "That's not the problem, Ms. McCloskey," she replies. "In the Hmong culture the home is kept very neat and free of clutter. Papers and other clutter are gathered and thrown away each day."

"OK, now I see the problem," says Ms. McCloskey thoughtfully. She immediately begins formulating a plan. She gathers cereal boxes for each of her students and covers them with contact paper, labeling them "My Reading Books," with each child's name on a box. She then meets with her students to explain the purpose of the reading boxes.

"These reading boxes are yours to take home. You are to put your little reading books in them each night so your mother will not throw your books away. When you take your box home tonight, explain to your mother that the box is for your reading books and that you will keep all your important school things in the box so they won't get thrown away. Then it will be your job to make sure your books are safely put into your reading box each night before you go to bed. It is also your job to practice your reading each night. I don't want to hear any more excuses about your mother throwing away your books."

Ms. McCloskey's students nod solemnly after she explains the purpose of the boxes. They take their boxes home, and she sends books home weekly. Because she has researched the root cause of the home reading difficulty, she has been able to establish that it was not a behavior problem. She responded by managing to find a solution that benefited both her students and their families.

Mr. Townsend has a bright student, Brian, who is making class discussions very difficult. Brian is very enthusiastic and shouts out the answer to every question Mr. Townsend asks before anyone else has a chance to respond. Mr. Townsend is torn because he admires Brian's interest and quick mind. However, the rest of the students aren't even attempting to answer questions. They are sitting back and allowing Brian to take over the discussions.

Mr. Townsend decides to take action. He has a private chat with Brian. "Brian, we have a problem," he begins. "None of the rest of the students are getting a chance to participate in class discussions. They are all sitting back and letting you answer all the questions. I need your help. Instead of answering questions, I need you to stop and raise your hand. I'll give you a signal that I see your hand by nodding my head. That means, 'I know you know the answer, Brian. I want to see if anyone else knows.' You need to help me by *not* shouting out the answer. I'll call on someone else, and then if you have anything else to add to the discussion, I'll give you a chance to talk."

Brian agrees to the plan, and Mr. Townsend is extremely consistent in following the new procedure. He sometimes has to remind Brian by putting his finger to his lips and shaking his head when Brian shouts out an answer, but he doesn't allow Brian to answer unless he's called on. Gradually the other students begin to take a more active part in class discussions, and Brian learns to listen to his peers and add information based on their responses. Mr. Townsend creates a win-win situation by carefully observing and analyzing the situation before formulating a plan of action. Instead of reacting in a negative manner, he is able to respond positively by giving Brian the recognition he needs while encouraging more diverse responses from other students.

 ## CONCLUSION

As both Ms. McCloskey and Mr. Townsend have demonstrated, analyzing, researching, and troubleshooting classroom problems can result in effective interactions to make classrooms a more responsive place for students. Both teachers have learned to search for possible causes for inappropriate behavior rather than simply react on a personal level and punish students.

References

Powell, R. R., McLaughlin, H. J., Savage, T. V., & Zehm, S. (2001). *Classroom management: Perspectives on the social curriculum.* Upper Saddle River, NJ: Merrill/Prentice Hall.

Stein, H. (2001). Dealing effectively with children's mistaken goals [Handout for Classic Adlerian Child and Family Therapy]. San Francisco: Alfred Adler Institute, Distance Learning Program.

Suggested Reading

Chernow, F., & Chernow, C. (1981). Handling specific discipline infractions. In *Classroom discipline and control: 101 practical techniques* (pp. 29–39). West Nyack, NY: Parker.

WHEN AND HOW TO ASK FOR HELP WITH DIFFICULT STUDENTS

No matter how well you organize your classroom, set up rules and routines, and teach students to respect one another, there will be times when students will misbehave. Teachers who are prepared for this can be consistent in their responses. Being consistent supports students in their understanding of the class expectations and logical consequences for their actions.

Occasionally you will have students in your classrooms who struggle with rules or don't respond in the ways you expect. Good teachers plan in advance for these types of students by using a discipline plan. In some schools there is a schoolwide discipline plan that is the same for all classes. In others, teachers are responsible for setting their own. See Figure 16.1 for an example of a discipline plan.

It should be noted that any student who harms or threatens to harm any teacher or other student should be removed from the classroom immediately and parents should be notified. District policies should be clear on such matters, and the implementation should be swift and complete. In other cases, the teacher must document the problem and any interventions that have been tried.

 ## STEP BY STEP

The steps for referring and documenting serous misbehavior in the classroom:

• **Keep records of student behavior**   Teachers have different ways of organizing behavior records. Some teachers use note cards and file them in a file-card box. Others use a clipboard and write observations and notes on peel-off mailing labels. When they have completed an observation, they peel off the label and place it on a behavior record page in the student's folder. It is important to keep records of incidents of misbehavior to be able to examine patterns. The record should include information such as time of day, interactions with certain students, or frequency of misbehavior. See Figure 16.2 for suggestions on keeping good records.

Figure 16.1   Preventive Discipline Plan

Students are expected to follow rules and routines in the classroom and other areas of the school. Teachers are responsible for helping students to understand their school responsibilities:

- Mutual respect
- Attentive listening
- Active participation

Infractions of the school rules or responsibilities are classified in three levels.
Level I infractions:

- Any behavior that disrupts the learning environment
- Showing disrespect, not listening attentively, or not participating in classroom activities
- Acting in a harmful way (pushing, shoving)

Level I consequences:

- Teacher and student confer to discuss the expectations that have been difficult for the student to meet.
- Teacher fills out a reflection form. The student reflects on his or her behavior and teacher and student decide on a plan for remediation.
- Reflection form with student's response is sent home for parent signature.

Level II infractions:

- Insubordination, defiance
- Bullying, harassment, verbal/sexual/racial comments
- Verbalizing or writing profanity, using foul language and/or gestures
- More than three Level I infractions

Level II consequences:

- Principal and student confer to discuss the problem.
- Reflection form is completed.
- Reflection form is sent home for parent signature.
- Additional logical consequences are assigned (behavior contract, loss of privileges, in-school suspension).

Level III infractions:

- Repeated Level II infractions
- Theft
- Damaging property
- Threats of harm to others
- Possession of a firearm, lighter, matches, knife, firecracker, or any weapon
- Computer misuse or Internet violation

Level III consequences:

- Principal and student confer.
- Reflection form is completed.
- Education team confer (includes teacher, principal, counselor, parents, student).
- Level II notice is given and explained to parents.
- Appropriate consequences are determined by the education team (behavior contract, probation, in-school suspension, out-of school suspension, expulsion, law-enforcement intervention).

Figure 16.2   Guidelines for Writing Discipline Records

Behavior or discipline records should be factual, actual, concise, and sensible.

Use facts,
  Write facts, not opinions:
  Billy broke all his crayons after Jenny told him his picture was ugly.
  Not: Billy had a temper tantrum and broke all his crayons for attention.

Write what you *actually* observed, not what was reported to you:
  Billy slapped George across the face.
  Not: George reported that Billy slapped him.

Be *brief* and to the point:
  When we returned to the room from recess, Billy tripped three children as they passed
  his desk.
  Not: Billy is always disruptive. He baits the other children and seems to get pleasure out
  of seeing them cry. Today he tripped three children as they passed by his desk.

Be consistent in keeping records. Only when you keep records on a regular basis can
you examine the frequency of the incidents.

• **Document interventions**   Equally as important as the behavior records are intervention records. Note the date that interventions were started, exactly what is being done, and the student's progress. If you set up the intervention with a student conference, keep a record of the date of the conference, the decisions that were made, and the terms of the intervention. If the need arises and you have to refer the student to a student study team, members will require that you share the interventions you have tried, the length of time they were tried, and the results.

FOCUS ON ENGLISH LEARNERS

English learners often need some quiet time, not so much for discipline purposes but to rest their ears and brains from concentrating on a new language. A cool-down spot can also serve as a quiet spot.

• **Work with parents**   When you put a student on interventions, the parents should be aware of the reasons for the intervention, exactly what is being done, and the student's progress. It is always helpful if the parents support the approaches being tried in the classroom. Having a conference with the parents with the student present helps the student recognize that all the significant adults in his life are making attempts to support him as he learns to become a more productive and responsible student.

• **Complete referrals**   If you have tried some interventions and feel that the student needs more than you can do in the classroom, the time has arrived to file a referral to the student study team. Every school has a different process for making referrals, but most require records of exactly why the student is being referred and what interventions have already been tried. See Figure 16.3 for an example of a study team referral.

• **Participate in the student study team process**   When a student of yours is to be discussed at the student study team meeting, you should come thoroughly prepared. Bring copies of your behavioral records, documentation of the interventions you have tried, report cards, attendance records, parent conference notes, and any student conferences and goal-setting you've done. Be prepared to present the situation concisely and professionally. The study team may decide to refer the student for further testing, and the school psychologist will need copies of all that has been done to date. The team may decide to try a different intervention before referral. Since you, the teacher, will probably

Figure 16.3 Student Study Team Referral Form

Student's name _____ Date of birth _____

Teacher's name _____

Educational history: Has the student been in this school throughout his school career?
If not, please give a list of schools attended in the past, with dates of attendance.

_____   _____

_____   _____

Did the student attend preschool? _____

Has the student been retained? If yes, at what grade level? _____

Is the student enrolled in any special programs? _____

Briefly state the reason for the referral.

Please list any interventions already tried and their duration.

Please attach copies of discipline records and parent permission for this referral.

---

be responsible for implementing the intervention with support from the team, make sure that you understand exactly what is expected of you and what help the different members of the team will provide. The parents should be actively involved in supporting the intervention as well.

• **Carry out intervention strategies** When carrying out an intervention recommended by the study team, try to be as exacting as possible. Keep good records of exactly what you are doing and the student's responses.

• **Monitor and document progress** It's highly important that you keep records of the interventions implemented and the student's progress. (Refer to Figure 16.2 to make sure your records are factual, actual, concise, timely, and sensible.) Celebrate even small signs of progress with the student and make every attempt to be positive with her. The study team will probably want you to report progress to them on a monthly basis.

Applications and Examples

Mrs. Tuttle is very concerned about her second-grade student Christopher. Christopher comes into the class with a positive attitude each morning, but by 10 o'clock he is argumentative and often engages in aggressive behaviors such as pushing and hitting. He is also verbally abusive to other students, calling them names and telling them that they're ugly and mean.

Mrs. Tuttle has conducted individual conferences with Christopher on a regular basis. She has restricted his freedom in the class by seating him away from the other students whenever he becomes aggressive. Mrs. Tuttle has had several conferences with Christopher's parents, and they, too, have observed this behavior at home with his siblings and friends. They seem to be at a loss as to what to do. Mrs. Tuttle decides to take Christopher's case to the student study team.

At the student study team meeting, Mrs. Tuttle presents her documentation of the interventions she has tried. The parents talk about the approaches they have tried at home. The counselor, upon looking over the behavior records and the time of day when Christopher begins having difficulty, suggests a physical examination. He also suggests that the parents share Mrs. Tuttle's behavior records with his pediatrician. The parents say they have discussed his behavioral problems with the doctor in the past but they will certainly try this new approach.

A week later Mrs. Tuttle receives a phone call from Christopher's mother. The doctor, after looking over the behavior records, scheduled a diabetes test for Christopher. The test reveals that he has hypoglycemia and must be allowed to snack every 3 hours to keep his blood sugars elevated. Christopher's mom suggests that Mrs. Tuttle schedule a snack break about 10 A.M. She volunteers to send graham crackers for the entire class so that Christopher's snacking will not be disruptive to the other students. Mrs. Tuttle eagerly agrees. Christopher's behavior problems seem to disappear almost immediately.

Christopher's parents are extremely grateful to the school for their help with his behavior problems and their suggestions for a remedy. Christopher's classmates now invite him into their activity groups with a smile

---

Darla is an eighth-grade student in Mrs. Franklin's language arts class. Darla is known throughout the school as a difficult student. Her teachers note that she is often defiant, refuses to follow directions, and when confronted, "goes limp," giving the appearance of fainting, although she is wide awake and able to use abusive language with the teacher. The doctors say there is nothing physically wrong with her to cause the fainting-like behavior.

Mrs. Franklin has heard about Darla from her seventh-grade teachers but is determined to keep an open mind and to begin the new year with positive interactions. She has a two-part plan in mind. Because Darla is known to rebel at direct instructions, Mrs. Franklin structures the assignments in her class to include choices. She also makes sure to talk pleasantly to all her students about topics other than schoolwork. Mrs. Franklin plans to make sure that these two approaches are used with Darla daily.

This approach seems to be working for a while, but then one day Darla refuses to change activities when time for transition arrives. She becomes abusive when Mrs. Franklin insists that she move to the next activity. Because Mrs. Franklin knows of Darla's past problems, she goes immediately to the school counselor that afternoon to discuss the problem with her. Mrs. Franklin brings her behavior records and has some positive things to share from her two-part intervention. She also notes that Darla has great difficulty staying on task when she's completing assignments and often stops her work to watch others or to disrupt with loud talk.

Ms. Grey, the guidance counselor, suggests trying the Attention Training System (ATS) (Gordon, Thomason, Looper, & Ivers, 1991; Polaha & Allen, 2000). ATS is a battery-operated module that displays points being earned (per minute or per 4 minutes) when on task. When an agreed-on number of points is reached, the student is able to do something special that she and her teacher have agreed on, such as play a computer game. If the student is off task, the teacher can use a remote control to subtract a point and send a visual, silent signal to the student to get back on task.

Ms. Grey shows Mrs. Franklin how to use the ATS device, and Mrs. Franklin schedules a private conference with Darla the next day. She explains that she wants to help Darla to learn study habits that will help her to succeed in school. Darla seems distrustful but brightens up when Mrs. Franklin demonstrates the ATS device. "You mean I can earn computer time?" she asks.

"Yes," Mrs. Franklin responds. "And you'll be getting your work done in the process."

"Cool," is Darla's only reaction.

The ATS intervention is progressing well, and Darla's other teachers have all adopted it. Ms. Grey is working with Darla to teach her socially acceptable ways of expressing her needs and concerns. Darla still has occasional problems, but her behavior is improving each day.

 # CONCLUSION

Teachers must have a number of strategies at their disposal when planning discipline interventions. It is important that teachers know the available resources at their schools, the process for obtaining support, and their responsibilities in documenting behavior that may require intervention strategies.

Students with aggressive behavior that may prove to be a threat to the teacher's or other students' safety must be removed from the classroom immediately. Most schools establish a panic code that teachers use when immediate help is required. All schools have a version of the student study team, though it may be called by another name, such as discipline committee, intervention planners, or referral team. It is important to become familiar with the protocol your school follows, the forms required, and expectations for the teacher in the process.

References

Gordon, M., Thomason, D., Cooper, S., & Ivers, C. (1991). Nonmedical treatment of ADHD/ hyperactivity: The Attention Training System. *Journal of School Psychology, 29,* 151–159.

Polaha, J., & Allen, K. (2000). Using technology to automate off-task behavior: Classroom management made simple. *Proven Practice, 2,* 52–56.

Suggested Reading

Fad, K., Patton, J., & Polloway, E. (2000). *Behavioral intervention planning: Completing a functional behavioral assessment and developing a behavioral intervention plan.* Austin, TX: PRO-ED.

Liaupsin, C., Scott, T., & Nelson, C. (2000). *Functional behavioral assessment: An interactive training module; User's manual and facilitator's guide.* (2nd ed.) Longmont, CO: SoprisWest.

Sugai, G., & Horner, R. (1999). Discipline and behavior support: Preferred processes and practices. *Effective School Practices, 17*(4), 10–22.

INTEGRATING ACTIVE LEARNING EXPERIENCES, AUTHENTIC PRACTICE, AND ASSESSMENT

Think of the times you've made new friends and colleagues. Usually you've been actively involved in a project that required collaboration, shared planning, and plenty of verbal interaction. Through these interactions you've built a shared understanding with a new group of people who have become friends or colleagues in the process. Rarely did your learning take place in a single, isolated discipline. You learned skills, vocabulary, social interaction strategies, and concepts related to many subject areas.

This section addresses the integration of learning and the use of authentic assessment. Since the adoption of standards-based education nationwide, many teachers are concerned about finding ways to meet the standards for which they are responsible while keeping the rich, integrated units they know support a depth of understanding in their students. This can be done and is well worth the effort it takes in planning. However, it is not a haphazard endeavor. Teachers must be knowledgeable about the standards they must meet in all the curricular areas they teach. They must find ways to integrate studies in several disciplines in order to utilize classroom teaching time wisely. They must build on the interests and strengths of their students and document their growth in order to write report cards and growth reports.

The first chapter in this section introduces multiple ways of documenting growth in students. The focus is on teaching the students to self-reflect and work with others to accomplish goals. By looking at student assessment through different lenses—self-reflection, goal-setting, and classroom support—the seeds of collaboration and authentic learning are sown. Teaching students to recognize growth and strengths in themselves and others begins to set the stage for the community atmosphere necessary in a collaborative classroom. By using multiple approaches to assessment, students are given an opportunity to document their learning in ways not possible with the use of more traditional evaluations such as true-false and multiple-choice tests.

Learning centers designed to give students an opportunity to learn through their strongest intelligences are explored as well. Howard Gardner (2000) and Thomas Armstrong (2000) have helped educators recognize that students possess multiple intelligences in various strengths. As teachers, we need to be aware of the multiple intelligence strengths of our students and plan learning and assessment activities that enable our students to use their strongest intelligences.

The strategies that follow the learning-centers strategy build on the use of differenti-ated instruction using techniques that address many intelligences. The use of manipula-tives, physicalization, the arts, technology, and the blending of multiple approaches and disciplines is explored in depth. See Figure V.1 for more information about Gardner's theory.

Figure V.1   Important Theory

Howard Gardner (1943–present)

Howard Gardner is a professor of cognition and education at Harvard University. He is the author of more than 20 books translated into 23 languages and several hundred articles. He is best known for his theory of multiple intelligences. For the past 20 years, Dr. Gardner and his colleagues at Project Zero have been working on the design of performance-based assessments, education for understanding, and the use of multiple intelligences to achieve more personalized curriculum, instruction, and assessment.

Gardner initially identified seven intelligences rather than the one, more traditional, IQ score. He has since added an eighth intelligence to the list and is currently researching a ninth. He believes that students learn through many intelligences, that people learn best through their stronger intelligences, and that schools have traditionally taught only to the linguistic and logical/mathematic intelligences. To improve a student's ability to process academic material and demonstrate his or her knowledge, Gardner suggests teaching strategies designed to meet the individual needs of students based on their intelligence strengths.

The intelligences Gardner has identified and their teaching implications are listed below:

Intelligence	Teaching/Learning Strategies
Linguistic (word smart)	Reading, writing, interviewing, discussing
Logical-mathematical (number/reasoning smart)	Problem-solving, logic and reasoning, math calculations
Spatial (picture smart)	Drawing, graphing, creating webs, building models
Bodily kinesthetic (body smart)	Enacting, miming, demonstrating
Musical	Singing, rhythms, rap
Interpersonal (people smart)	Verbal interaction, group collaboration
Intrapersonal (self smart)	Independent study, individual projects, personal reflections
Naturalist (nature smart)	Observing laws of nature, demonstrating understanding through natural phenomenon

References

Gardner's published works include the following:

Gardner, H. (2000a). *The disciplined mind: Beyond facts and standardized tests: The K–12 education every child deserves.* New York: Penguin.
Gardner, H. (2000b). *Intelligence reframed.* New York: Basic Books.
Gardner, H. (2001). *Good works: When excellence and ethics meet.* New York: Basic Books.
Gardner, H. (2004). *Changing minds: The art and science of changing our own and other people's minds.* Boston: Harvard Business School Press.

Figure V.2   Important Theory

Lev Vygotsky (1896–1934)

Lev Vygotsky was born in Russia and received a law degree from Moscow University. In Russian society of his day, individuals were expected to sacrifice their personal goals for the improvement of society. Sharing and cooperation was stressed, and personal success was equated with its contribution to society as a whole. Vygotsky incorporates both of these elements into his sociocultural theory of human development.

Vygotsky looks at human mental development in terms of thought, language, and reasoning. He sees these abilities as developing through social interactions with others. He states that the child's cultural development occurs twice: first between people (interpsychological) and then inside the child (intrapsychological). Vygotsky states that intellectual abilities are specific to the culture to which the child belongs. He sees culture as affecting intellectual ability in two ways. In Vygotsky's theory children acquire much of their thinking, the processes of their thinking, or intellectual adaptation from their own culture and from their surrounding cultures.

Vygotsky is best known for his ZPD theory (zone of proximal development). ZPD refers to the gap between what a given child can achieve alone, his or her potential development by independent problem solving, and what he or she can achieve under adult guidance or in collaboration with more capable peers. The child's full development in the ZPD depends upon social interaction and requires that teachers identify the child's actual level of development in order to provide support at the proper levels.

Vygotsky also stresses the importance of the learning environment in providing opportunities for maximum development. The placement and style of furniture needs to support peer instruction, collaboration, and small-group instruction. Instructional materials and teaching should also focus on interaction and collaboration in order to foster a community of learners.

References

Vygotsky's published works were not translated into English for years after his death. Those translated works include the following:

Vygotsky, L. (1962). *Thought and language.* Cambridge, MA: MIT Press.
Vygotsky, L. (1971). *The psychology of art.* Cambridge, MA: MIT Press.
Vygotsky, L. (1978). *Mind in society.* Cambridge, MA: MIT Press.

Vygotsky (1978), in his theory related to the zone of proximal development (ZPD), helps us to understand the importance of knowing exactly what our students know and can do. See Figure V.2 for more information about Vygotsky's theory.

The use of multiple measures in assessing our students' understandings and growth is a vital part of planning and implementing effective instruction. In order to do this type of assessment well, teachers must use a wide variety of assessment strategies in the classroom on a daily basis. These assessments may take the form of observation as students interact in a discussion or group project. Sometimes the assessment will be a more traditional test. No matter which approach is used, the teacher must be aware of the strengths and weaknesses of the various forms of assessment in order to make sure the student is given an opportunity to reliably demonstrate his or her growing skills and abilities.

References

Armstrong, T. (2000). *Multiple intelligences in the classroom* (2nd ed.). Alexandria, VA: Association for Supervision and Curriculum Development.
Gardner, H. (2000). *Intelligence reframed.* New York: Basic Books.
Vygotsky, L. (1978). *Mind and society: The development of higher mental processes.* Cambridge, MA: Harvard University Press.

RELATING NEW SKILLS TO PRIOR EXPERIENCES

Piaget's (1979) schema theory is a widely accepted tenet in educational methodology classes across the nation. This theory tells us that we build new knowledge on schema, or concepts, that we have established in our brains and adapt new ideas based on our past experiences. New teachers are reminded always to activate prior knowledge as a beginning step in any lesson, but little attention is given to two important facts: (1) not all students possess the same prior experiences; and (2) as teachers we need to have methods for exploring individuals' experiences and relating them to the new concepts and ideas to be studied.

In order to fully relate lessons to students' prior knowledge, teachers must have approaches for getting to know their students and understanding their experiences as well as possible sources of misconceptions. To gain this knowledge of individuals' background related to an area of study in the classroom, teachers must plan assessment strategies that can be implemented before the lesson is taught. They need to plan ways in which to relate the background knowledge in authentic ways so that students can build on their existing schema (Richard-Amato, 1996.)

 ## STEP BY STEP

The steps for relating new skills to prior knowledge in the classroom:

- **Identify a strategy to determine background understandings** Identify a strategy to be used to determine what, if any, background knowledge students possess that relates to the topic of study. The best strategy should match the focus of the lesson to be taught while identifying the background knowledge of individual students. It must support the students in learning how to identify and make connections of their own and still be flexible enough to adapt to follow-up instruction. See Figure 17.1 for possible strategies to be used for this purpose.

FOCUS ON ENGLISH LEARNERS

English learners often need background and vocabulary-building activities before they can successfully participate in classroom instruction.

Figure 17.1   Strategies for Identifying Student Background Knowledge

Individual KWL charts	Teacher introduces topic and holds a brief discussion to help students identify possible experiences and knowledge they may have. Students fill out the K section of the chart, telling what they think they know about the topic. After another brief discussion, students suggest questions they have about the topic by writing the questions under the W section of the chart, signifying things they want to know. The teacher reviews the charts to determine the range of background knowledge and plans ways to connect the students' experiences and questions to the lesson to be taught.
Discussion with student response cards	Teacher initiates an introductory discussion of the topic to be studied. A response card is prepared for each student on which the teacher lists possible experiences the student may have had that relate to the topic of study. As the discussion takes place, the teacher stops occasionally to ask students to mark their cards to show whether or not they have ever had the experience being discussed. The teacher collects the response cards and uses them to plan the lesson based on the students' range of experiences.

- **Use the information gathered to determine the range of experiences in the class and build common understandings**   After gathering information on the background experiences of all the students, analyze this information, looking for background knowledge, concepts that seem to be lacking in all students, and the range of understandings within the group. If there are basic experiences or concepts that seem to be missing in all students, plan introductory activities to build these understandings. Such things as reading informational books aloud to the class and engaging them in discussions, showing videos to build background knowledge, or bringing in a guest expert are all ways that can be used for this step.

Sometimes you will identify only a small group of students who will need this background building and can give the others another assignment related to the topic of study that enriches and builds on their already existing knowledge. Sometimes there are groups of students with varying levels of background experiences, and the background-building activities must be done in several groupings. This step is vital in setting the scene for success for all students. In addition, having the groups share the results of their background-building activities with the whole group helps build shared knowledge across the board.

- **Plan a lesson introduction and sequence to maximize connections**   Once the basic background understandings are built, plan an introductory lesson to get the students engaged in the study, build interest and enthusiasm, and help students make connections to their background knowledge. In addition to the introductory lesson, plan the sequence of lessons to be implemented, making sure that there is a logical progression of skills and concepts. See Figure 17.2 for suggestions on connecting activities and sequence building.

- **Assess the students' understanding of the concepts and skills being taught**   Periodically throughout the sequence of lessons, you must check for understanding. These checks can be informal, such as discussions in which you make notes of students who have acquired basic concepts and those who need more teaching or experience. Checks for understanding can also be assessments, such as performance tasks, tests, or oral reports.

The timing and choice of checks for understanding are both vital. Whenever a concept is taught that is necessary for the next lesson or activity in the sequence, you must plan some way to determine which students are ready to move on and which students will require additional instruction before moving to the next step. When you determine

Figure 17.2 Connecting Activities and Sequence Building

Activity	What It Does	Implementation
BCA— background, concept, activity	Builds on background, introduces new concept, uses concept in active engagement	1. Build background 2. Introduce new concept 3. Provide an active learning experience to use the new concept
RLCR— review, learn, check understanding, repeat	Helps sequence learning, making sure basic concepts are understood along the way	1. Review previous knowledge and basic concepts 2. Teach new information 3. Assess for understanding 4. Repeat with new concept
Learning cycle	Builds basic concepts in sequence, allows student to make connections to new learning	1. Build background knowledge on basic concepts 2. Introduce basic concepts 3. Model the use of basic concepts 4. Give students guided practice in basic concepts 5. Check for understanding 6. Give students time to practice what they've learned 7. Introduce new concept building on the one taught previously
Double-entry journal	Gives students an opportunity to reflect on material being studied and relate it to past experiences	1. Students create a T chart with "New Information" at the top of the left side of the chart and "My Experiences" at the top of the right side of the chart. 2. Students write a quote from reading material or an idea that's been discussed on the left side of the chart and reflect on their experiences related to the quote or idea on the right side. 3. Students discuss their entries. 4. Teacher encourages sharing and points out differing points of view based on exprience.

that some students need more instruction you also must plan for learning experiences for the other students to continue broadening their knowledge and involvement in the course of study.

• **Plan reteaching based on the assessment data**   If the checks for understanding have been made specific to necessary skills, you can easily identify exactly what must be retaught. Academic vocabulary, basic concepts, basic operations in such subjects as math and science, and basic reading and writing skills must all be considered.

Figure 17.3 Reteaching Formats

Target	Format	Preparation
Individual	Tutorial	Teacher prepares a series of activities on the computer or in a programmed learning format, gradually giving the student practice in basic skills or introducing basic concepts.
Small group	Learning center	Teacher prepares material to be explored in a learning center by the group. They work through the material collaboratively and support one another in their exploration. The students can use the listening center and the computer, filmstrips and videos can be viewed, and follow-up activities can be done by the group.
Small group or individual	Teacher-led guided practice	Teacher walks individual or group through direct instruction, providing guided practice in the skills or strategies needed.
Small group	Reciprocal learning	Small group explores resource material using the following reciprocal learning sequence: 1. Forming a group and numbering the members. 2. Reading—each group member reads the material. 3. Summarizing—member 1 summarizes the section just read. 4. Questioning—member 1 questions other members of the group about the reading. 5. Clarifying—member 1 clarifies any questions the other members have. 6. Problem-solving—the group discusses possible solutions or strategies that can be used. 7. Predicting—member 1 makes a prediction about what will happen next. 8. The process is repeated with member 2 as leader.

Once the teacher is aware of exactly what must be retaught, she plans small-group instruction to build the missing knowledge. It is important to look at basic skills needed and use approaches that will support the students in gaining these skills. See Figure 17.3 for suggestions on reteaching formats.

Applications and Examples

Mrs. Bendel is planning a science unit on tide pools for her second-grade class. To determine the background knowledge of her students, she makes some overhead transparencies of photos of tide pools that she downloads from the Internet (www.calstatela.edu). Before Mrs. Bendel shows the transparencies to her class, she builds a checklist of basic experiences and knowledge to use in order to keep a record of her student's responses. See Figure 17.4 for the checklist Mrs. Bendel constructs.

Mrs. Bendel numbers the transparencies and shows them to her class. As she shows each transparency, she asks questions from her checklist and notes the students who seem to lack certain understandings. With several of the transparencies she asks the students

Figure 17.4 Checklist of Basic Tide Pool Information

Names	Ann	Bob	Carla	Fred	Jose	Ken	Liz	Maria	Mario	Oscar	Pat	Pete	Rita	Rosy	Sergio	Shane	Tina	Tomas	Violet
Tide pool info	✓																		
How formed?	✓																		
How animals get there?		✓																	
How animals survive?																			
Recognize some animals?																			
Know some facts about animals?																			

+ = Strong understanding
S = Some knowledge
N = No knowledge
M = Misinformation

to write words they know that relate to the picture. After the whole-group activity she meets in small groups with the students who seem to lack experience with tide pools and beaches and talks to them about the topic to determine their levels of understanding. While she is meeting with the small groups, the other students are looking through some of the resource books she has gathered for the study, searching for vocabulary words related to the beach and tide pools.

After the initial assessment activities, Mrs. Bendel decides that many of her students have limited experience with tide pools. She plans a sequence of activities using a videotape she makes at the beach to prepare the class for an upcoming field trip. After showing the videotape, she meets with the group of students who have never seen a tide pool and conducts a vocabulary-building lesson with them using shells, seahorses, and photos. The other students are engaged with some of the same realia but are writing brief sentences describing what they know about the objects and photos.

Instead of waiting until the end of the unit to visit the tide pools, Mrs. Bendel decides to visit the beach at the beginning of the study. She does a series of lessons focusing on building vocabulary and concepts before the field trip. She plans several follow-up lessons after the trip to connect the students' background knowledge, real-life experiences, and the knowledge they are gaining by reading about tide pools.

During the field trip, Mrs. Bendel asks a parent to videotape the tide pools and the discussions that take place for use in follow-up lessons. She also prepares an information sheet for the students to use as they acquire new concepts on the trip. See Figure 17.5 for an example of this field-trip information-collection sheet.

Figure 17.5   Field-Trip Data-Collection Sheet

What I Saw (Draw a Picture)	What I Learned
Tide pool	
Crab	
Anemone	
Starfish	
Urchin	
Limpet	
Algae	

Before the field trip, Mrs. Bendel conducts a check for understanding by giving the students a diagram of a tide pool for them to label with vocabulary that has been discussed in the introductory activities. This gives her information so that she can do some brief reteaching activities with the group of students who need more vocabulary support. She does several read-aloud activities to further build vocabulary and concept knowledge as well.

During the field trip the students take notes on their information-collection sheets, and Mrs. Bendel plans several activities after the field trip so they can share their information sheets and collectively celebrate new understandings.

As a culminating activity, Mrs. Bendel and her students draw and label a large mural showing the parts of a tide pool. Each student is assigned one tide pool creature to research and explain to the class. Mrs. Bendel videotapes the mural and the oral report projects and shows the videotape at the spring open house.

Mr. Goede's 11th-grade language arts class is preparing for the high school exit exam on which they must write a five-paragraph essay. He begins to collect information about their knowledge of paragraph writing by conducting a discussion about Mardi Gras, which has recently been celebrated. After the discussion, Mr. Goede asks the class to write a paragraph about Mardi Gras and examines the student responses using a basic paragraph checklist. See Figure 17.6 for an example of this checklist.

Using the results of this assessment activity Mr. Goede briefly reviews paragraph format with the whole class and provides more specific examples for the group that lacks this basic writing skill. Instead of reteaching before any additional instruction, Mr. Goede moves forward with his step-by-step plan of five-paragraph essay lessons but pulls the

Figure 17.6   Basic Paragraph Checklist

Names					
Writes complete sentences					
Begins with a topic sentence					
Builds on the topic sentence					
Stays on the topic					
Ends with a concluding sentence					
Uses punctuation correctly					
Uses capitalization correctly					
Uses a variety of sentence structures					
Uses connectives and segues					

group needing extra support aside as the others work independently each day. He provides this group with additional guided practice and works more collaboratively with them to build their writing skills.

After teaching each new element of the essay format, Mr. Goede conducts a check for understanding by having the students write a new part of their essay demonstrating their understanding of the essay elements. He uses their ongoing essay writing as assessment to determine when reteaching or clarifying is necessary.

After the majority of the class has mastered the essay format and Mr. Goede moves on to another topic with the entire class, he walks through an additional essay assignment with the group that needs more experience. He uses class time when the rest of the class is engaged in independent reading and writing to provide more structured support in the form of guided practice for this group.

 CONCLUSION

Both Mrs. Bendel and Mr. Goede are aware of the need to build on their students' prior experiences. They plan a series of classroom activities to expand their students' knowledge and understandings. They check for understanding at key points in their instruction and plan to give further instruction to students who need it. They are extremely aware of the wide range of abilities within their classes and take responsibility to meet the needs of their individual students. Because the students feel supported and safe in the classroom, they are more willing to put forth effort in the tasks assigned to them.

References

Piaget, J. (1979). *The development of thought.* New York: Viking.

Richard-Amato, P. (1996). *Making it happen: Interaction in the second language classroom.* White Plains, NY: Addison-Wesley.

Suggested Reading

Dixon-Kraus, L. (1996). *Vygotsky in the classroom: Mediated literacy instruction and assessment.* White Plains, NY: Longman.

Herrell, A., & Jordan, M. (2004). *Fifty strategies for teaching English language learners* (2nd ed.). Upper Saddle River, NJ: Merrill/Prentice Hall.

18

USING THE LEARNING CYCLE
TO ENHANCE ACADEMIC SUCCESS

In the previous chapter we discussed the importance of identifying the background knowledge and skill levels of your students when planning a lesson sequence. This is an important consideration for lesson planning. However, there is additional thought that must be put into planning an effective lesson. Motivation theory supports the concept that students learn new skills best when they understand the importance of the skills to the accomplishment of behaviors and understandings that are a important to them (Bandura, 1997). Using purpose-setting to arouse student interest and begin lessons enables the teacher to create interest in the topic and helps students maintain focus. When students are connected to the learning process, they are more likely to benefit and less likely to involve themselves in behavior that is detrimental to the community of learners.

Research in intrinsic motivation suggests that certain elements must be present to enable students to build their self-confidence and maintain enough interest to successfully complete learning tasks (Ryan & Deci, 2000). These are defined in relation to specific actions that teachers can take, such as:

- Explaining or showing why particular content or skills are important
- Creating and/or maintaining curiosity
- Providing a variety of activities and sensory stimulations
- Providing games and simulations
- Setting goals for learning
- Relating the learning to student needs
- Helping students develop a plan of action

Since the teacher is responsible for planning the sequence of activities in most lessons, these required elements can be built into the planned learning cycle, beginning with making connections to real-life needs for the content or skill to be studied. This is then followed by teaching (defined as explaining, modeling, and providing guided practice) and a variety of independent practice activities that require the use of the new content or skill. These activities should include goal-setting and relating the learning to student needs and past experiences. Many of these things are intertwined, so the process is not really linear in nature.

The cycle continues with giving the students opportunities to use the new content or skills in authentic practice, such as student-planned projects. Once again, this allows the students to use and appreciate the importance of the new content or skill in real-life situations.

 ## STEP BY STEP

The steps for utilizing motivation theory in the learning cycle:

- **Set purposes for learning** Begin the lesson by discussing what will be learned in the lesson sequence and making it clear how the students will benefit from this new knowledge. Relate the new concepts and skills to future endeavors, whether in school or in life, and give several examples of how these skills are used. The best purpose-setting is related to desires, interests, and goals that the students have themselves identified. In other words, the teacher must know her students and build on their interests.

- **Relate the new material to past experiences** As discussed in Chapter 17, it is important to bring students' past experiences to mind. You can do this by relating this new lesson to prior classroom activities or experience that you know most of your students have had. Again, you need to have knowledge of your students' backgrounds. See Chapter 26 for suggestions on how to gain this knowledge.

- **Explain the skill or content** Explain the content or skill to be learned, give examples, and relate the skill to interests and needs of the students. If the students are going to be asked to complete a task in relation to this lesson, explain that task.

- **Model the use of the skill or content** Move from talking about the skill to demonstrating its use. Accompany this demonstration with a more detailed explanation. Again, the purposes of the content or skill should be made clear. If the students are expected to complete a task or activity, then the task or activity should also be modeled, step by step, so that the students can see and hear what they are expected to do.

FOCUS ON ENGLISH LEARNERS

Multiple approaches enable English learners to explore topics with visual and physical support.

- **Provide guided practice** Engage the students in an exercise in which they practice what you have just demonstrated. The students complete several examples under your guidance. Feedback and correction is given until you are confident that the students can move into independent work. Guided practice is also the place where you observe and identify any students who will require reteaching and additional guided practice before they can be successful with independent practice.

- **Utilize the new content or skill in authentic ways** Give the students opportunities to practice their newly acquired content or skills. Every attempt should be made to make this practice as authentic as possible. Think of ways in which they will be needing the skills in future educational or employment situations and encourage the students to practice the skills in that context or a close approximation. Rarely will students be asked to complete worksheets in the real world. They should be given the opportunity to practice in more authentic ways. This is another point at which you can assess the students' understandings and plan reteaching where necessary.

- **Make connections to real life** As a part of the lesson closure, support the students in understanding the real-life connections to the content and skills they've learned. This can be done by relating the authentic practice to real life and asking how the use of the skill will differ from the practice activity. It can also be done as a reflective journal activity in which the students think about the lesson and reflect on ways they will be able to use their new knowledge in the future.

Applications and Examples

Mrs. Milsovic's third-graders have been learning to add, subtract, and solve word problems dealing with money. In order to give them motivation for mastering their manipulations of problems involving money, Mrs. Milsovic plans an activity that will give them experience with budgeting, money problems, and collaborative decision-making.

She begins the activity by asking the students, "How many of you know how your parents pay the bills for groceries and rent?"

"My mom writes checks at the grocery store," offers Helena.

"How does that work, Helena?" asks Mrs. Milsovic.

"Well, she puts her paycheck in the bank, and then she writes checks and the bank pays the grocery store for the check," replies Helena.

"That's just right," Mrs. Milsovic replies with a smile. "How did you learn that?"

"My mom took me to the bank one day and explained it all," says Helena.

"So do you think you'll write checks someday when you're grown up?" asks Mrs. Milsovic.

"Oh, yes," replies Helena. "But I don't know how to do it yet."

"Well, with this next project, we are going to learn how to write checks," explains Mrs. Milsovic. "We're also going to work with a budget. That's like an allowance."

Mrs. Milsovic can see that the students are excited about this prospect. They are sitting up straight and tall and asking lots of questions.

Mrs. Milsovic has gotten packs of sample checks from her local bank. She has also purchased spaghetti and miniature marshmallows to use as building materials. She explains the project and demonstrates some basic building principles.

The students are arranged into construction companies and instructed to build a house for their clients. Gummy bears are used as potential clients, and the groups have a choice as to whether to build a house for a couple or a family. Each group has a construction manager, an architect, a materials person, and a money person (an accountant). Mrs. Milsovic serves as the owner of the materials store and sells building materials (spaghetti and marshmallows).

After Mrs. Milsovic explains and demonstrates how to write a check, the students practice with her guidance. She then explains their budget and the cost of the building materials. Because she wants the students to practice adding and subtracting decimals, she gives each group a budget of $100.00 and prices the spaghetti at $1.29 per strand and the marshmallows at $1.09 each.

Each group decides on a name for their construction company and then works together to draw a plan for the house they will build. The architect is responsible for making the actual drawing with input from the group. The construction manager writes down the supplies needed as the group examines the plan and counts the necessary materials. The materials manager comes to Mrs. Milsovic to purchase the materials. The money person (accountant) writes the actual check to pay for the materials after the group works together to determine the exact amount to be paid. Mrs. Milsovic explains that the groups should buy only as many materials as they need to begin their construction because they can always come back for more as long as they still have money in their account.

After the houses are completed, each group must decide on a method for advertising its house. Some groups write ads for the newspaper; others write advertising jingles. They all put up "For Sale" signs. Each group conducts an open house, giving the other students a tour of the house and telling about the special features included. Some of the groups have built two-story houses; some have swimming pools, gardens, spas, fences, and even treehouses.

The students have used found materials like construction paper, paper clips, and even erasers to represent features for their houses. They also set the prices for their houses.

Each group reviews its budget, brings its check register up to date, and submits financial records to Mrs. Milsovic. At the conclusion of the project Mrs. Milsovic takes pictures of each group with its completed structure for the class newspaper.

Ms. Newsome's 10th-grade language arts class is working on a standard related to the writing of descriptive paragraphs. To help the students understand the importance of this skill in everyday life, Ms. Newsome shows a brief video clip of an automobile accident and asks the students to write a paragraph describing the accident.

After they write their descriptions and read them aloud, the class discusses occupations in which employees have to be able to write descriptive paragraphs. Their list consists of

Police officers—descriptions of accidents, crime scenes

Newspaper reporters—descriptions of sports plays, accidents, community events

Teachers—descriptions of behavior for discipline referrals

Realtors—descriptions of property for sale

Store owners—descriptions of property for sale

Online sellers—descriptions of their products

Advertisers—descriptions of their products

Car salespeople—descriptions for ads and commercials

Ms. Newsome then explains the components needed in a good descriptive paragraph and models the writing of one, being sure to include all the components by referring to her list. The class then works together to write a description of one of their peers, pretending to write a missing-person report.

Ms. Newsome distributes pictures she has clipped from newspapers and magazines. Some of the pictures show accidents; others are sporting or cultural events. As the folder comes around, each student chooses a photograph and then proceeds to write the description of the event, employing the components listed on the board:

Who

What

When

Where

How

Specific physical features

The students' paragraphs are passed around the class. Ms. Newsome shows each picture on the overhead projector, and the student who has the description of that event reads it aloud. Some of the descriptions are quite innovative, and the class enjoys several hearty laughs.

Ms. Newsome assures the class that there are even more occupations in which descriptive writing is important. "Ask your parents tonight if they ever have to write descriptions in their jobs," she challenges the students. "Let's see if we can add to our list tomorrow."

CONCLUSION

Teachers who use motivation theory and the learning cycle to help them plan innovative lessons find their students engaged in authentic practice that supports their learning and often exceeds the standards because of their interest level. The active learning planned by both Mrs. Milsovic and Ms. Newsome show that learning can become useful and exciting when this approach is used. These activities are much more interesting for students and help them make connections between school and real life while addressing academic standards.

STRATEGY ON VIDEO
Using the Learning Cycle to Enhance Academic Success

Using the learning cycle to enhance academic success is demonstrated on segment 6 of the DVD that accompanies this text. In this segment a new concept is being introduced in a fourth-grade science lesson. As you watch this segment, consider the following:

- Identify alternative ways in which the procedure could be presented.
- Identify ways in which the teacher could determine the students' background knowledge about the concept being taught.

References

Bandura, A. (1997). *Self-efficacy: The exercise of control.* New York: Freeman.

Ryan, R., & Deci, E. (2000). Self-determination theory and the facilitation of instrinsic motivation, social development, and well-being. *American Psychologist, 55,* 68–78.

Suggested Reading

Corbett, D., Wilson, B., & Williams, B. (2005, March). No choice but success. *Educational Leadership.* Reprinted in *The Best of Educational Leadership, 2004–2005.* Alexandria, VA: Association for Supervision and Curriculum Development.

Rimm, S. (1995). *Why bright children get poor grades.* New York: Crown.

19

BUILDING RESOURCES FOR USING MANIPULATIVES, REALIA, AND VISUALS

Active learning often requires interaction with materials. Teachers sometimes recognize this need but find that collecting realia (real objects) is time-consuming and expensive. Accumulating realia, manipulatives, and visuals for use in learning experiences is a vital concern for teachers of children whose native language is not English (Krashen, 1988) but is also highly supportive of learning for native English speakers.

As beginning teachers slowly collect resource and professional books for their teaching libraries, it is also important for them to begin to collect props for the purpose of contextualizing language in lessons. When new vocabulary is introduced in context, connecting the unfamiliar words with a visual or real object makes them more easily understood. When new concepts are explored through the manipulation of objects called manipulatives, the concepts become clear.

Teachers often look for inexpensive sources for building a library of manipulatives, realia, and visuals by searching through thrift stores, garage sales, or dollar stores. They can also make wonderful color transparencies using the Internet, their computer, and a printer. But collecting the materials brings about another problem: storing all these objects so that they are readily available takes some planning.

Because teachers are innovative people, they often find inexpensive ways to store materials and yet make them available for lessons and even accessible for the use of the students. See Figure 19.1 for examples of these innovative storage ideas.

One of the goals of active learning is to encourage active engagement by all students. One way to do this is to design activities where all students respond to all questions. Show-me cards are easily made and can be used in almost every curricular area. Each student has a show-me card (an individual pocket card) and a set of response cards. For a math lesson all they need are number cards; for phonics lesson they need letter cards; for other lessons they may need a set of *yes* and *no* cards, cards with all the continents and ocean names on them, or whatever the topic of the lesson may be. The teacher asks all students to respond to questions by placing cards in their show-me card and then turning the card around when the command, "Show me." is given. For directions for making show-me cards, see Figure 19.2.

Figure 19.1 Manipulatives, Realia, Visuals, and Storage Solutions

Material	Use	Storage Ideas
Color transparencies	Helping students visualize vocabulary or settings	Using a three-ring binder, store transparencies in clear plastic sheet protectors, three-hole punched. Organize in alphabetical order or in groups related to subject matter.
Puppets or plastic realia	For story reenactment, language practice, contextualizing new vocabulary	Put objects into jumbo-sized reclosable plastic bags; store by hanging the bags on a PVC chart holder using plastic skirt hangers.
Small objects such as beans or blocks	Math manipulatives	Collect small containers such as plastic medicine bottles, film canisters, yogurt containers, or milk cartons and store manipulatives in sets that individual children can use.
Costumes	Story reenactment or dramatizing student writing	Use labeled plastic or cardboard storage boxes or jumbo plastic bags as described above
Show-me cards	Allowing all students to respond to every question	These fold flat and can be stored in a legal-sized envelope along with the cards needed for the activity. See Figure 19.2 for directions.

FOCUS ON ENGLISH LEARNERS

Using manipulatives, realia, and visuals support English learners in understanding and building language skills.

Collecting and storing the manipulatives, realia, and visuals to support lessons is important, but not worth the time and effort unless they are used. Teachers must think about active learning as they plan lessons in order to provide more opportunity for active engagement in the classroom.

 STEP BY STEP

The steps for collecting, storing, and using manipulatives, realia, and visuals:

• **Identify curricular topics to be studied in the near future** Rather than trying to collect manipulatives for the entire year, start with the studies you will be exploring in

Figure 19.2   How to Make a Show-Me Card

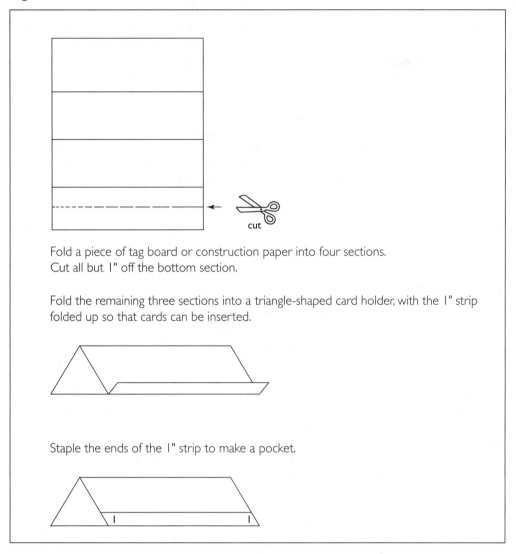

Fold a piece of tag board or construction paper into four sections.
Cut all but 1" off the bottom section.

Fold the remaining three sections into a triangle-shaped card holder, with the 1" strip folded up so that cards can be inserted.

Staple the ends of the 1" strip to make a pocket.

the near future. List the areas you will be addressing in math, science, social studies, and the stories your students will be reading.

• **Brainstorm manipulatives, realia, and visuals to enhance instruction** Working with the list you made, brainstorm materials that would help you to make the information clear, and materials the students could use to explore the topics through active engagement. Don't censor your list because things are expensive. Write everything down and then try to think of inexpensive substitutes for the expensive items.

• **Locate inexpensive materials**   Get to know the bargain stores in your town. Visit thrift shops, junk stores, dollar stores, and yard sales to see what you can find. Even though you are working on building resources for specific lessons, don't pass up bargains that you know you will be able to use in future studies.

• **Involve parents**   Let parents know that you will be using materials that they can supply. Ask them to save things such as plastic milk-carton lids (for counters), plastic yogurt cups and lids, film cans, old medicine bottles, shoe boxes (for storing manipulatives), fabric remnants, leftover wallpaper (for binding student-made books), and leftover art supplies such as paint, glue, and newspapers.

- **Use the Internet to create visuals**   Use websites such as google.com and altavista.com to locate photographs that can be downloaded and printed onto transparency film. Be sure to use the correct transparency film for your printer, or the ink will run right off the transparencies.

- **Organize and store materials**   Create a system for storing materials so that they are accessible at all times. Before you ask parents to donate items, have your storage system in place. See Figure 19.1 for some suggestions.

- **Continue to build your resources**   As you build your storage system and begin to collect materials, always stay on the lookout for new resources. When you visit businesses, look for items that can be used in the classroom. Stores often throw away cardboard display cases that can be used. Printing businesses will keep scraps of paper for teachers if the teachers leave a container with a phone number on it so the business can call when the container is full. Things that are often discarded such as the small paper circles that are created when paper is hole-punched make wonderful materials for teaching. Those leftover hole-punch circles can be glued onto letter and number forms to make outstanding tactile teaching aids for your children, for example.

Applications and Examples

Mrs. Talbert knows that second-graders get wiggly when they have to wait their turn, so she tries to plan lessons in which everyone can respond to questions. She makes show-me cards with her students, showing them how to fold, cut, and staple the cards to make individual pocket cards for use in lessons (see Figure 19.2). Because she has been working with her students on the spelling of word families, she designs a lesson to help them manipulate letters to create words. She gives the students pieces of card stock and markers, and together they create the letter cards they will need. Since the introductory lesson will focus on the short "a" sound, they create a set of 10 letters for each student. After the students make a set of letters including *b, c, f, m, p, r, s, t, v,* and *th,* Mrs. Talbert begins the lesson. She gives each student a card with the word "at" written on it and asks them to put this word into the pocket of their show-me card. "We will be building words that belong to the 'at' family," she announces.

Instead of telling them which word she wants them to build, she gives them clues. This will help them think about the meanings of the words. Her first clue is "I'm thinking of an animal that has whiskers and says meow." She observes as the students build their word. She is able to tell which students can quickly build the word and which have to think about it or even look to their neighbor for help. As she observes, she makes notes about which students may need additional instruction after the lesson.

The students wait for the signal, "Show me," after they have built their word. When they hear the signal, they turn their card around so that Mrs. Talbert can see their responses. When the students reveal their responses, she notes that one child has built the word "rat." She asks, "Kevin, you are right that rats have whiskers, but do they say 'meow'?"

Kevin laughs and says, "No!" and quickly substitutes the first letter of his word. After they have built all the "at" family words, Mrs. Talbert has them place an *n* over the *t* in "at," and then they build "an" family words.

To follow up on this lesson, Mrs. Talbert has designed a sorting center for the students to use later. To strengthen their skills in discriminating among beginning sounds, she has collected a number of small objects from around the house. She has also visited a craft store and a party-supply store to find small objects to place in the sorting center. From around her house she collects a Band-Aid, a small ball, a bracelet, a barrette, a stamp, a sock, and many other small objects. From the craft store she collects a small plastic pumpkin, some buttons in the shape of teacups, windmills, wheels, nuts, and other objects. From the party-supply store she collects small baby bottles; plastic forks, spoons, and knives, whistles, tops, and other party-favor objects. She places all these objects at the sorting center along with empty pint-sized milk cartons labeled with the letters of the alphabet. The students then spend their time at the center sorting the objects into the correct cartons. After they complete their sort they must review it with one of the student helpers whom Mrs. Talbert has appointed to this job because she knows they already know their initial consonant sounds. Mrs. Talbert stores these small objects in reclosable plastic bags labeled with the initial letter. The bags are stored in a large shoebox placed on a low bookcase where students can reach it.

Mr. Sanderson's 10th-graders are studying *Julius Caesar* by William Shakespeare. To assist the students' understanding of this difficult text, Mr. Sanderson downloads pictures of theatre productions of this work showing the characters in costume. He creates color transparencies of the various scenes to display as the class reads the scenes aloud. Instead of having the students sit at their seats to read, he has them dress in costume whenever possible using a collection of old bed sheets he has saved over several years of shopping yard sales and thrift shops. He has also collected olive-leaf headpieces made from bargain leaves he has found at his local craft store.

Because Mr. Sanderson is required to teach this play every year, he has accumulated most of the props he needs for the students to act out the scenes. His students tell him that their older siblings told them about this practice before they got to 10th grade. They seem to look forward to the activity each day.

In high school classrooms the storage is meager, so Mr. Sanderson has had to be innovative in storing the costumes and props for his literary activities. He stores the costumes and small props in jumbo reclosable plastic bags. These are all placed in a large cardboard box labeled with the name of the play. The box is placed in the bottom of the coat closet, where students can get to it easily.

He has also researched a number of the props and found pictures of them on the Internet. He then created transparencies to show the students and they have made replicas from cardboard, papier-mâché, or plastic. This was not all accomplished in one year. Mr. Sanderson started the productions with very basic props and costumes, which have been augmented over the years, sometimes from parent donations. One mother came in with four white bed sheets that were very worn but usable. "I was going to throw these away," she said, "But I thought about your plays. I thought you might like to add them to your costume box."

Another student and her mother made costumes for some of the other roles in the play when they heard about his projects. A number of parents have shared their appreciation for his approach to Shakespeare, saying, "I wish it had been taught that way when I was in school. It was many years before I learned to appreciate the bard."

 ## CONCLUSION

Teachers who use manipulatives, realia, and visuals to support student engagement in their classrooms add to their students' understanding in many ways. The props help make new vocabulary and concepts come to life. Active learning approaches help students learn through their stronger intelligences. These approaches support motivation by making lessons accessible to students (Bandura, 1997; Brophy, 1987). It's also very difficult to avoid active participation in highly engaged classrooms.

STRATEGY ON VIDEO
Building Teaching Resources

Strategies for building teaching resources are demonstrated on segment 7 of the DVD that accompanies this text. As you watch this segment, keep a list of the suggestions the teacher makes about ways to collect resources and store them. Also think about the following:

- The teacher's philosophy of teaching and how it is made evident by the resources she uses

- How the materials needed to support learning might differ in a classroom when the students are older or the curriculum is different

References

Bandura, A. (1997). *Self-efficacy: The exercise of control.* New York: Freeman.

Brophy, J. E. (1987). On motivating students. In D. G. Berliner & B. V. Rosenshine (Eds.), *Talks to teachers* (pp. 201–245). New York: Random House.

Krashen, S. (1988). *Second language acquisition and second language learning.* New York: Prentice Hall.

Suggested Reading

Gibbons, P. (1993). *Learning to learn in a second language.* Portsmouth, NH: Heinemann.

Meyers, M. (1993). *Teaching to diversity.* Toronto: Irwin.

USING SIMULATIONS IN THE CLASSROOM

There's an old adage that says, "Tell me, I forget. Show me, I remember. Involve me, I understand." Classroom simulations provide an avenue for totally involving students so that they can understand complex situations that are sometimes difficult to explain without having been there.

Simulations are activities in which students role-play either real persons or characterizations of people or situations in history. There is a wide range of possibilities for classroom simulations, such as historical events, literary scenes, real-life situations, or actual conflicts that have occurred in history or in the students' lives.

There are also a number of websites available on the Internet to support teachers as they begin to integrate simulations into the classroom. Examples of simulations available online are shown in Figure 20.1.

Because simulations place students into environments and interactions often unfamiliar to them, teaching and research is involved in preparing students to participate. Teachers explain the scenarios, build background knowledge, and only then run the simulation. The students learn about the dynamics of complex or historical situations by experiencing them.

 ## STEP BY STEP

The steps for implementing classroom simulations:

- **Prepare a simulation**   Explore the possibilities for situations that can be investigated, and choose a simulation that supports the curriculum and standards for which you are responsible. (See the websites listed in Figure 20.1 for suggestions.) Gather the materials you will need, and prepare the introductory lessons that will ensure your students' successful participation. Don't try to teach everything before the role-play. Encourage students to research the scenario, incorporating simulation preparation into their assigned reading. Establish a sequence of events for your study.

Figure 20.1 Examples of Simulations Available Online

Simulation	Website
Debbie's Desert—explore a desert ecosystem *Grades K–2*	www.interact-simulations.com
Friends—live as a member of an ethnic family *Grades K–3*	www.interact-simulations.com
Lewis & Clark—explore with the famous expedition *Grades 4–8*	www.interact-simulations.com
Apple Valley School—pioneer life in a one-room schoolhouse *Grades 4–9*	www.interact-simulations.com
Personal Finance—financial activities in everyday life *Grades 5–10*	www.interact-simulations.com
The Cambodia Peace Settlement—negotiating a peace agreement *Grades 9–12*	www.usip.org/class/simulations/ (United States Institute of Peace)
The Israeli-Palestinian conflict—lead and participate in a U.S.-led peace discussion *Grades 9–12*	www.usip.org/class/simulations/
Alive Maths—math problem activities *Grades 6–9*	www.enc.org/welinks/classroom/simulations/

• **Provide space, materials, and time**   Because simulations involve active participation and group planning, making space in the classroom is an important issue. You may even want to find some break-out space for small groups to work without disturbing other groups. Many materials can be helpful in planning, preparing, and researching the project: e.g., an overhead projector, flip charts, and markers. Computers with printers and Internet access are also vital for gathering the information necessary for the simulation. Though none of these things are mandatory for using simulations in the classroom, they can play a large role in motivating and engaging the students. Finally, teachers need to allocate blocks of time for the research, writing, and practicing involved in simulations.

- **Choose and research roles** The number of roles in the simulation should be adapted for your class size. Not everyone must have a speaking role, but everyone must be actively involved. Some web-based simulations have background information for the players. Some of the information may be read by all players. Other information is available only to certain players to ensure the authenticity of the situation. Be careful not to cast your most verbal students in the lead role as they may tend to overpower the others. Give students adequate time and resources to thoroughly research their roles.

- **Run the simulation** Begin by distributing information to all participants. Explain the situation and the approach that will be taken. Learning from simulations takes place in many different ways. Students learn through firsthand experiences, by observing, and also from reflection and discussion of the scenarios. While running the simulation, the teacher roams and observes, taking notes to facilitate discussion after the role-play.

- **Debrief the simulation** The purpose of the debriefing is to allow students to reflect on their experiences, feelings, and lessons learned. The teacher should avoid telling the students what happened. Begin by asking an open-ended question such as "What happened in the simulation?" Follow that discussion with a question such as "What was the outcome?" Feel free to ask participants how they felt during the interactions. Use this opportunity to link the simulation to ideas, concepts, and behaviors studied elsewhere. For example, "Did you see an example of conflict management in today's simulation?"

A follow-up assignment can be made to support connection of the simulation to other academic content. The students might write reflections comparing the simulation to an actual event in history or to a scene from a literary work.

Applications and Examples

Mrs. Gengosian's fourth-graders are studying California history and are reading books about the Gold Rush. Mrs. Gengosian begins the unit by reading aloud the book *Nine for California* (Levitin, 1996). This book tells the story of a family traveling by stagecoach to join their father, who is prospecting in the gold fields. As the students read more about the Gold Rush and all the activities involved, Mrs. Gengosian decides that they need to plan a simulation of life in the gold fields and the small towns that sprang up as a result of the gold seekers' rush to California. The students read a number of books and then plan activities, such as panning for gold, staking claims, bringing gold to the assayer's office, and mapping areas to determine where next to explore. The students read about the economy of the time and enjoy the companion books to *Nine for California—Boom Town* (Levitin, 1998) and *Taking Charge* (Levitin, 1999)—which explore the development of a town based on supplying the needs of the prospectors and the daily life of the families. Students work in groups to create simulations of the gold fields, town life, and family life of the time.

FOCUS ON ENGLISH LEARNERS

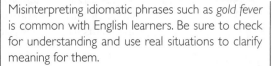

Misinterpreting idiomatic phrases such as *gold fever* is common with English learners. Be sure to check for understanding and use real situations to clarify meaning for them.

As Mrs. Gengosian observes the preparations for the simulation, she becomes aware of a growing misconception. The students read about *gold fever* and assume it is a disease the prospectors suffered. To give the students a chance to experience gold fever, Mrs. Gengosian plans a little simulation of her own. She finds some rocks and paints them gold. She hides the rocks around the classroom one day while the students are at lunch. When the students return from lunch, Mrs. Gengosian meets them at the door and explains the activity: "You are entering a gold field. I am giving you each a piece of yarn with which to stake your claim. You can look around the room and find gold. When you find gold you may stake your claim by circling the location with your piece of yarn. Once you have staked your claim, you must then guard it to avoid letting anyone else jump your claim."

While the students search frantically for gold in their classroom, Mrs. Gengosian videotapes their actions. After they each find their gold, she assembles the class to view the videotape. The students watch themselves dash around and search madly for gold and laugh at their antics. Mrs. Gengosian then asks them, "What happened in this activity?"

Matthew responds first. "We looked like we were all crazy. We ran around like chickens with our heads cut off, and it wasn't even real gold."

"That's exactly right, Matthew," Mrs. Gengosian comments. "Why do you think you acted that way?"

"Well, I wanted to make sure I found gold," says Terri. "I didn't want to be the only one who didn't find any."

"How did you feel while you searched?" asks Mrs. Gengosian.

"I was excited and nervous, and I just kept looking, even after I found gold. I kept looking for other places the gold might be hiding, but I didn't want to leave my claim," Terri answers.

"What do you suppose was wrong with all of you?" asks Mrs. Gengosian.

"Oh . . . ," Rena responds tentatively. "Did we all have gold fever?"

"That's exactly what was wrong with you," says Mrs. Gengosian.

"Oh, so gold fever isn't a disease where you really get a fever and have to go to bed," says Rena. "You just can't help yourself. You go crazy looking for gold."

"I think you have all experienced gold fever today," says Mrs. Gengosian with a smile. "Now you know how the prospectors felt so many years ago."

Miss Young's ninth-graders are studying the westward movement. Because this is her first attempt at running a simulation, Miss Young decides to use one from the Internet that has already been planned. She uses the Pioneer simulation available at www.interact-simulations.com.

In this simulation the students participate as members of four wagon trains headed west in 1846. The wagon trains face many challenges along the way, and the students must make life-and-death decisions. The students assume roles as members of families and work cooperatively to select supplies and track their progress on a map. They must solve problems such as weather crises, broken wagon wheels, snake bites, and flooding rivers. To move their wagons west, the students complete tasks that earn them travel points. Travel points are translated into miles along their journey.

As a part of their assignments, students keep a travel diary and use math and writing skills for authentic purposes. Miss Young is pleased with the enthusiasm of her students and plans to use many more simulations during the school year.

 ## CONCLUSION

Simulations offer opportunities for students to actively engage in learning about complex situations and interactions (Van Ments, 1989). Simulations can be used effectively in kindergarten through 12th grade and even in college classrooms. They engage students in research, writing, speaking roles, and discovering unique approaches to complex problem-solving. Simulations require planning and the allocation of time and materials while benefiting the students in many ways. The content standards in any curricular area can be addressed through this highly interactive process.

References

Van Ments, M. (1989). *The effective use of role-play*. London: Kogan Page.

Suggested Reading

Ellington, H., Gordon, M., & Fowlie, J. (1997). *Using games and simulations in the classroom.* New York: Taylor & Francis.

Freckleton, J. (1981). *Practicing real-life skills: An ungraded classroom simulation.* Pittsburgh: Hayes School Publishing.

Hare, P. (1985). *Social interaction as drama.* Beverly Hills, CA: Sage.

Levitin, S. (1996). *Nine for California.* New York: Orchard.

Levitin, S. (1998). *Boom town.* New York: Orchard.

Levitin, S. (1999). *Taking charge.* New York: Orchard.

Taylor, J., & Walford, R. (1972). *Simulation in the classroom.* New York: Penguin.

Internet Resources

http://multimedialearning.org
http://www.todaysteacher.com/Simulations
www.usip.org/class/simulations/
http://caho.columbia/edu/main/sim/
www.enc.org/weblinks/classroom/simulation/
www.interact-simulations.com

DOCUMENTING LEARNING

Helping students recognize their strengths and areas of need is important in establishing their active involvement in learning (Cunningham & Allington, 2003.) In order to involve students in their own assessment they need to recognize their current level of functioning—in other words, be aware of what they know and can do. They also need to be taught to set goals for themselves. In a collaborative classroom students are taught to give encouragement to one another and to celebrate their own accomplishments and the accomplishments of their peers.

There are multiple ways of documenting growth in students, which provide a variety of opportunities for self-reflection and celebration. Some students will not be able to demonstrate their growth in classrooms that use limited approaches to assessment (Herrell & Jordan, 2003). Introducing collaborative assessment procedures in a classroom is a gradual process. The teacher must explain and model what she expects of the students and be extremely supportive throughout the process.

 ## STEP BY STEP

The steps for implementing collaborative assessment in the classroom:

• **Identify the approaches to be used**   Identify the assessment approaches to be used in the classroom and plan the steps for involving the students. See Figure 21.1 for suggested approaches.

• **Introduce the assessment strategies one at a time**   Introduce each of the strategies to be used, carefully explaining and modeling how they will be implemented in the classroom and the students' roles in the process. See Figure 21.2 for an explanation of the strategies and the student roles.

 FOCUS ON ENGLISH LEARNERS

English learners benefit from being allowed to demonstrate their knowledge and skills without depending entirely on language.

Figure 21.1 Assessment Procedures and Their Uses and Purposes

Procedure/Use	Purpose
Portfolios—collections of work samples taken periodically; assessment relates to grade-level standards and goals set collaboratively between teacher and student	Allows students to see their own growth. Provides students with very authentic assessments, work done in class, and how this work meets the grade-level standards
Running records—documentation of a student's reading on a given day; provides evidence of reading strategies used and needs for instruction	Allows students to become aware of the reading strategies being used and those that need more practice
Writing samples—periodic samples of a student's writing; usually taken several times during the year for evaluation and planning future instruction	Allows students to collaboratively evaluate writing skills based on a grade-level scoring rubric
Skills checklists—a list of skills being taught and practiced, with space for documentation when a student uses the skills effectively	Allows students to see which of the skills being taught have been mastered and which need more practice; helps the teacher and student to work together to set learning and teaching goals
Scoring rubrics—descriptive scoring standards set up to help teachers, students, and parents see where a student is working in relation to grade-level standards	Sets clear expectations for the student so the current level of functioning is identified in relation to what needs to be done to improve the score on the next assignment
Narrative summaries—a verbal summary written to document a student's growth in a certain area; the summary usually identifies the former level of functioning, the progress that has been made, and a comparison of the progress with the grade-level standard to be met	Points out the progress that has been made in very understandable terms

- **Begin the process with baseline assessments** To begin the process, obtain baseline assessments for each of the students. These document current functioning and will allow the students to see and celebrate future growth.

- **Share the baseline assessments and set goals with individuals** Meet individually with each student at this phase. The discussion involves evaluating what the student knows and can do at this point in time based on the baseline assessment. Involve each

Figure 21.2   Student Roles in Assessment

Assessment	Student Role
Portfolios	Student chooses work to be included in the portfolio to show individual growth. Student can write a brief cover note for selected pieces to document why that piece was chosen. Student shares portfolio with parents at student/teacher/parent conferences and in periodic portfolio sharing in the classroom.
Running record	Student reads aloud while running record is taken and engages in discussion with teacher related to the running record once it has been scored. Student identifies, with teacher support, reading strategies to be practiced.
Writing samples	Student produces a writing sample, usually based on a provided topic but occasionally on a topic of the student's choice. Student engages in discussion with teacher related to assessment of the writing, identification of writing strengths, and needs for improvement and works with the teacher to set learning/teaching goals.
Skills checklists	Student and teacher work collaboratively to identify the skills the student has accomplished and to set future learning/teaching goals.
Scoring rubrics	Students can be actively involved in building scoring rubrics. Once built, the rubrics help make the expectations clear, identify the student's level of functioning, and what must be done to ensure improvement.
Narrative summaries	Student reads and discusses the teacher's narrative summary and works collaboratively to set goals for the future. Student shares progress from the narrative summary in celebration circles and parent conferences.

student in identifying areas that need improvement and steps to be taken to ensure progress.

• **Collect periodic work samples to monitor and celebrate growth**   Repeat the assessment/goal-setting steps regularly throughout the school year based on timely assessments of current work. Take work samples periodically and engage students in discussion, celebration of progress, and goal-setting in an ongoing manner. See Figure 21.3 for an example of a schedule that demonstrates how this is done.

• **Conduct class celebration circles**   Each time students are reassessed and engage in new goal-setting sessions, recognize their progress in a classroom celebration circle. This is an informal celebration but encourages public recognition of each student's progress. It also models ways for other students to recognize and congratulate their peers.

Applications and Examples

Mrs. Leonard's third-graders are gathered on the carpet at the front of the room. Mrs. Leonard is showing them their new portfolio folders, which she has color-coded into four different groups so the students can locate their own more easily.

Figure 21.3   Example of an Assessment/Goal-Setting Schedule

Group	Week	Assessment/Goal-Setting
1	1	Running records/writing samples/reading and writing goal-setting
2	2	Running records/writing samples/reading and writing goal-setting
3	3	Running records/writing samples/reading and writing goal-setting
4	4	Running records/writing samples/reading and writing goal-setting
1	5	Portfolio selections/skills checklists/math and science goal-setting
2	6	Portfolio selections/skills checklists/math and science goal-setting
3	7	Portfolio selections/skills checklists/math and science goal-setting
4	8	Portfolio selections/skills checklists/math and science goal-setting
		REPEAT PROCESS

"We will be choosing some work to go into our portfolios each week," she explains. "I am putting the list of language arts standards for third grade into each of your folders to help you select papers to include."

Mrs. Leonard then chooses an example from the language arts standards and brings Jeremy up in front of the class. "Jeremy has a writing paper from yesterday that shows that he has met one of the standards. The standard says that students will include similes in their writing. Jeremy, read what you wrote yesterday."

Jeremy reads, "I was as sad as an awful thunderstorm."

Mrs. Leonard says, "That's exactly what this standard is talking about. You used a wonderful simile to tell how sad you felt when your rabbit died."

"That was great, Jeremy!" chimes in Vanessa. "Similes really help us understand how the writer feels."

"Exactly," says Mrs. Leonard. "Now this week I want you all to begin to select papers that show how you are meeting the third-grade standards. I will be meeting with three of you each day to look over your portfolios and help you set goals for yourselves. When you have a paper selected, sign up for a goal-setting conference."

Mr. Castle teaches ninth-grade algebra in a large urban middle school. Because he wants his students to become more responsible for their own learning, he is using skills checklists aligned with the ninth-grade mathematics standards. Each student is keeping a work folder and documenting his or her progress toward meeting the standards in algebra. Mr. Castle holds small-group meetings on Fridays where the students share the progress they made that week and discuss the standards they plan to meet in the following week. Each student is responsible for selecting a paper to document the skills they check off on their checklists. The group talks about the different ways that they can meet and document the standards. Several students have used tests to document their standards. Others have used classwork or even homework. The group holds a lively discussion and talks about how some of the standards must be met in a specific order. Students are very good at using positive talk to support one another because they've been practicing this all year.

Mr. Castle is pleased with the progress his students are making. He is especially excited when one student suggests something another student has accomplished but forgotten to document. The students seem to be supporting one another and a community feeling is developing in this group, even though they meet together for only 50 minutes a day.

CONCLUSION

Both Mrs. Leonard and Mr. Castle are using multiple assessments to monitor and document their students' growth. They have found ways to involve their students in self-assessment and become aware of their own personal growth. Although both teachers still give traditional tests, they offer their students other opportunities to document their understanding. They are instilling skills in organization, summarization, and record-keeping as well. By using things such as portfolios, standards checklists, and work folders, both teachers have authentic examples to share with parents during conferences and to use when writing comments on report cards.

STRATEGY ON VIDEO
Documenting Learning

Strategies for documenting learning in a fourth-grade classroom are demonstrated on segment 8 of the DVD that accompanies this text. You will see how one teacher progresses from just collecting student work to selecting items for a portfolio and using the portfolio for assessment and goal-setting. As you watch this segment, think about the following:

- How are the students involved in the process?
- How does the verbal interaction between the students and the teacher enable them to use conferences to establish goals and expectations?

References

Cunningham, P., & Allington, R. (2003). *Classrooms that work: They can ALL read and write.* (3rd ed.). Boston: Allyn & Bacon.

Herrell, A., & Jordan, M. (2003). *Fifty strategies for teaching English language learners.* (2nd ed.). Upper Saddle River, NJ: Merrill/Prentice Hall.

Suggested Reading

Stowell, L., & Tierney, R. (1995). Portfolios in the classroom: What happens when teachers and students negotiate assessment? In R. Allington & S. Walmsley (Eds.), *No quick fix: Rethinking literacy programs in America's elementary schools.* New York: Teachers College Press.

22

ESTABLISHING AND MAINTAINING READING AND WRITING WORKSHOPS

The workshop format for reading and writing instruction involves students in following the stages in process writing; prewriting, drafting, revising, editing, and publishing using self-chosen topics. Reading workshops also involve self-chosen books but add follow-up projects employing what is learned through the study of good literature. These follow-up activities often involve writing projects. The implementation of reading and writing workshops allows the teacher to use large blocks of time usually allotted to these two disciplines.

Reading and writing workshops are among the most successful ways to provide students with authentic practice in reading and writing skills, collaborative learning, connections among past experiences, new skill achievement, and applications to life (Tompkins, 2005). These workshops incorporate all of Cambourne's (2002) conditions for learning literacy:

- Immersion in literacy
- Modeling of literate behaviors
- Learner expectations of success
- Individual responsibility
- Successive approximations toward a standard
- Employment of skills being acquired
- Formal and informal feedback and authentic engagement in learning and practicing new, literate behaviors

These workshops also provide opportunities for genuine collaboration in the form of student-led writing conferences where students support one another's efforts to improve their writing. This contributes to the feeling of building community in a classroom.

STEP BY STEP

The steps for implementing and maintaining reading and writing workshops:

- **Develop a schedule for gradual implementation** To avoid being overwhelmed by the planning involved in reading and writing workshops, develop a schedule that allows you to implement the elements one at a time. Teachers often introduce the elements in mini-lessons related to the steps in the writing process. They support this approach by reading aloud quality literature to demonstrate the goal of the student authors. Since a main tenet of this approach is the self-selection of reading and writing topics by the students, they must have available to them a variety of leisure reading materials as well as a wealth of writing materials such as scrap paper, writing folders, dictionaries, thesauruses, and computers with word-processing capability.

- **Plan and teach mini-lessons** Start the process of implementation by examining the reading and writing standards for your grade level. Also examine writing samples from your students and choose a mini-lesson that will help the students make progress toward the standard. Plan, teach, and model a short lesson (10–15 minutes) related to the topic you have chosen, and then give the students time to practice under your guidance. Once the students are ready to practice independently, give them time (30 minutes or more) to practice what you've taught them. If they have a piece of writing they're already working on, encourage them to examine it and see if they can add the element you've just taught. For students who do not have an idea about what to write, post some photographs for them to use as topics. Model the use of self-talk (thinking aloud about a photograph and what might be written about it) and list the ideas on the board.

FOCUS ON ENGLISH LEARNERS

Breaking English writing tasks into small steps with modeling and explanation is very supportive to English learners.

- **Teach the writing process** Schedule mini-lessons to gradually teach the writing process. Explain each stage, model it, and walk the students through the process. Using a piece of writing you have created, model how the author goes through the prewriting process, coming up with possible topics and choosing one to web, outline, or illustrate. After these mini-lessons give the students time to practice the step you have demonstrated.

- **Build reading and writing folders** Provide a special folder for each student. Choose folders with three-hole brads and pockets in the front and back. Encourage the students to keep a list of possible writing topics in the front pocket and a list of books they have read in the back pocket. Students keep drafts of writing they're working on in this folder as well as records of the steps in the writing process they've completed and the dates. They may even use notebook paper in the center of the folder as a reading journal. See Figure 22.1 for an example of a workshop record sheet.

- **Schedule time for quality work** Since the reading/writing workshop will use the time allotted for instruction in both areas, block out the time in increments in order to give the students structure to their workshop. See Figure 22.2 for an example of this type of schedule.

- **Teach and practice conferring skills** After you've taught prewriting and drafting using your own writing as an example, make a transparency of your story, leaving spaces between lines of print. Explain to your students that you always skip lines when writing your drafts because that allows you to go back and make revisions. Read your story aloud to your students and ask them to tell you what parts they like. Explain that it's important to start with the good parts because the author needs to know which sections to keep. After they tell you what they like, ask them if there are parts that are not clear or parts that they'd like to know more about. As they give you suggestions, write the suggestions on lines near where they need to be placed in the text. You are modeling what they, as authors, will be doing when their peers give them suggestions to improve

Figure 22.1 Workshop Record Sheet

Date Begun/Pub.	Project	Prewriting	Drafting	Conference	Revising	Editing
4/18/05 5/3/05	Cugo, my dog	4/19	4/20	4/25 4/28	4/26 4/29	4/30

Books Read	Author	Title	Begun	Completed	Project	Date
4/18/05	Gardiner	Stone Fox	4/18	4/22	diorama	4/28

their work. Make this clear to the students, and tell them that this process is called a writing conference. They will be reading their own work and asking their peers to give them suggestions as soon as they complete their first draft. They will then go back to their seats and revise their work according to the suggestions that were given to them. They may want to schedule another conference after they've made revisions. Once they've finished the revision, they can take their work to the editing table. Make it very clear that correcting spelling, punctuation, and other mechanics are part of editing, not revising. Revising deals with the flow of the story, the way the story develops, the main ideas and supporting details.

• **Set up the editing station** The editing station is the location in the room where the students take their work to be edited once the draft is revised and ready to prepare for publication. It should be a table where two students can work together. The table should be supplied with dictionaries, thesauruses, colored pens and erasers. Students work here to read drafts together and make notations about corrections that need to be made. Some teachers like students to circle misspelled words for the author to look up in the dictionary. With very young children, it's sometimes helpful to have an older peer editor work with them.

• **Publish student work** There are many different ways of publishing student work. The students themselves can word-process their work, print it out, and bind it using cardboard and leftover wallpaper. Some teachers like to publish classroom anthologies: books

Figure 22.2   A Third-Grade Reading/Writing Workshop Schedule

Time	Activity
8:30–9:00	Mini-lesson and guided practice
9:00–9:45	Quiet writing time Teacher monitors and teaches a reading group.
9:45–10:30	Quiet reading time Teacher monitors and teaches a reading group.
10:30–11:00	Students meet in student-led literature circles or writing and editing groups to discuss their reading or writing. Teacher teaches a reading group.
11:00–11:30	Celebration circle Students read completed writing or share an especially interesting book with the group. Progress is celebrated. The status of the class is taken. (Students report their progress in moving through the writing process and where they plan to work tomorrow.)

that contain the writings of a number of students in the class. Once the final draft is rewritten in neat penmanship or word-processed, it can then be displayed on bulletin boards, on cardboard easels, or in any way that encourages students to read it.

• **Schedule celebrations**   Once a piece of writing is completed, the student should be given an opportunity to read it aloud. This might be done while sitting in the author's chair, in a celebration circle in the classroom, to the principal, or another class. Some schools announce newly published authors' names in the lunchroom during lunch and have a special table for newly published authors so they can sit together and talk about their new books.

• **Read aloud to provide quality models of good writing**   Teaching the genres of literature fits into the structure of the reading/writing workshop very well. Read aloud examples of good children's or adolescent literature that provide the students with a better understanding of the genre being studied. After reading several examples, present a mini-lesson on how to write in the genre. Students still choose their topic, but they practice writing in the genre being studied, whether fairy tales, biography, historical fiction, or nonfiction. The same approach can be used when teaching story structure. Begin by reading some stories that have a distinct beginning, middle, and end, others that have a cumulative structure, and others with a circular structure. After reading several books in the same structure, the students write their own book using the modeled structure.

• **Integrate the teaching of reading**   The integration of reading instruction into the workshop is easily done. Once students understand the workshop structure and the activity is running smoothly, you have the opportunity to work with small groups for reading instruction. There is no need to plan seatwork for the students in a workshop classroom. The students are practicing reading and writing in an authentic way.

• **Monitor student progress** Review the reading/writing folders to note the progress the students are making in completing reading and writing projects. If you note a student who is not using time wisely or not progressing through the writing process, schedule an individual conference with that student to set more specific daily goals. You might need to be more directive with that student for a while, assigning tasks for the morning and then checking on progress periodically throughout the workshop.

Applications and Examples

Mrs. Martin's first-graders are reading and writing about farms. They read books about farm animals, and each day Mrs. Martin walks them through an exercise in which they read a book about a specific animal and then talk about the animal as a prewriting strategy for their writing for the day. Mrs. Martin draws a big picture of the animal, and the students help her label its unique parts. They then make a list of all the things they have learned about the animal to help them plan what to write.

"What we have done today is to get ready to write about cows," Mrs. Martin tells them after they've labeled a large picture of a black and white cow. "When you go back to your seats today, you can use some of the books you've been reading and you can use the labels and ideas we've written down. I want you to write an informational piece about cows. Who remembers what an informational piece is?"

"It's a piece that's true. It's facts and not a story," volunteers Frederic.

"That's exactly right, Frederic," responds Mrs. Martin. "So in your writing today, will your cows be talking?" she asks.

"No!" the students all chorus. "Cows can't talk."

The students go back and spend their reading/writing workshop time reading and writing about cows. Mrs. Martin asks them to turn in their stories for that day since she wants to use one of them for the mini-lesson on revising she's planning for the next day.

The following day, Mrs. Martin uses one of the student's stories as the basis of her mini-lesson. She writes the story on a chart tablet, leaving lots of room between the lines.

"I have a wonderful piece about cows that one of our friends wrote yesterday," she begins. "Today I want to show you how to help each other make your stories even better."

The class reads the story together and makes suggestions to improve it. Mrs. Martin shows them how to write the ideas onto the draft. She then walks them through revising the piece, using some of their suggestions and deciding not to use others. "Remember, it's your piece. You get to decide how to revise it," she reminds them. She then puts the students into pairs to work together on conferring and then revising independently.

Once the students complete their revisions, Mrs. Martin has them read their stories aloud to the class. Because they are only first-graders, she is introducing the steps in the writing process very slowly. She meets with the students to help them edit their drafts. The students recopy their edited stories, illustrate them, and Mrs. Martin publishes them in a class book.

Mr. Gonsalves and his eighth-graders are studying the formation of the nation and the writing of the Constitution after the Revolutionary War. In his block-scheduled class Mr. Gonsalves is responsible for addressing the social studies and language arts standards with his students in a 2-hour block each day. His students work in a reading/writing workshop and are reading biographies and historical fiction set during this time in history. As a culminating activity, the students are writing a piece in which they will speak as a person instrumental in the Revolutionary War or the writing of the Constitution. They base their soliloquy on the information they gain from reading biographies of the person they've chosen.

Mr. Gonsalves introduces a new prewriting technique in which students brainstorm the attributes of their character on an outline of the person's head. They put in the thought they want to convey to the class and then draw speech balloons to note any quotes they

Figure 22.3   Mr. Gonsalves's Status of the Class Chart

Names	9/2	9/3	9/4	9/5	9/6	9/9	9/10	9/11	9/12	9/13	9/15	9/16	9/17	
Arthur	PW	D	D	C	R	C	E							
Beatriz	PW	D	C	R	D	E	P							
Carlos	PW	D	D	C	R	E	P							
Danny	PW	D	C	R	C	R	E							

PW = prewriting D = draft C = conference R = revising E = editing P = practicing soliloquy

want to include in their piece. Once he demonstrates the technique, the students work on their "talking heads" until they feel they have enough ideas to get started on their drafts.

Mr. Gonsalves has groups of desks set up in his classroom and has identified two groups of desks for the students to use in conferring about their drafts, once they have written them. The students move through the writing process and note the steps they complete on a "status of the class" poster in the front of the room. See Figure 22.3 for the poster Mr. Gonsalves uses for this purpose.

Once the students have practiced their character presentations, they create a visual or prop to use. The class works together to create a narrative of the historical events to set the stage for the character presentations, and the class practices reading the narrative as a reader's theatre with the character presentations inserted in appropriate places.

The entire piece is published as a class book, with the group-written narrative setting the stage and the character pieces placed in context within the book. Mr. Gonsalves puts their publication into the class library and notices that the students often read it during their workshop free-reading time.

At the next faculty meeting, Mr. Gonsalves shows clips from the videotape he's made of their production. The other history/language arts teachers are very interested in how he got the students to produce such quality work. Mr. Gonsalves is convinced that the workshop format encourages quality and cooperation.

 ## CONCLUSION

There are many aspects of reading/writing workshop that make it worthwhile. Students are learning responsibility. They are given time to work through the steps of the writing process to constantly improve their writing under supervision and with peer support. They are learning communication skills as they confer with one another about their drafts. They are learning that quality writing involves writing more than one draft and that drafts can always be improved. Equally important is the fact that they are working and learning in a cooperative relationship and building a stronger class community.

STRATEGY ON VIDEO
Establishing and Maintaining Reading and Writing Workshops

Strategies for establishing and maintaining reading and writing workshops are demonstrated in a first-grade classroom on segment 9 of the DVD that accompanies this text. You will see a mini-lesson on prewriting and drafting. As you watch this segment, think about the following:

- How does the teacher support the students as they begin the process of learning to spell the words they need in order to write?

- How does the teacher provide support to those students who are not initially able to begin their drafts?

References

Cambourne, B. (2002). The conditions of learning: Is learning natural? *Reading Teacher, 55*(8), 758–762.

Tompkins, G. (2005). Writing workshop: Implementing the writing process. In G. Tompkins & C. Blanchfield, *50 ways to develop strategic writers* (pp. 152–153). Upper Saddle River, NJ: Pearson Education.

Suggested Reading

Cambourne, B. (1999). Explicit and systematic teaching of reading—a new slogan? *Reading Teacher, 53*(2), 126–127.

Fletcher, R., & Portalupi, J. (1998). *Craft lessons: Teaching writing, K–8.* York, ME: Stenhouse.

Gillett, J., & Beverly, L. (2001). *Directing the writing workshop: An elementary teacher's handbook.* New York: Guilford.

Holdaway, D. (2000). Affinities and contradictions: The dynamics of social or acquisitional learning. *Literacy Teaching and Learning, 5*(1), 7–25.

23

USING MULTIPLE INTELLIGENCES THEORY IN CENTERS TO SUPPORT LEARNING

Learning centers or stations are used in many classrooms. In kindergarten classrooms you often see block centers, art centers, listening centers, and library centers. In primary grades you may see some of the same centers as well as math and science centers. Unfortunately, you rarely see learning centers or stations in classrooms above the primary grades.

Learning centers, as defined in this section, are extremely appropriate at all grade levels, kindergarten through high school. Learning centers are used as opportunities for students to expand their experiences in authentic ways. It is important that the centers be presented as an important part of academic assignments and that the skills to be practiced have already been thoroughly taught. Centers serve as additional independent practice or even as extensions in academic skill building. They present an opportunity to integrate learning, and, in the case of Multiple Intelligence (MI) centers, they allow students to address new skills in a way that utilizes their strongest intelligences. They serve one more important function: they provide an opportunity to meet the wide range of individual needs and cognitive abilities present in every classroom (Owocki, 2005). They provide additional basic practice for some students, expanded practice for others, and an opportunity to use new skills in connection with higher-level thinking for others.

FOCUS ON ENGLISH LEARNERS

Multiple intelligences centers enable English learners to practice and demonstrate knowledge without always being hampered by their limited English proficiency.

Howard Gardner's (1999) multiple intelligences theory provides the structure on which to build learning centers. After teaching lessons that address academic standards, Gardner's eight intelligences are used to design extension and authentic practice activities to build students' understanding of the concepts that have been taught.

STEP BY STEP

The steps for implementing MI learning centers:

- **Identify the standards and concepts to be addressed**   Select major concepts that are being taught. The concepts to be practiced may be integrated across academic disciplines, but in the beginning it's best to keep it simple.

- **Think in multiple intelligences terms**   Taking each of the eight intelligences, think about the concept or skill to be practiced and identify ways in which students can interact with the concept or skill using each of the intelligences. See Figure 23.1 for suggestions.

- **Start simple**   Start with four centers instead of eight. Be sure to include some that encourage students to use more than the more traditional verbal-linguistic and logical-mathematical intelligences. If you have some very active students in your class, be sure to include the body-kinesthetic center.

- **Set up the centers**   Be sure to think about things such as material storage and access, the number of students to be included in each center, and expectations for behavior and interaction in the center. Allow students to use the centers after the routines and expectations are clear to them. As a part of the design, think about how the students will demonstrate their use of the center and their understanding of the concepts or skills being practiced. You will be involved in other things after the first few minutes of center time, so you want to make centers as self-directed as possible.

- **Involve students in setting up the routine**   As you explain the purpose and expectations for each center, involve the students in helping you to decide such things as:

  1. How many students can comfortably work in this center?
  2. How can we indicate the center capacity in some way?
  3. Exactly what will be required in this center?
  4. How can we post the expectation?
  5. How will the work done in this center be submitted?
  6. What are the expectations for cleanup and materials use?
  7. Can you move to another center once you finish your work?

Once these points have been discussed, the routine and expectations should be posted at each center.

- **Monitor center use**   For the first few minutes of center time, monitor the activity and make sure that students are on task. If anyone seems to be unsure about what to do, intervene and redirect. At this point, you can go on to conduct individual conferences or teach small-group lessons.

- **Promote responsibility**   Students should understand that centers are not play time. They have definite tasks to complete and should have responsibility for submitting a record of their accomplishments each day. (See Figure 23.2 for an example of a center record sheet.) When using the record sheet, students enter a notation for each center visited each day. They can use 1 = started, 2 = continued, and 3 = completed or just jot a short note about their activity. For kindergartners, omit the center names and put pictures corresponding to the center label on the record sheet. Students should be prepared to share their accomplishments with the class at the end of the center period.

- **Celebrate accomplishments**   It is vital to take a few minutes periodically throughout and at the end of center time to celebrate students' accomplishments. A few words of

Figure 23.1 Multiple Intelligences Learning Centers

Intelligence	What to Use	Suggested Centers
Verbal-linguistic	• Words • Reading • Writing	• Crossword puzzles with clues related to important vocabulary • Listening center with supplementary reading/written responses • Writing center—writing formula poems about the topic
Logical-mathematical	• Numbers • Logic • Problem-solving	• Math problems related to the topic • Logic conundrums that can be solved with numbers
Visual-spatial	• Pictures • Graphics	• Illustrating basic concepts taught • Creating graphs, posters, or murals related to the topic • Creating webs showing the connections among concepts or characters. • Designing flowcharts
Body-kinesthetic	• Movement games • Enactments • Mime	• Designing a game involving movement, to teach to the class, that helps us understand or remember the topic • Creating a skit, with or without words, that illustrates the concepts studied
Musical-rhythmic	• Song • Melody • Rhythm	• Creating a song or jingle related to the topic studied • Creating a rap related to the topic • Writing words to a familiar melody that helps us remember the topic
Interpersonal	• Conversation • Debate • Interview	• Creating, with a partner, the main points in a debate supporting or arguing against an issue related to the topic • Interviewing another student about his or her understanding of the topic; sharing your views with the person you interviewed
Intrapersonal	• Self-reflection • Working alone to create a project	• Responding to literary quotes related to the topic (in a journal or on a tape recorder) • Designing an advocacy project to gain support for the topic • Designing an original way to represent the concepts studied
Naturalistic	• Nature studies • Using nature to explain concepts	• Using natural materials to show how the concept works • Finding an example in nature that demonstrates the topic • Illustrating how the topic contrasts with natural phenomena

Figure 23.2   Example of a Center Record Sheet

Learning Center Record Sheet					
Student's Name _____ Week of _____					
Center	**Monday**	**Tuesday**	**Wednesday**	**Thursday**	**Friday**
Verbal-linguistic					
Logical-mathematical					
Visual-spatial					
Body-kinesthetic					
Musical-rhythmic					
Interpersonal					
Intrapersonal					
Naturalistic					

Note: A blank, blackline master of this form is included in the "Teacher Resources" section of this text.

encouragement as students are working diligently helps direct other students back on task. These celebrations need not be extensive. Just give a student or two a minute to share accomplishments.

  • **Include the center work as part of student work samples or portfolios**   To further validate center work, evaluate it and include it as part of the student's work folder or portfolio. If the student gets no feedback on center work, he or she quickly perceives it as busy work.

Applications and Examples

Ms. McCloskey's first grade is studying the life cycle of a frog. Students have read and written about frogs, observed frogs, seen videos about frogs, and even watched the life cycle progress from frog eggs, to tadpoles, to adult frogs. Ms. McCloskey is introducing multiple intelligences learning centers into their study to give them even more experiences related to their science/language arts unit. She begins by gathering the students on the carpet and introducing the concept of learning centers: "You remember last year in kindergarten you went to centers every day. We are going to begin to have center time in first grade now, but the centers are going to be just a little different. We are going to go on exploring frogs, but I want you to have some new activities to do as you explore frogs. For the first center I want you to learn a song about frogs. Listen to this music." Ms. McCloskey plays a tape, and the children learn a song about frogs.

"Now, you already know a lot of things about frogs, so I want you to make up some more verses for the frog song. This verse tells about a jumping frog. Think of all the other things frogs can do and add them to the song. After center time, you can sing your new verses. You can sing by yourself, or you can teach the song to the class and we can sing with you," Ms. McCloskey adds. For this center, she has recorded a tape that repeats the known verse of the song two times and then adds six additional verses of music without words so the children can sing their new songs along with the tape.

Ms. McCloskey goes on with her explanation: "Our next center is an art center. Here I want you to make a chart that shows the life cycle of the frog. I have included some pictures of all the different stages to help you remember them. There is poster paper here and markers, too. You can also use construction paper, glue, and scissors if you want."

"I have put some hula hoops over on this side of the room," she goes on. "This center will be where you can practice jumping like frogs. Each time someone jumps, you place a hula hoop where he lands and measure the jump using the big number line. We will keep a graph of how far people jump. And you can keep jumping to try to do better," she says.

"We will still have our regular reading center where you can read books about frogs and write in your reading journals," Ms. McCloskey continues. "We also have a listening center where you can listen to books about frogs that are too hard for you to read by yourself. But you still have to write a sentence in your reading journal after you hear the story," she reminds them.

"In the last frog center you will be doing math problems about frogs. There are little toy frogs in that center for you to use as you do the problems," she adds.

Ms. McCloskey passes out center report sheets with the children's names on them. Each center is listed on the sheet, and students will color in the box next to a center when they've completed it. They color the box green if they've started the center, yellow if they want to work there some more, and red if they've finished it.

"You are responsible for putting the materials away and cleaning up when you're done, though. I have some poster paper so we can make signs for each of the centers to remind you of what you're expected to do," Ms. McCloskey goes on. She and the children make posters for the centers. The children tell her what to write, and she does the writing. Each poster tells

1. What to do

2. How many people can work in the center at one time

See Figure 23.3 for an example of one of the posters they created.

Ms. McCloskey chooses to use free-flow centers. Her students can move from one center to another whenever they have completed work at a center. They are not required to do any certain number of centers for the frog study, but she may have "must do" centers in future studies. She never has all the centers designated as "must do" because she wants children to choose the centers that best match their strongest intelligences.

As the class begins centers, Ms. McCloskey observes their choices. These choices help her understand their strengths. She monitors behavior closely and has private conferences

Figure 23.3 Example of a Center Poster

Poster Center

Four people can work here.

1. Make a poster to show the life cycle of the frog.
2. Clean up and put away all materials before you move to a new center.
3. Put your poster on the chalk tray.

with children who are not making good choices. Occasionally she will assign a center for a child who is not using time wisely.

As the students work in centers, Ms. McCloskey calls reading groups to work with her. When a child is called to reading group, the child places his nametag at the center where he was working to save his place until he returns. Between reading groups, Ms. McCloskey circulates briefly, giving words of encouragement to students who are working well. At the end of the center time she gathers the students together for debriefing and celebration She talks about the good work that she saw being done, asks students to share what they accomplished, and they all sing the new verses to the frog song that the students have written. They are expanding their knowledge about frogs and celebrating their good work.

Mr. Frederick teaches high school physics and often hears questions about how students will be able to use "the stuff" they're learning in real life. To help them explore the principles they are learning and see real-life applications, Mr. Frederick teaches a principle or two for 4 days and then engages his students in learning centers on Fridays. Because he knows his students have differing intelligence strengths, he sets up the centers based on Howard Gardner's multiple intelligences.

For a week Mr. Frederick has been teaching lessons on force as it relates to water and atmospheric pressure. As he plans Friday's centers, he thinks about how students can explore these concepts and begin to recognize their importance in everyday life. Because the students have already taken a self-analysis to determine their strong intelligences, Mr. Frederick will allow them to choose their centers based on their two strongest intelligences.

At the math center he sets up a series of problems related to building a two-story house and designing the routing and size of the water pipes to be used in the house. The final problem is a project that he plans to have the students actually build the next week. He proposes a class fountain and gives the students the challenge of deciding what size water pump should be used for the fountain and what size pipes to buy to maintain the fountain at a particular height.

At the visual center the students are challenged to design a graphic illustrating the principles that were studied that week. At the conclusion of the center period they will be expected to present and explain their graphics.

At the interpersonal center the students are asked to work in groups of two or three to design a simple project that demonstrates the principles taught this week. They must

1. Discuss and plan the project together
2. Collect materials and build the project
3. Present the demonstration to the class

At the intrapersonal center students are to complete a personal reflection, finding ways in which the principles taught can be used in real life. They can write about the applications in a personal journal or talk about the ideas into the tape recorder.

At the musical center students are asked to create a song, rap, or jingle that will help the class remember the principles studied that week. They will then present their work to the class.

At the naturalistic center students are asked to find examples of the principles in nature and present them to the class. They can use photos from the Internet to demonstrate their points, downloading and using overhead transparencies printed from the class computers.

Before they begin the centers on Friday Mr. Frederick meets with the whole class briefly, reminding them of the expectations for center time. He asks the students to list the expected behaviors and calls attention to the posted center rules. As students choose their centers, he passes out task cards that outline exactly what must be completed in the center. During the center period Mr. Frederick circulates throughout the classroom, encouraging good work, and occasionally reminding students of their responsibilities.

Because the students are so actively involved in the centers on Friday, Mr. Frederick decides to let them work for the entire 2-hour period and present their findings on Monday. He's very pleased with the results, especially the actual demonstrations. He takes pictures of their projects and presentations with his digital camera and posts the pictures on the bulletin board. He notices that students stop, look at the pictures, and discuss the projects every day for weeks. The center work has deepened the students' understanding of the principles and their real-world applications.

 CONCLUSION

Multiple intelligences centers are very powerful at all grade levels. Secondary students are especially receptive to this approach because they spend so much time in classes where only the linguistic and mathematical intelligences are rewarded. Planning these centers is time-consuming at first but gets easier as the teacher gains more experience in creating them. Students respond well, and teachers often discover hidden talents in unique students.

STRATEGY ON VIDEO
Planning Multiple Intelligences Learning Centers
First-grade teachers work together to plan multiple intelligences learning centers on segment 10 of the DVD that accompanies this text. Watch to see how they begin the process of changing from generic learning centers to those based on Gardner's research. As you view this segment, think about the following:

• How do the teachers review their understanding of the multiple intelligences?
• Why do they feel the need to make this change in their learning centers?
• How do they manage to integrate curriculum in their learning centers?

References

Gardner, H. (1999). *Intelligence reframed: Multiple intelligences for the 21st century.* New York: Perseus.
Owocki, G. (2005). *Time for literacy centers: How to organize and differentiate instruction.* Portsmouth, NH: Heinemann.

Suggested Reading

Diller, D. (2003). *Literacy work stations: Making centers work.* York, ME: Stenhouse.
Marks-Tarlow, T. (1996). *Creativity inside out: Learning through multiple intelligences.* New York: Addison-Wesley.
Marriott, D., & Kupperstein, J. (Eds.). (1997). *What are the other kids doing while you teach small groups?* New York: Creative Teaching Press.
Opitz, M. (1994). *Learning centers.* New York: Scholastic.

DESIGNING EFFECTIVE HOMEWORK ASSIGNMENTS

"Data show that homework accounts for about 20 percent of the total time the typical American student spends on academic tasks. . . . considering this fact, it is surprising how little attention is paid to the topic in teacher education" (Cooper, 2000).

Homework is defined as the out-of-class assignments that students are given as extensions of their schoolwork. Three types of homework are commonly assigned (LaConte, 1981):

• Practice assignments reinforce newly acquired skills and knowledge. These tasks are most effective when

They are carefully evaluated by the teacher.

They are matched to the abilities and backgrounds of the student.

Students are asked to apply recent learning directly.

• Preparation assignments are intended to build background knowledge by reading, researching, or collecting materials. These types of tasks are most effective when the student is given guidelines indicating why and how the assignment should be completed.

• Extension activities encourage individualized and creative learning that emphasizes the student's initiative and interests.

The research on homework effectiveness demonstrates that the amount of time spent on homework increases as students move into higher grades (Cooper, 2000). Students who do more homework tend to be more successful in school, but researchers quickly disavow a cause-and-effect connection due to many intervening variables (Walberg, 1991). International studies indicate that either too much or too little homework may be counterproductive to academic success (Sharp, 2001).

Parents are almost always involved in homework activities and often require support with effective strategies they can use at home to make their involvement a positive factor. If the homework interactions at home are negative, this can impact students' attitudes toward school and learning.

Teachers must have a clear understanding of the purposes of the homework they are assigning, the amount of time it will take to accomplish, and how it will be evaluated. Planning an effective homework program should not be taken lightly. It involves making many decisions.

STEP BY STEP

The steps for designing and implementing effective homework:

- **Set standing assignments**   Students should have required assignments that they complete each night. This may be reading from a self-chosen library book or from a text-book that will be used in class the next day. They may also have standing assignments such as reworking math problems they worked incorrectly.

- **Help parents understand the expectations**   At the first opportunity, communicate in writing and in parent-teacher meetings that parents have several responsibilities related to their students' homework assignments:

  1. They should provide a quiet place for the student to do homework.
  2. They should maintain a designated time for homework.
  3. They should expect homework every night, even if it's just reading.
  4. They should document the starting and ending time their student spends on homework and sign a daily homework journal.
  5. If the homework is taking the student longer to finish than the time set according to the student's grade level, that fact should be noted in the student homework journal as well. (See Figure 24.1 for time allocations for homework, grade by grade.)

  For students who see different teachers each day, devise a system for coordinating homework assignments should be devised so that time-consuming assignments are not assigned by several different teachers on the same night.

- **Match homework assignments to the abilities of the student**   Students should never be asked to practice skills for homework if they do not fully understand them. Make sure that you have taught the skill, provided guided practice, and are reasonably sure that the student is ready for independent practice. Give the students time to work on the problems or skills independently before they take them home for homework. This gives them an opportunity to ask questions if they are still not sure of what to do. Parents should not be placed in the position of having to teach skills. If students get home and find they cannot complete the homework because they don't know what to do, they have backup homework in the form of standing assignments such as reading or correcting math problems.

FOCUS ON ENGLISH LEARNERS

Many English learners have no one to assist them with homework at home. Be sure to make sure they understand what to do and how to do the assignments before sending them home.

  In the event that you have students who really don't need more practice on a skill, give those students assignments that extend their knowledge, provide opportunities to make real-life connections to their schoolwork, or create something innovative in relation to the topics studied in school that day.

- **Make students accountable**   Let students know that they are responsible for doing their homework each night. Explain the benefits of daily reading, reworking problems that have given them difficulty, or practicing newly acquired skills. Have the students make homework journals in which they keep track of their assignments, the amount of time spent on homework, and any problems they encounter. See Figure 24.2 for an example of a homework journal.

- **Establish a routine for submitting and evaluating homework**   Students should have a set place to submit their homework when they enter the classroom. When possible,

Figure 24.1   Homework Time Allocations

Grade Level	Homework Assignments Should Take No Longer Than ...
Kindergarten	15 minutes
First Grade	20 minutes
Second Grade	25 minutes
Third Grade	30 minutes
Fourth Grade	40 minutes
Fifth Grade	45 minutes
Sixth Grade	45 minutes
Middle School	60 minutes (must be coordinated by all teachers)
High School	90 minutes (must be coordinated by all teachers)

they should have the opportunity to self-check the accuracy of their own work. As a general rule, homework is not evaluated and given a grade but the fact that it is completed should be recorded. Make sure you check homework and give students feedback. Otherwise, they may feel that it's simply busy work and has no connection to the learning process. Also quickly review homework journals for problems or parental questions. Some teachers have the students keep their homework in folders for a period of time so that the work can be reviewed in individual conferences.

• **Adjust homework assignments**   Teachers should monitor the students' responsibility and success in completing homework assignments. Teachers and students should engage in periodic evaluations related to homework, the length of time it is taking, and any adjustments that might need to be made. Adjustments are not always made on the recommendations of students, of course, but teachers should be open to their concerns. Teachers should also be aware of activities in the school and community that will affect the students' availability to complete their assignments. Some teachers have been successful in giving students homework-free days when they have successfully completed their homework for a period of time. These should come as surprises, however, and not be promised as rewards.

• **Work with students who don't do their homework**   When you have students who regularly do not do their homework, the first thing you need to do is determine the cause. Sometimes students live in a very chaotic environment where they have no place to work and no materials to use. Schedule a private conference with the student and talk to him calmly about your concern that he is not completing assignments. Encourage the

Figure 24.2   Example of a Homework Journal

Date	Time Started	Time Completed	Assignments	Parent's Signature Any Problems?
9/2	5:00	5:28	• Read library book. • Rework math problems. • Write three descriptive sentences.	*Mother Bear* *Had to recopy* *sentences . . . messy!*
9/3	4:55	5:32	• Read library book. • Rework math problems. • Write a descriptive paragraph.	*Mother Bear* *Didn't get to read today.* *Spent too much time on* *writing assignment.*
9/4	4:30	5:05	• Read library book. • Rework math problems. • Work on draft of story started in school	*Mother Bear* *Spent all his time on* *writing. Is this OK?*

student to talk about why the homework is not getting done and ask if there is any way you can help solve this problem. Schedule a parent conference if the student indicates that he has no place to work. Suggest alternative places where the student might work and send home pencils and paper for the student to use, if materials are the problem. Give the student the firm message that you expect him to do his homework, that you'll help as much as possible, but that it is his responsibility. If this first conference produces no change, schedule a follow-up parent conference and require the student to come into class as soon as he arrives at school each day to complete his homework assignment. Restrict his free-time activities within the class to give him class time to complete the work, or have him eat lunch in the classroom while working on his homework. This is, of course, more difficult with older students since their assignments take so much longer to do, but find a way to hold students responsible, even if it means keeping them after school for a private homework club.

Applications and Examples

Mrs. Pender's second-graders are working very hard to improve their reading and writing skills. They are also working on mastering their addition and subtraction facts so that they will be ready to learn multiplication next year.

Mrs. Pender is preparing a presentation for the parents at the fall open house. She wants everyone to understand the expectations for student homework this year. She prepares a handout that explains the homework policy and helps the parents to understand what the students will be bringing home for homework. Figure 24.3 shows the handout Mrs. Pender shares with the parents.

Mrs. Pender has designed a series of math-facts folder games that she sends home with the students at the beginning of the year. As they make progress in math, she substitutes games. This is done on an individual basis so the students work hard to pass their timed math-facts tests so they can take home new games. The games are simple adaptations of old favorites such as Concentration, Go Fish, Lotto (Matho), and Chutes and Ladders. The

Figure 24.3 Mrs. Pender's Homework Handout

Second-Grade Homework—Should take no more than 25 minutes per day

Please provide a quiet place for your child to do homework and set a time for homework to be competed each evening.

If there is any reason why your child can't complete homework, please send me a note with your child. If homework is taking more than 25 minutes to complete, please let me know.

Thanks!
Mrs. Pender

Monday	Tuesday	Wednesday	Thursday	Weekend
• Read and write in reading journal. • Play math-facts game 1—Students can play this game alone or with siblings or parents.	• Read and write in reading journal. • Play math-facts game 2.	• Read and write in reading journal. • Play math-facts game 3.	• Read and write in reading journal. • Play math-facts game 4.	• Read for at least 15 minutes each day. • Please sign your child's reading journal each night to confirm that he or she has complete that day's reading/writing.

games require students to use addition and subtraction facts which get progressively harder as the year moves on.

The students submit their reading journals as they enter the classroom each day. As the students make progress in reading, the books they bring home get more challenging, and Mrs. Pender always sends a note of celebration home with the students when they move up a level in reading. They all work very hard to get to bring home higher-level books. The class celebrates together by moving a symbol up a step on the reading ladder each time a group or individual moves to a higher level.

Mr. Strang's seventh-grade prealgebra students do all their homework on the computer. Mr. Strang discovered that all his students have computers and Internet connections at home, so he has designed a homework site using Blackboard (2006). He designs several levels of homework for each assignment, and the students work from level 1 up to level 3 according to their accuracy scores. They can choose to complete one level or all three. When students have reached level 3, they can choose to complete challenge activities. Most of the students work through at least two levels, and many work through all three and the challenge activity. Once they have established a pattern of working at level 3 and beyond, he no longer requires them to complete levels 1 and 2. This is determined on an individual basis.

Most of the students complete and e-mail their assignments to Mr. Strang, which gives him the opportunity to look over the assignments and send an e-mail of congratulations when the work is done well.

Mr. Strang used to have difficulty getting his students to complete homework before he began to use the computer-based approach. About halfway through the year, he issues a challenge to students who are working on level 3 assignments: "I would like those of you who are interested to submit some challenge activities for the others to try. The only catch is that you must submit your activity to me for approval first. You must also submit the solution to your challenge before we can post it."

Mr. Strang is inundated with student-written challenge problems. He is very pleased with his students' involvement.

 ## CONCLUSION

Teachers who think reflectively about their homework find that they can make the assignments more meaningful for their students. Tailoring the assignments to the needs of the students is vital, as is finding ways to make the assignments interesting and challenging without making them too difficult for the ages and abilities of the students. Homework expectations support the development of students' responsibility and enhance their learning.

References

Cooper, H. (2000). Homework research and policy: A review of the literature. Minneapolis: University of Minnesota, Center for Applied Research and Education Improvement. Electronic document retrieved April 30, 2005, from http://education.umn.edu/CAREI.

LaConte, R. (1981). *Homework as a learning experience: What research says to the teacher.* Washington, DC: National Education Association.

Sharp, C. (2001). Review of studies on homework. Review commissioned by the National Foundation for Educational Research. Electronic document retrieved April 30, 2005, from www.nfer.ac.uk/

Walberg, H. (1991). Does homework help? *School Community Journal, 1*(1), 13–15.

Suggested Reading

Blackboard Learning System (2006). www.blackboard.com

Knorr, C. (1981). A synthesis of homework research and related literature. Paper presented to the LeHigh Chapter of Phi Delta Kappa, Bethlehem, PA, January 24, 1981. (ERIC document ED 199 933).

Sharp, C., Keys, W., & Benefield, P. (2001). *Homework: A review of recent research.* Slough, UK: NFER.

25

MAKING CONNECTIONS TO THE ARTS

Most states have adopted curricular standards in many areas, including reading/language arts, mathematics, science, and history/social sciences. Teachers are expected to address the grade-level standards in all of these areas. That focus is emphasized in teacher education programs. The standards in visual/performing arts, technology, and physical education are not as widely addressed in classrooms today due to the emphasis on standardized assessment and meeting goals for raising test scores (Considine & Haley, 1999). However, these areas are important to the process of creating well-rounded students. They are also areas in which students have an opportunity to demonstrate their unique abilities. The good news is that visual and performing arts, physical education, and technology can all be easily integrated into units of study to bring all students a rich diversity of experiences.

Integrating visual and performing arts and physical activities into units of study gives students many ways in which to explore a topic. This integration also allows them to pursue a personal interest or passion while examining required curriculum (CNAEA, 1994). Consider the student interested in art who chooses to explore the art of a specific period to add to a study of history. That student can bring a dimension to the study that may also appeal to others and will certainly deepen everyone's knowledge of the historical time. The same can be said for a student interested in sports who researches the sports played during a given historical time.

FOCUS ON ENGLISH LEARNERS

Dance, music, art, and dramatic arts often give English learners an excellent way to become active contributors to the classroom community.

To set these pursuits in motion, the teacher need only give students opportunities to explore these areas. Avid readers and writers can use their skills to create scripts to provide an additional glimpse of the topic under study. History, a scientific discovery, or a practical math application can all be included in the dramatic presentations.

STEP BY STEP

The steps for integrating visual/performing arts and physical activities into the curriculum:

- **Identify the topic to be studied**   After examining the standards to be addressed, identify standards in two or more curricular areas that can be integrated. In addition to examining the standards in the main curricular areas, also explore the standards in visual/performing arts and physical education to determine which of them can also be addressed.

- **Plan ways to integrate**   As you plan the sequence of study, look for ways to address standards in many modes See Figure 25.1 for examples.

- **Identify integration points**   Points of integration can sometimes be identified in advance, but other times they arise naturally when you are aware of the standards and the interests of the students. If a student is interested in art or music, it is natural to suggest some activities related to the study that will bring those interests into play. If you

Figure 25.1   Integrating Visual Performing Arts and Physical Education into Units

Integration	Explanation
Art appreciation	Students explore art of a certain period by searching the Internet, downloading examples and creating color transparencies to share with the class. Art books can also be used on opaque projectors. Students relate art to literary studies and scientific discoveries.
Murals	Students create a visual representation in the form of a large painting on butcher paper. This is especially effective as a culminating activity in which all they have learned is represented.
Reader's theatre	Students create a script reviewing the events in a topic of study. Roles are read rather than memorized.
Scriptwriting	Students use the information they are acquiring to create a script to reenact a time in history, a scene from literature, a scientific discovery, or a mathematical principle.
Mime	Students create a silent, physical enactment to demonstrate an element of the topic being studied.
Dance	Students research, learn, and perform a dance from a historical period. They can also design a dance that demonstrates a scene from literature or an element of nature.
Music	Students research and find examples of music created or popular during a specific historical period. They can also create original songs, jingles, or raps that review facts related to a topic of study.

have students who are avid readers, asking them to create a script for a reader's theatre or play related to literature that adds to the study is another natural. Another time for integration is at the conclusion of the study. Culminating activities may involve murals, reader's theatre productions, or even museum days when students explore art and music from the period under study, present a student-written play, or demonstrate and teach games and leisure-time activities related to the study.

• **Find ways to expand the study**   After the study is completed, you may want to expand on the interests of the students by appointing an art-appreciation director, a music-appreciation conductor, and a physical games coordinator. All of these students should be interested in these areas of study. They should keep the class aware of any connection that can be made to their area of responsibility. For example, one second-grade art director added to the discussion of fractions in math by explaining the fractions used in creating colors in a palette. The students then had the opportunity to create color fractions during learning center time and were given time to display and explain their results at the end of the activity. If you have several students with similar interests, they can serve as co-chairs for an area or alternate duties.

Applications and Examples

In Chapter 23 we visited Mrs. McCloskey's first grade and read about their frog unit. To integrate standards from the visual/performing arts into her study, she planned to integrate activities into her science/language arts unit. She brought in books that displayed nature photographs, many of them containing pictures of frogs. The class talked about photography as a form of art and looked at the photographs in relation to art elements such as color, line, shape, and balance. Since they had many real frogs living in their classroom during the study, Ms. McCloskey brought in some disposable cameras for the students to use to capture the frogs on film. After the students took their photographs, she had them transferred to a CD at the local drugstore so she could then make color transparencies for the class to examine. As they looked at the photographs, they again discussed the art elements. Ms. McCloskey allowed each child to choose one of their photos and print it. The students then wrote brief captions for their photos, chose mounting colors, and mounted the photos with the help of some sixth-grade helpers.

Ms. McCloskey then displayed the student photos in the hallway outside her classroom and invited other classes to visit their art gallery. Every time a class came to visit the gallery, two children were chosen to explain their project to the visiting class, addressing another of the language arts standards—oral explanations.

At the conclusion of the frog unit the students created a wall-sized mural depicting all they had learned about frogs. They showed the stages in the life cycle, the environment, what frogs eat, and different species and labeled all of the parts. Their label read, "We learned about the life cycle of a frog."

For back-to-school night Ms. McCloskey invited the parents to view a videotape of the activities the students had experienced during the unit. The video included

- Students reading and writing about frogs
- Students imitating frogs jumping
- Students taking photos of frogs
- Students observing tadpoles in the child-sized swimming pool used as a pond
- Students working on the mural and explaining what they were doing
- Students explaining the frog art gallery of photos
- Students singing songs about frogs
- Students playing board games using frog facts and lima beans painted to look like frogs

The parents enjoyed seeing their students in action in the classroom and were impressed by all they had learned about frogs.

We visited Mr. Rowell's seventh-graders in Chapter 5 as they studied the Middle Ages. As a part of their study, Mr. Rowell encouraged them to integrate arts and physical education elements. Because Mr. Rowell had grouped the students to explore areas of feudal life in depth and challenged them to create visuals and demonstrations for a museum day, the students were motivated to use many different approaches in creating their displays. Mr. Rowell encouraged the group that investigated the religion of the period to look at the art of the period. At first they were confused, but soon saw the connection to their goal. They downloaded copies of many of the paintings of the day and created a display. The paintings all depicted religious topics that related to the primary religion of the day, Catholicism. They also created a model of a cathedral that was built during the Middle Ages and researched the locations of the major cathedrals of Europe built during that time. They then created a map indicating the locations.

The group investigating homes of the period also created a model. But theirs was a typical home, that of a serf. They researched the dress of the period and actually created costumes to wear on museum day when they made their presentation.

The group investigating clothing of the time also created costumes. This group chose to create clothing of the aristocracy. They required some help from the sewing arts teacher and some very innovative substitutions for the rich fabrics and jewelry of the time. They especially enjoyed creating visuals showing pictures of the elaborate head-dresses shaped like hearts, butterflies, or turbans. They also created replicas of the habits and robes worn by priests and sisters of the Catholic church.

The arts and entertainment group found pictures on the Internet of period instruments. They also found some chants that were used in celebrations during the Middle Ages and performed them for the class. They found that most of the dramatic presentations of the day enacted scenes from Scripture and discovered some beautiful photographs online as examples. They researched the games that the children played and taught them to the class. Several members of their group dressed as jesters and juggled as a part of their museum day display.

The group that investigated town life wrote a wonderful script that encompassed many of the occupations and pursuits of the day. They acted out how the people obtained water, exchanged goods, and generally created a very thorough image of feudal life.

Because Mr. Rowell encouraged his students to approach their assignments with creativity and include the arts and physical activities, they enjoyed their projects. They seem to include much more than he would ever require of them.

 ## CONCLUSION

Because of the focus on academic skills and raising test scores in today's standards-based schools, teachers are finding ways to integrate the teaching and exploration of the arts into class projects. Although many schools still teach art, music, and physical education, these curricular areas do not receive the financial support they need to provide students with consistent instruction for the development of interest and excellence. By including instruction, attention, and respect for the arts in the mainstream curriculum, teachers are able to plant a seed. They can often encourage students who have talents and passion in these areas as well.

References

Considine, D., & Haley, G. (1999). *Visual images: Integrating imagery into instruction* (2nd ed.). Englewood, CO: Teacher Ideas Press.

Consortium of National Arts Education Associations (CNAEA). (1994). *National standards for arts education: What every young American should know and be able to do in the arts.* Reston, VA: Music Educators National Conference.

Suggested Reading

Booth, D. (1994). *Story drama: Reading, writing, and roleplaying across the curriculum.* Markham, ON: Pembroke Publishers.

Booth, D., & Neelands, J. (Eds.). (1998). *Writing in role: Classroom projects connecting writing and drama.* Hamilton, ON: Caliburn Enterprises.

Page, N. (1995). *Music as a way of knowing.* York, ME: Stenhouse.

Wormeli, R. (2006). Differentiating for tweens. *Educational leadership, 63* (7), 14–19.

26

USING TECHNOLOGY TO SUPPORT LEARNING

Teachers use technology in many forms in the classroom. Overhead projectors, video players, television sets, and computers are now standard equipment in most classrooms. In most states, teachers in training are now required to take technology courses as part of their teacher education programs. Even with all this emphasis on technology in education, however, there are still classrooms where technology is not being used to its potential or even at all.

For many students technology adds motivation for learning (Roblyer, 2004). It makes record keeping and report writing easier for teachers. It can enhance learning in many ways. But it can also be overwhelming for teachers who are not comfortable integrating it into their classrooms.

The Internet is a great boon to teachers and students who are conducting research. Many websites are available online to support units of study, provide programmed skills practice, and encourage innovative ideas. The responsible and ethical use of technology in the classroom is important and should be taught as part of any curriculum in which technology is integrated. See Figure 26.1 for sites related to this vital issue.

There are several important elements of technology use to consider when making decisions about how and where to infuse it into your classroom:

- How can I use technology to improve my teaching and knowledge base?
- How can I use technology to support motivation and learning in my students?
- How can I evaluate the technology that is available to me and my students?

These points must be considered carefully in making decisions about technology use, but don't let them scare you. Help is available in the form of educational resource books and websites. See Figure 26.2 for a partial listing of these resources.

Beyond the Internet and computer programs, there are many other technologies available to teachers. Teachers effectively use video in teaching, create PowerPoint presentations for presenting information, and engage students in creating video productions to

Figure 26.1 Websites with Information About Ethical Computer Use in Education

http://www.nelliemuller.com/Ethics_and_Technology_in_Education.htm
http://lrs.ed.uiuc.edu/wp
http://rgfn.edu/programs/trainer/ethics.htm
http://www.aect.org/About/Ethics.htm

help the curriculum come alive (Herrell & Fowler, 1997). The possibilities are almost endless. See Figure 26.3 for some suggestions.

As you can see, technology in education is not a topic that can be discussed in depth in one chapter of a book. There are many books with resources and approaches for teachers. See suggested readings at the end of this chapter for a few of the best.

Figure 26.2 Teacher Resource Sites

Help surfing the Internet for the beginner
http://ozline.com/learning/stumble_js.html

The role of technology in education
http://www.nap.edu/readingroom/books/techgap/index.html

Technology standards in education
http://cnets.iste.org/index.html

Finding e-mail pals for your students
http://www.siec.k12.in.us/west/slides/penpal/index.html
http://web66.coled.umn.edu/schools.html
http://www.epals.com
http://www.globalschoolhouse.com

Free Internet access
http://www.freei.com/
http://www.custtechnst.homestead.com/

PBS resource collections for teachers
http://www.pbs.org/teachersource/teachtech.htm

The best of the web according to teachers and media specialists
http://scout.cs.wisc.edu/index.html

Web-based learning activities
http://edweb.sdsu.edu/webquest/webquest.html

Finding educational freebies on the web
http://www.thegateway.org/

Finding resources by grade level and subject
http://www.teachersfirst.com/matrix-f.htm

K–12 science instruction
http://www.sciquest.com/k12/

To read the current issue of *Learning and Leading with Technology*, published by the International Society for Technology in Education
http://www.iste.org/L&L/archive/vol28/no1/index/html

Figure 26.3 Suggestions for Technology Use in the Classroom

Technology	Suggestions for Use
Video cameras	Have students create a video production, writing, acting, and editing using the computer.
	Videotape group interactions, view as a class, and discuss expectations.
	Videotape student presentations, view, evaluate using a scoring rubric, and share with parents.
Digital cameras	Create transparencies for teaching or student presentations. Take pictures to provide motivation for writing. Illustrate student-written books.
Presentation software such as PowerPoint	Create slide presentations for teaching. Students can create presentations for oral reports.
Computer-downloaded photographs	Using search instruments on the computer such as google.com or altavista.com, download pictures for student reports, lessons, or a library of teaching resources.
Flat-bed scanners	Scan student work to be included in student portfolios. Work can then be sent home.
	Scan photos for making transparencies.
Videos	Collect videos from educational television programming, personal vacations, or commercial sources. Always show videos with learning in mind, stopping and discussing as appropriate.
Overhead projectors	Use manipulatives made from clear plastic on the overhead. Show transparencies made from downloading or scanning photos.

 ## STEP BY STEP

The steps for integrating technology into your classroom:

• **Do your homework**   Explore the resources that are available to you as a teacher. Look over the Internet sites that sound promising, always previewing them before recommending them to students. Talk to other teachers about how they use technology in their classrooms. Be open to new ideas.

• **Start small**   If you're new to using technology in your classroom, choose one approach and investigate it. If you start with computer software, be sure to review and

Figure 26.4   Evaluating Educational Software

Element	What to Look For
Instruction	Will it hold the students' attention? Look for color, action, challenges. Does it provide reasonable opportunities to be successful? Does it provide cognitive curiosity? Look for challenges and surprises. Does it support goal-setting and scoring? Look for expectations for success and indications of how you're doing. How long does it take to complete an activity? Align with the age of your students.
Interaction and feedback	Does it reinforce the correct answer with positive feedback? Does it supply the correct answer? Does it evaluate the student's answer? Does it explain why the student's answer was incorrect? Does it provide recommendations for special help? Does it offer a variety of ways to respond?
Learner control	Are users free to discover the program, or is it linear?
Time-worthiness	Does the activity enhance the student's learning? Is the activity worthy of the time needed to complete it?

evaluate it before you use it with your students. See Figure 26.4 for guidelines to use when evaluating educational software.

• **Involve students**   Students can often serve as technology experts in the classroom. They frequently have a lot of experience in computing, videotaping, or digital photography. Don't be afraid to use their expertise. Students can also be involved in making decisions about the use of technology. Give them options that involve technology for their presentations and projects. Encourage students who are not comfortable with technology to work with others who are.

• **Move forward**   Once you are comfortable with one application in technology, keep trying other approaches. Get in the habit of doing an Internet search every time you plan a lesson. You will be amazed at the resources you will find.

Applications and Examples

Mr. Thele's fifth-graders have been participating in literature circles all year. As a culminating activity, he plans to encourage them to choose their favorite book and produce a video depicting their favorite scenes. Mr. Thele begins by asking the students to choose among the books they've read this year. He then allows them to work in groups to create a storyboard showing the scenes they will include in their video. Mr. Thele demonstrates the use of computer software to build their storyboard. Using this software (Script Werx) the students plan the scenes and the dialogue (audio) they will include in their video production.

After the students have completed their storyboards, Mr. Thele gives them time to plan their production and costumes and rehearse the dialogue. When each group is ready, Mr. Thele videotapes their production. Once the video footage is taped, he works with each group, showing them how to use the computer to edit the raw footage and complete their production. They add titles, credits, and musical background using a digital editing system that allows them to select scenes and place them into the order that matches their storyboards (Pinnacle Studio).

Once the project is complete, Mr. Thele brings all the groups together, and they pop popcorn. They view all the video productions, eat popcorn, and celebrate all the learning they've accomplished during the project. The students are so pleased with their productions that they ask Mr. Thele if they can have copies of their videos. As a final project, Mr. Thele shows a small group how to save copies of the videos on CD-ROM disks, and they each get a copy to take home as a memento of their fifth-grade year.

Mrs. Caldwell's 12th-graders are working on their senior projects. Their school requires that they complete an in-depth research project and present it to their classmates along with a PowerPoint presentation. To support her students in completing this assignment, Mrs. Caldwell plans to walk them through the use of the Internet. Although they have been using this tool all year to research topics being studied in the classroom, she wants to extend their search abilities to help prepare them for college or employment requirements. She also wants to demonstrate the steps in completing a PowerPoint presentation and give them suggestions for making their presentations more interesting.

Mrs. Caldwell begins the project with a PowerPoint presentation of her own to give her students an example of how effective this tool can be. Her presentation walks them through the use of the Internet, the ethics of Internet use, and ways to narrow their Internet searches. She also provides them with a website to use in getting themselves more familiar with this valuable tool (http://www.ozline.com/learning/stumble.html).

FOCUS ON ENGLISH LEARNERS

Creating a PowerPoint presentation provides visual cues vital to English learners who are speaking in front of a group.

Once the students have completed their basic research, Mrs. Caldwell walks them through the steps of creating their own PowerPoint presentation, demonstrating each step and giving the students ideas for ways to make their presentations more interesting and informative. She cautions them about the tendency to overuse many of the "whistles and bells" of the program, de-emphasizing the importance of the information for the sake of creating a flashy presentation. She then creates a schedule for using the available computers. She sets a requirement that students must complete their research and write a draft of their report before they can schedule computer time for creating their presentations, hoping this will motivate them to get the research done in a timely manner.

 ## CONCLUSION

Mr. Thele and Mrs. Caldwell are examples of teachers who have discovered the power of integrating technology into their classrooms. They use technology on a regular basis and keep challenging themselves to find new ways to enhance the learning in their classrooms. Neither teacher uses technology simply for the sake of using technology. They both find technology helpful for motivating students and allowing (sometimes surprisingly) students to shine in their classrooms.

References

Herrell, A., & Fowler, J. (1997). *Camcorder in the classroom.* Upper Saddle River, NJ: Merrill/ Prentice Hall.

Roblyer, M. (2004). *Integrating educational technology into teaching* (3rd ed.). Upper Saddle River, NJ: Prentice Hall/Pearson.

Suggested Reading

Roblyer, M. (2002). *Starting out on the Internet: A learning journey for teachers* (2nd ed.). Upper Saddle River, NJ: Prentice Hall/Pearson.

Sandholtz, J., Ringstaff, C., & Dwyer, D. (1997). *Teaching with technology: Creating student-centered classrooms*. New York: Teachers College Press.

Stempleski, S., & Arcario, P. (1992). *Video in second language teaching: Using, selecting, and producing video for the classroom*. Alexandria, VA: Teachers of English to Students of Other Languages.

BUILDING COMMUNITY THROUGH COLLABORATION

In today's competitive world students need instruction in cooperation and collaboration. Classroom communities provide the perfect setting for introducing students to collaboration and the value of learning to work as a team. Many of today's employers (including Donald Trump) decry the lack of team players available in the workforce (SCANS, 2000). Traditionally, boys have had an edge in teamwork due to their more frequent involvement in team sports (Butler, 1996). With the advent of Title 9 programs, girls are being provided with more and more opportunities to participate in team sports and similar cooperative activities.

Although many school settings have encouraged competition over the years, teachers often find it challenging for some of their students. Some studies (Kohn, 1992) have shown that classroom competition is beneficial only to a limited number of students. (See Figure VI.1 for more information about Kohn's theories.) Students must see themselves as capable of competing before competition can be motivating (Krashen, 1996).

Teachers can encourage all their students by building a supportive classroom community. For this to be successful, however, the students need to experience everyday activities and routines that succeed through teamwork. Every student must feel that he or she has a vital part in the community and contributes to the success of the activities. All this requires a teacher's planning and vigilance in observing and recognizing students' individual differences and strengths.

Successful participants in a rich classroom community recognize that "not everyone is good at everything, but everyone is good at something" (Cohen, 1994). For more information about Cohen's theory, see Figure VI.2.

The teacher provides the key to community building through verbal interactions and frequent recognition of individual contributions and by planning activities that require collaboration. In this section of the book, we explore strategies for implementing a collaborative classroom and steps for using cooperative learning. Strategies include teaching classroom routines that encourage collaboration, exercises in supporting students as they learn to cooperate, and techniques for helping students understand everyone's role in cooperative learning groups. The section also explores the teacher's important role in providing status for all students, supporting them as they learn to work well in a group

Figure VI.1 Important Theory

Alfie Kohn

Alfie Kohn is a noted author and lecturer whose research addresses ways in which students can be taught to be responsible and respectful. He focuses on this goal in his research and teaching and believes that, once students develop these two attributes, all learning takes place at a more reasonable rate and in a more efficient manner. "Adults who are respectful of children are not just modeling a skill or behavior, they are meeting the emotional needs of those children, thereby helping to create the psychological conditions for children to treat others respectfully" (Kohn, 1997b, p. 27–28).

According to Kohn, students have potential as long as they are given the opportunity to be active meaning-makers. He urges teachers to take risks based on the needs of their students and leave traditional grading and reward systems behind. In *The Schools Our Children Deserve* (1999b), he states that, when curriculum is engaging, students who are not graded do just as well on proficiency exams as those who are. "Students' interests may therefore help shape the curriculum, and a growing facility with words and numbers derives from the process of finding answers to their own questions" (Kohn, 1997c, p. 41–42.).

Kohn is perhaps the most outspoken critic of rewards, gold stars, and extrinsic motivation in the United States today. His books cite many research studies that support his position. He believes, instead, that all children should be educated and schooled in a way that encourages "exploration, discovery, and curiosity." "The act of learning ideally is its own reward" (Kohn, 1997c, p. 42).

References

Kohn's works include the following:

Kohn, A. (1990). *The brighter side of human nature.* New York: Houghton Mifflin.
Kohn, A. (1992). *No contest: The case against competition.* New York: Houghton Mifflin.
Kohn, A. (1997a). How not to teach values: A critical look at character education. *Phi Delta Kappan,* 79(2), 37–42.
Kohn, A. (1997b). *The limits of teaching skills: Reaching today's youth.* New York: Houghton Mifflin.
Kohn, A. (1997c, September 3). Students don't work: They learn. *Education Week,* pp. 5–6.
Kohn, A. (1999a). *Punished by rewards.* New York: Houghton Mifflin.
Kohn, A. (1999b). *The schools our children deserve: Moving beyond traditional classrooms and tougher standards,* New York: Houghton Mifflin.

Figure VI.2 Important Theory

Elizabeth Cohen (1931–2005)

Drawing on years of research and teaching experience, Elizabeth Cohen provides us with a rich look at the experience of cooperative learning. Her background in sociology has given her a unique perspective on the group-learning process, particularly as it applies to skills and procedures for succeeding in a broad environment of group tasks and interaction. She reminds us that students are naturally drawn toward learning from each other, no matter what their levels of ability or place within a social setting might be.

Her work focuses on the use of cooperative learning throughout the curriculum to enhance learning and develop social skills, academic achievement, and higher-order thinking skills in heterogeneous settings. She reminds us of the importance of emphasizing the appropriateness of group-work tasks, the assignment of specific roles for group participants, and the skills that must be taught to make these interactions efficient and productive.

Not every task works well as a cooperative learning project. For this purpose we must establish tasks that

1. Do not necessarily have a single right answer
2. Cannot be done more quickly and efficiently by one person than by a group

Figure VI.2 Continued

3. Are appropriately challenging and not too low-level
4. Do not involve simple memorization or rote learning

The task could be some culminating activity that helps students synthesize what they have learned throughout a unit of study. It might give them an exciting opportunity to apply and demonstrate concepts or skills. In any case, accomplishing the task requires the use of multiple abilities and a wide range of social skills.

Cooperative group work involves a great deal of planning. Students are generally oriented to the project: the teacher explains not only goals but also the processes and norms students might follow during their group work to arrive at conclusions and findings. The teacher may give specific instructions for the task or perhaps write them out on activity cards, with one or more students given the task of using these written instructions to guide the group's participation. Finally, a wrap-up session follows the activity in which the students are given an opportunity to report on their conclusions and findings. This wrap-up session is essential, and the teacher may also use it to talk about processes and review the norms and behaviors that the groups were expected to follow. It's an excellent opportunity to point out those students who were particularly good at using the group process and contributing to their group's success.

According to Cohen (1994), groups should be mixed in regard to achievement, sex, race, ethnicity, and possibly even level of English acquisition. She points out that it is not necessary to balance every group in every way but that grouping homogeneously low-achieving students should be avoided so that everyone will be successful at the task. It is most important to reasonably balance the groups so that children who need assistance in any realm will have access to the task, possibly through the intervention of another student in the group.

Cohen reminds us that every member of the group should have a specific task or role in the group. Their jobs have specific names, such as facilitator, materials manager, clean-up supervisor, or reporter. The teacher may also create other positions as called for by the assigned task. To ensure group success, teachers must carefully teach students the duties related to the roles and offer specific training in accomplishing them. With the whole class or with individual students, the teacher can discuss the various roles that one might have in a group. In either case, students should never have to guess what their duties entail. Cohen tells us that "members feel very satisfied with their part in the group process in groups with different roles and/or jobs to do; such groups can work efficiently, smoothly, and productively. The use of roles alleviates problems of nonparticipation or domination by one member" (Cohen, 1994, p. 87).

FOCUS ON ENGLISH LEARNERS

Ensuring that English learners make a viable contribution to the group helps them be included in the process.

Cooperative learning through the use of academically complex tasks is a challenging yet fulfilling approach to learning in the classroom. Teachers can benefit from further study of the work of innovative researchers like Elizabeth Cohen in their quest for instructional techniques for enhancing learning in the classroom and preparing children to work in a constructive, collegial fashion with others in their groups and with society as a whole.

References

Cohen's published works include the following:

Cohen, E. (1994). *Designing groupwork: Strategies for heterogeneous classrooms.* New York: Teachers College Press.

Cohen, E., & Lotan, R. (1997). Operation of status in the middle grades: Recent developments. In J. Szmatka & J. Berger (Eds.), *Status, network, and structure: Theory development in group processes* (pp. 222–240). Stanford, CA: Stanford University Press.

Cohen, E., Lotan, R., Scarloss, B., & Arellano, A. (1999). Complex instruction: Equity in cooperative learning classrooms. *Theory into Practice, 38,* 80–86.

Lloyd, P., & Cohen, E. (1999). Peer status in the middle school: A natural treatment for unequal participation. *Social Psychology of Education, 4,* 1–24.

setting, and sharing the knowledge gained through group interactions. Once students are working well in groups and supporting each other's efforts, the teacher can begin to set up collaborative workshop structures in the classroom to maximize the authentic learning that is taking place. This is addressed in the section's final chapter.

References

Butler, A. (1996, April 16). Study: Employers now encouraging teamwork. *Daily Egyptian,* p. 13.

Cohen, E. (1994). *Designing groupwork* (2nd ed.). New York: Teachers College Press.

Krashen, S. (1996). *The natural approach: Language acquisition in the classroom.* Upper Saddle River, NJ: Prentice Hall.

Kohn, A. (1992). *The case against competition.* New York: Houghton Mifflin.

Secretary's Commission on Achieving Necessary Skills (SCANS). 2000. *Report for America 2000.* Washington, DC: U.S. Department of Education.

TEACHING CLASSROOM BEHAVIORS AND ROUTINES THAT ENCOURAGE COLLABORATION

Classroom routines are the heart of the classroom community. The teacher sets the stage for community building by creating expectations for collaborative behavior and involving the students in everyday decision-making and classroom maintenance (Powell, McLaughlin, Savage, & Zehm, 2001). The teacher's role in a community of learners is to model acceptable behavior, clarify expectations, and monitor student behaviors.

From the very first day of school the teacher must make it clear to the students that they are members of a supportive community and their involvement is vital for the community to flourish (Bridges, 1995). Model encouraging words daily and make cooperative routines part of everyday life. Setting the stage for community building requires an investment of time in the beginning of the year but pays off handsomely. As the year moves on, the students will begin to accept and perform many daily maintenance chores, such as taking roll and lunch count, setting up classroom centers, making learning materials available when needed, putting materials away, emptying pencil sharpeners, and cleaning white- or chalkboards. To encourage an atmosphere of collaboration, pairs or small groups of students should share these chores and rotate them on a regular basis so that everyone in the class has an opportunity to be an active participant. Many teachers assign chores using an assignment board that is changed daily or weekly. Some teachers have found that creating teams or tribes that are rotated monthly also works well (Gibbs, 2001).

 ## STEP BY STEP

The steps for establishing collaborative routines and behaviors:

- **Brainstorm the classroom needs** Engage the students in a brainstorming session in which you collaboratively list all the classroom routines and jobs and then take suggestions about how the students can work collaboratively to accomplish them. See Figure 27.1 for the results of one class's brainstorming session.

Figure 27.1 Brainstorming Tasks

Job or Routine	Pair or Team?	Plan
Taking roll	Pair	Students place name into a roll container as they enter the classroom each day. Pair fills in numbers on roll sheet and takes it to the office.
Collecting homework	Pair	Students place homework into a homework tray as they enter the classroom. Pair enters the homework onto a homework check sheet and alphabetizes and places it into the teacher's homework folder for teacher perusal.
Taking lunch count	Pair	Students place their names into the hot lunch or lunchbox container as they enter the classroom. Pair counts names in each container, fills out the lunch count form, and takes it to the cafeteria.
Filing papers	Team	Teacher leaves papers to be filed in a "to be filed basket." Team works together to file papers in alphabetic file folders for students to look over and place in their work folders or portfolios.
Distributing materials	Team	Teacher gives directions regarding materials to be distributed. Team works together to make sure all students have necessary items.
Emptying pencil sharpener	Pair	Pair is responsible for making sure that the sharpener is emptied as needed (at least once a day).
Cleaning white- or chalkboard	Team	At the teacher's signal throughout the day, team erases board and cleans the rail at the end of the day.
Emptying trash cans	Pair	Pair is responsible for making sure trash cans are emptied as needed (at least once a day).
Setting up stations/centers	Team	At a signal from the teacher, team sets up materials at centers while the class is given instructions for work to be done at the centers. Team also puts materials away at end of center time.
Putting up chairs	Team	As students line up for dismissal, team places chairs onto desks for room cleaning.

Figure 27.2   Example of Collaborative Planning Pocket Chart

Name	Week 1	Week 2	Week 3	Week 4
Arnold	Pair with Bruce	Team with Carol, Ben, Frank	Team with Joan, Lisa, Ken	Pair with Mona
Bruce	Pair with Arnold	Team with Mona, Carol, Joan	Pair with Nathan	Team with Dan, Ken, Paul

- **Encourage suggestions for making the collaboration work**   Ask the students for ideas about how the jobs and routines can be shared to make sure that all class members are fully involved. This is a good time to discuss assignments of teams or partners and to consider how often these teams might need to be changed to make sure that everyone gets to work with different teams and partners during the year. See Figure 27.2 for one class's solution to this dilemma.

- **Make time to evaluate the plan**   Discuss the need to evaluate the plan, and set aside time periodically to involve everyone in discussions to reveal any problems. Sometimes it is helpful to have a class suggestion or problems box so that all students feel free to express concerns and ideas.

- **Conduct periodic class evaluation discussions**   Following the schedule that is suggested in the original plan, involve students in discussing how the plan is working and brainstorming solutions to problems. Be sure to remain open to innovative suggestions and student solutions, but hold the students responsible for making sure that the jobs and routines are being performed effectively.

Applications and Examples

Mrs. Frederick has taught first grade for several years. She loves the way in which her students come into class not knowing how to read and write and exit as readers and authors. The one thing she doesn't like about six-year-olds is their egocentricity. As Mrs. Frederick prepares to begin a new school year, she is determined to find a way to help her students learn how to work together.

On the first day of the new school year, Mrs. Frederick gathers her students together on the carpet in front of the whiteboard and engages them in a brainstorming session in which they build a list of all the jobs that need to be done in the classroom each day. Because she knows that beginning first-graders have trouble working in teams, Mrs. Frederick decides to begin with partners and gradually move into larger teams.

The class begins with a list of jobs:

Taking attendance
Taking lunch count
Collecting homework
Passing out paper
Passing out books
Collecting library books
Taking notes to the office
Cleaning the whiteboard
Emptying the pencil sharpener
Emptying the trash can

Passing out snacks

Cleaning up after snacks

Being line leader and ender

Putting up chairs

Because the class has brainstormed 14 jobs and there are only 24 students in the class, Mrs. Frederick suggests that they combine some of the jobs so that there will only

FOCUS ON ENGLISH LEARNERS

For English learners, working with partners helps them gain confidence.

be 12. Each job will be assigned to one pair of students, which will give everyone in the class a job. The students decide that one pair can empty the pencil sharpener and the trash can. They also decide that another pair can collect library books and take notes to the office. This reduces the list of jobs to 12.

Mrs. Frederick then asks how the students think she should assign jobs and how often the jobs should be changed. After some discussion, the students decide that they should change jobs each Monday and that names should be drawn to decide which job each student will do that week.

"What shall we do if someone gets the same job 2 weeks in a row?" asks Mrs. Frederick.

"Put their name back into the can and draw again," suggests Daniel. "That will be fair."

The rest of the students agree, and Mrs. Frederick prepares a list of jobs and name cards to be used for drawing and posting jobs. A few weeks later she reconvenes the groups to discuss how things are going.

"Some of the jobs are harder than others," says Annette.

"But since we take turns, that doesn't really matter," adds Juan.

"I don't like to empty the pencil sharpener and trash," says Maria.

"I don't either, but we all need to take turns to make it fair," says Jeanie.

"It's our classroom, and we all need to help," insists Mathew.

A few weeks later Mrs. Frederick asks the students to identify the hard jobs and asks if it would help to have more than two students working on those jobs. She is testing to see if they are ready for teams. No one seems to think that increasing the number of people assigned to do the jobs is necessary. Mrs. Frederick decides to use the team approach in some training exercises before she uses them for classroom jobs.

Mrs. Salazar is having difficulty keeping up with the task of filing all the paperwork generated by her six sections of seventh- and eighth-grade literature classes. Her colleague, Mrs. Martin, has the students do all the filing, so Mrs. Salazar decides to give this approach a try.

While she is assigning paper filers, Mrs. Salazar decides that maybe the students can do some of the other classroom tasks also. She sets up six filing crates with different-colored file folders. Once she has this system in place, she decides to color-code some of the tasks.

Working with each class, Mrs. Salazar and the students decide that each period should have pairs or teams of students assigned to perform classroom tasks. Mrs. Salazar shows the students the file boxes, and the students ask if assigning each period a color for other things would help her also.

Students are assigned to collect papers each period, which are alphabetized and filed in a colored folder that matches the color of their period's file folders. Another pair takes the graded papers and returns them to their owners. Papers that are to be kept in the student portfolios are collected by yet another pair and filed in the color-coded file crates.

Teams of students are assigned to distribute materials, set up learning centers, put materials away, take attendance, and place attendance reports on the appropriate hook outside the door. After filling out the form in duplicate they file the teacher's copy in the folder color-coded for their period.

Mrs. Salazar is very pleased that so many responsibilities have been taken off her shoulders. "I don't know why I didn't set up this system years ago," she says. See Figure 27.3 for the plan Mrs. Salazar's class adopted.

Figure 27.3 Plan Adopted by Mrs. Salazar's Class

Plan: Both pairs and teams are needed. The pairs and teams need to be changed weekly and rotated so that everyone gets a chance to work with everyone else. Use a pocket chart to keep track of changes.

 ## CONCLUSION

Both Mrs. Frederick and Mrs. Salazar recognize the importance of involving their students in planning for classroom management chores. Because the ages of their students differ, their abilities to plan and implement necessary tasks also differ. Students gain ownership of the classroom and its maintenance by helping to solve the maintenance problems and devise a plan. By taking the students through the problem-solving and planning processes, both teachers are teaching valuable life skills as well.

References

Bridges, L. (1995). *Creating your classroom community.* York, ME: Stenhouse.

Gibbs, J. (2001). *Tribes: A new way of learning and being together.* Windsor, ON: Centersource Systems.

Powell, R. R., McLaughlin, H. J., Savage, T. V., & Zehm, S. (2001). *Classroom management: Perspectives on the social curriculum.* Upper Saddle River, NJ: Merrill/Prentice Hall.

Suggested Reading

Herrell, A., & Jordan, M. (2003). Predictable routines and signals: Reducing anxiety. In *Fifty strategies for teaching English language learners* (2nd ed.), (pp. 15–18). Upper Saddle River, NJ: Merrill/Prentice Hall.

Eby, J., & Herrell, A. (2005). *Teaching in the elementary school: A reflective action approach* (4th ed.). Upper Saddle River, NJ: Merrill/Prentice Hall.

TRAINING STUDENTS TO RECOGNIZE AND RESPOND TO THE NEEDS OF THE GROUP

Students are not innately capable of working successfully in cooperative learning situations. They must be trained in the process and taught the skills necessary for succeeding in cooperative group environments. One of the classic errors that teachers, particularly new teachers, make is assuming that children know how to work with each other cooperatively. Without previous training and success, students will inevitably fall back into their comfort zone of independent work without regard to the collegial process. Teaching these initial skills and setting the norms for behavior is a crucial step toward successful group projects and the key to accomplishing group tasks smoothy in a cooperative environment. Teachers must systematically teach the process, and students must practice the norms and procedures prior to attempting collegial work on a new product or concept. A great vehicle for teaching awareness of group needs is a group exercise called broken circles, adapted in the work of Nancy Graves and Ted Graves (1985) from an exercise called the broken squares problem (Pfeiffer & Jones, 1970).

 ## STEP BY STEP

The steps in training students to recognize and respond to the needs of the group, using the broken circles exercise:

• **Prepare a set of broken circles** See Figure 28.1 for the pattern for a set of advanced broken circles suitable for use with older children and high school students. The circles should be reproduced in a size that students can easily manipulate. The best way to make the circles might be to simply enlarge the circles in the figure to a suitable size, using a copy machine with an enlarging capability, and cut them into their various pieces. Each set might be a different color; this will help keep the sets together and simplify sorting the pieces for the exercise.

• **Sort the pieces of the circles for distribution to each group** Figure 28.2 provides a set of circles that can be used with six-, five-, or four-member groups, depending on

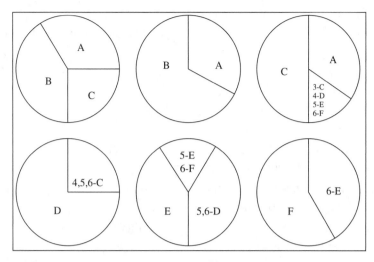

Figure 28.1   *Advanced Circles Patterns*

the makeup of the classroom. The lettered pieces are placed into their corresponding lettered envelopes, depending on the size of the group. For instance, if you are using a six-person group, the piece marked *6-F* goes into the *F* envelope, the piece marked *6-E* goes into the *E* envelope, and so on. A five-member group uses neither the *F* envelope nor those pieces marked as strictly *F*. A four-member group uses neither the *F* envelope nor the *E* envelope. So the pieces are sorted into their appropriate envelopes according to the size of the group, either four, five, or six. If you have extra children, they can be paired with other children to assist the group. Once the pieces are sorted into their appropriate envelopes, place all the envelopes into a larger single envelope. They are now ready for distribution.

• **Give instructions to the class for the exercise**   Tell the students that they each receive an envelope that contains two or three puzzle pieces. They should not open their envelopes until told to do so. The object of the exercise is to put pieces together so that *each member of the group* ends up with a completed circle. There are some rules to follow. Display a poster that you've made in advance to remind students as they work, or write the rules on the board as you explain them. The rules are

FOCUS ON ENGLISH LEARNERS

Modeling behaviors as you explain helps English learners understand what you expect of them.

1. No talking at all. Play in silence.
2. You may not signal to your teammates in any way.
3. Each player must put together his or her own circle.
4. This is an exercise in *giving*. You may not take a piece from another player, but you may *give* one or more of your pieces to another player at any time. If you want to give a piece to another player, just place it next to that person's work space.
5. Remember that the task is not complete until everyone in your group has a completed circle in front of him or her.
6. You may take your pieces out of your envelope now and place them colored side up in front of you. Remember, *no talking!*

• **Monitor the exercise**   Circulate during the exercise, noting students who are giving pieces, and make sure there is no signaling or talking. When you note a group that has completed, give it a thumbs-up signal and a smile. You can ask students to mix the pieces up again and see if they can come up with an alternate way to group the pieces into circles. (It can't be done, but it keeps them busy until the other groups have finished.)

• **Debrief after the activity**   Once all groups have completed the task or at the end of a prescribed time limit, ask the students to identify some important things that happened in their group. Make sure that you don't lead the discussion to the correct answers but allow them to discuss the process. You can ask questions like these:

Did you find this difficult or easy?

Why was it difficult or easy for you?

How do you feel about the group effort?

What did you learn about working in a group?

What would have helped your group?

• **Identify the key behaviors**   In the debriefing discussion, make sure that the students identify two key behaviors that support group success:

Pay attention to what other members of the group need.

No one is done until everyone is done.

It isn't necessary to state these conclusions in this exact wording, but the students need to make these connections.

• **Adapt this exercise for younger students**   Advanced broken circles is an appropriate exercise for fifth grade and above, but you can make simpler versions for younger students. The rules and approach are the same. See Figure 28.2 for patterns for a simpler version for use with grades K–4 in groups of three.

• **Provide additional training exercises**   Observe your students very carefully as they engage in broken circles. If you feel that they need more training before moving into their first experience with cooperative learning, give them one or two more exercises. See Figure 28.3 for suggestions of additional training activities.

Applications and Examples

Mrs. Andrew's first-graders have completed the simplest broken circles activity as their first training exercise in cooperative learning. During the activity and debriefing discussion, Mrs. Andrews realized that they would need more training before really understanding the importance of being sensitive to the needs of others in the group. So Mrs. Andrew purchases some 20-piece jigsaw puzzles of fuzzy animals for a second group training activity.

She divides each puzzle into five bags of four pieces each and puts the pieces into reclosable plastic bags. Because her students are so young, she decides to let them see the picture on their puzzle boxes to help them complete the task (something she would not have done with older students).

She explains the activity to the group, reminding them of the rules of yesterday's broken circles game. Her groups are much more successful in noticing the needs of others as they put the puzzle together. They are much quicker to give one of their pieces to another person when a spot is created in the puzzle that requires a piece from their bag.

During the debriefing the students are very excited about the activity and proud of the fact that they have helped each other. They want to play the game again.

On the third day, Mrs. Andrew uses the same puzzles but gives each one to a different group so that they are not reassembling a puzzle they have already done. "Today," she starts, "we are going to be allowed to talk while we are doing the puzzle. I want you to remember to use your respectful language, though. You may suggest that someone place a piece into the puzzle, but you may not ask for a piece from another player or take one from another. Just use your words to help someone find the places for his or her pieces if you can see where they go."

The students work very well together and practice their respectful language well. The debriefing discussion focuses on how much easier it is to do the puzzles when students are allowed to talk.

Mr. Gardner is introducing his eighth-grade social studies class to cooperative learning in preparation for working on group projects. He has done advanced broken circles with them

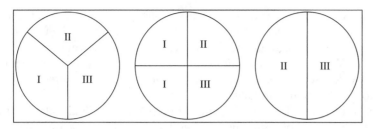

Figure 28.2   Patterns for Simpler Broken Circle Exercises

Figure 28.3   Additional Training Exercises

Activity	Explanation
Puzzle pieces	Purchase jigsaw puzzles appropriate for the ages of your students. Buy enough for the number of groups you plan to use, making sure all the puzzles have the same number of pieces. Divide the pieces into small packets according to the number of students you will place in each group and package the pieces into small plastic bags. The team must assemble the puzzle using the same rules as in broken circles: no talking; giving but not taking. Student can use the puzzles for a second time or use a different set of puzzles with talking allowed to help them see the advantage of verbal interactions.
Master designer	Each student receives a set of geometric shapes in various sizes and colors. The master designer constructs a design behind a screen and then gives directions to the other players about how to place their pieces on their desks. Each player has a screened space in which to build in so that the other players can't see the design. When players feel they have completed the design, they raise their hands, and the master designer checks all of them for accuracy and gives directions for correcting them, if necessary.
Architect	Using building blocks and craft sticks, one student serves as architect by giving the team directions to build a structure one step at a time. Students have individual materials so that everyone can contribute to the building. One student may have all the red blocks, one all the green, etc. Others may have short and longer sticks. *Please note that debriefing discussions should follow all training exercises.*
Artist	Using pencils, markers, crayons, etc., one student draws a landscape and colors it. He or she then gives directions to the team about to how to duplicate the drawing. Each member of the team can add different elements as they are described by the artist, or they can complete their own individual pictures following the artist's directions.

and decides to work on their verbal interaction skills using a master designer activity. He prepares sets of geometric shapes for each student and introduces the task by walking the class through a simple design, giving the directions himself. Because his school has purchased small trifold boards for use during standardized testing, he uses them during this exercise to provide a screen for each student. Before he begins, he stresses the importance of listening to the directions carefully.

Once the students understand the rules of the game, he divides them into groups of five by numbering them off. Student number 1 begins the game by quickly building a design and giving directions for replicating it. Mr. Gardner has allotted time during this period so that each student gets an opportunity to play the role of master designer.

After each student has had a turn at being the master designer, he engages the class in a debriefing discussion. He is very pleased with the results of the discussion because his students were very complimentary about each other. They also recognized how difficult, but necessary, it was to give exact and precise directions. He feels they are ready to work in cooperative groups on a more challenging task.

CONCLUSION

Teachers all over the nation have discovered the power of cooperative group work. They find that their students develop critical thinking skills, are able to work more cooperatively with others, and become actively engaged in cooperative group assignments. However, some of them discover that they are trying to start academic group-work tasks before thoroughly training their students in positive group-work behaviors. To quote one second-grade teacher, "I became impatient and tried to move my students into group work too quickly. Once I backed up and provided more training activities, I found the process worked like clockwork . . . well, as clockwork-like as seven-year-olds get."

Strategy on Video
Cooperative Learning

Strategies for using cooperative learning are demonstrated in a middle-school classroom on segment 11 of the DVD that accompanies this text. Watch as the students participate in a training exercise to help them understand the power of working together. As you view this segment, think about the following:

- How does the teacher prepare the students for the task?
- How does the teacher support students who may not initially be accepted into the group?
- How does the teacher help the students understand the purpose of the exercise?

References

Graves, T., & Graves, N. (1985). *Broken circles* [Game]. Santa Cruz, CA: Educational Games.

Pfeiffer, J., & Jones, F. (1970). *A handbook of structural experiences for human relations training* (Vol. 1). Iowa City: University Associated Press.

Suggested Reading

Cohen, E. (1994). *Designing groupwork: Strategies for the heterogeneous classroom* (2nd ed.). New York: Teachers College Press.

Oakley, B., Felder, R., Brent, R., & Elhajj, I. (2004). Dynamics of peer education in cooperative learning workgroups. *Journal of Student Centered Learning, 2*(1), 9–34.

ESTABLISHING THE RULES AND EXPECTATIONS FOR COOPERATIVE GROUP WORK

Once you have provided your students with training in cooperative behaviors and you feel they are ready to begin to work in cooperative groups, you have some decisions to make. Based on your objectives and the ages of your students, you must begin to choose activities for them to complete as teams of learners. The complexity of the tasks you will assign should gradually increase, so don't start with multiweek projects. To begin with, find a task that can be completed in a class period. Make sure you structure the tasks so that each student must contribute to the outcome. Questions to ask yourself when selecting a task include

Is there more than one answer or more than one way to solve this problem?

Will my students be interested in this activity?

Will this activity enable different students to make contributions?

Can the students include multimedia when completing this activity?

Does the activity require a variety of skills and behaviors?

Does it require reading and writing?

Is it challenging? (Adapted from Cohen, 1994)

After choosing the cooperative task, you need to establish the rules and expectations for the activity before you get your students started. Some rules will be standard for all cooperative tasks, but others will change with each activity. Make these points clear in the beginning. In addition to the basic rules and expectations, you also need to share your plan for evaluating and grading the groups and individuals.

 ## STEP BY STEP

The steps for establishing the rules and expectations for cooperative group work:

• **Set and share your expectations** Once you have chosen an activity, you need to decide on your expectations. Do you want your students to do individual pieces of research to bring together a product that they will present to the class? Do you want them to be able to share their findings with the class individually? Do you want them to include a multimedia presentation in their report to the class? Do you want them to solve a problem using multiple approaches? Once you decide what you expect from the students, prepare a poster or a handout that will remind them of the expectations.

 • **Design the activity**   As you design the activity, think about the individuals who will work as a group and find a way to distribute the information they will need so that they become interdependent. You don't want one student to solve everything. If no one student has all the information needed, they will all have to work together. For some ideas on beginning activities for cooperative group work, see Figure 29.1

Additional suggestions for cooperative group-work activities can be found at http://ncsu.edu/felder-public/Cooperative_Learning.html.

 • **Make the rules explicit**   Once you decide on the activity, prepare a poster, a visual, or a handout listing the rules. The rules should help the students decide how to proceed with the activity and ensure that all students participate actively. See Figure 29.2 for an example of rules for a cooperative scriptwriting activity.

 • **Design and explain the grading procedures**   The best approach to evaluating and grading cooperative group work is to use both group and individual grades (Cohen, 1992). This ensures that everyone plays a part in the group elements of the assignment but encourages individuals to do good jobs on their individual responsibilities to the group. Creating a cooperative rubric for scoring the contributions and final product is a worthwhile activity. To do this, engage the students in a discussion of the expectations for the activity and ask for descriptions of examples of outstanding work. For an example of a scoring rubric, see Figure 4.2 in Chapter 4.

Figure 29.1   Suggestions for Beginning Cooperative Group-Work Activities

Activity	Explanation
Reader's theatre script and props	Each student takes responsibility for writing dialogue for one character. Students write a reader's theatre script and create simple props to enact a scene from a favorite piece of literature.
Create a timeline	Each student takes responsibility for researching one time span. Students work together to create an innovative representation of a timeline for the period.
Create a mural or diorama	Students take responsibility for researching different elements in the mural or diorama. They each create pieces to be included, and the group works together to create the arrangement and oral presentation of their findings.
Science project	Students are given some materials and a question. They find the solution through research, reading, and sharing from a variety of materials. (Each student has one source to use and contribute to the group knowledge.) Students work together to demonstrate what they have learned. They must include some type of visual to support their explanation.

Figure 29.2   Rules for Cooperative Scriptwriting

Everyone in the group is responsible for supporting the rules!

1. Remember to use respectful language.
2. Each student writes the dialogue for one character.
3. One student serves as secretary.
4. Group works together to decide on props needed.
5. Students work cooperatively to create the props. Everyone must contribute!
6. Work together to practice reading the script.
7. Help one another make the dialogue sound real.
8. No put-downs allowed! Be supportive!

• **Provide access to resources and materials**   Once you have designed the activity and expectations, decide on necessary resources and materials. Find a way to provide them in an accessible way. Some teachers like to prepackage materials for each group. Other like to store all materials on shelves and allow students to choose their own materials from whatever is available. Think about computer and Internet access as well. If you have only one or two computers in the classroom, how will you allow all groups access to this resource? Some teachers schedule groups; others assign computer helpers and have the groups request searches from the helper. Still others reserve the computer for word-processing or visuals once the groups reach this step.

Applications and Examples

Mr. Meadow's fifth-graders have been studying the Revolutionary War. He would like to have them create a presentation to culminate their unit and decides to use cooperative groups. His students have been reading Jean Fritz's biographies of famous Revolutionary War heroes in small groups, so these literature groups will serve as the cooperative groups as well.

In thinking through his plans, Mr. Meadows decides to have each student responsible for one aspect of the group project and each group responsible for creating a timeline of the events in the Revolution in which their hero was instrumental. After the group timelines are complete, the whole class will work on integrating them into a timeline of the entire war.

The final presentations will involve short reports on aspects of each hero's life written by individual students. The group timeline will determine the group grade, while individual reports will be graded separately.

Mr. Meadows plans to present his expectations for the individual reports as well as his expectations for the group timeline using posters that he creates. See Figure 29.3 to see these posters.

FOCUS ON ENGLISH LEARNERS

English learners benefit by rehearsing oral reports with teacher support prior to classroom presentations.

Mr. Meadows plans to present the posters and collaboratively construct scoring rubrics for both the individual and group assignments with his class. He then thinks through the aspects of the heroes' contributions that he wants the students to research and additional resource materials that he can provide. He decides that he needs to provide additional biographies of the men and women to be researched, a list of good Internet sites, and some samples of timelines for the students to use. He plans to provide computer time for each group outside of the allotted time for the project to make sure that all groups have access to Internet materials.

Figure 29.3 Mr. Meadow's Posters of Expectations

Individual reports:	Group timelines:
• Should address the aspect that you are assigned • Should be word-processed • Should include a picture or visual • Should be free of spelling and other errors	• Should include points to illustrate the major contributions of your hero to the Revolutionary War • Should be large enough to be easily read from the back of the room • Should contain the major points from the individual reports • Should be colorful and attractive

He decides that he wants to students to research the following:

1. Information about where and when the hero was born and his or her education and profession
2. Information about how and when the person became involved in the Revolution
3. Information about times and dates of interesting events involving the hero
4. Information about how the hero was involved in the formation of the new government after the revolution
5. Interesting information about the hero that is not commonly known (Jean Fritz's books are full of this type of information)

The groups have been reading about Ben Franklin, John Adams, Thomas Jefferson, Paul Revere, and King George, so the groups will focus on those heroes—or antihero, in King George's case.

Mrs. Sparks's 11th-grade homeroom class is responsible for planning and making the decorations for the junior-senior prom. She decides to use this opportunity to encourage them to work in cooperative groups. She divides the task into small parts and plans to give one part to each of five groups. They are to work together to create a plan. They must divide the task so that they determine how much material they will need, the cost of the material, a plan for creating their part, and a timeline for completing the work. Each group should plan two approaches to present, and the class will decide as a whole on which plan works best to contribute to the overall decorating scheme.

The group assignments look like this:

1. Favors
2. Table decorations
3. Hanging decorations
4. Special lighting
5. Wall decorations

Mrs. Sparks plans to explain the task and the budget to the students. She wants to ask each group to research the materials they can use, some inexpensive options, and even some merchants who might donate materials. She will ask each group to divide the duties and submit a plan to her. She wants to make sure every student is actively involved in the project.

CONCLUSION

Cooperative groups serve as authentic practice in critical thinking skills and teamwork. Students work together, which is a natural way for students to get to know one another and learn about hidden strengths of their fellow students.

To be successful, cooperative group activities take careful planning. Teachers should give practice in cooperative behaviors, establish clear expectations, and monitor student interactions during the process. Evaluation and grading of the group and individual projects are important as well. The standards for this grading should be very clear before the students begin working.

References

Cohen, E. (1992). *Restructuring the classroom: Conditions for productive small groups.* Madison: University of Wisconsin—Madison, Center for the Organization and Restructuring of Schools.

Cohen, E. (1994). *Designing groupwork: Strategies for the heterogeneous classroom* (2nd ed.). New York: Teachers College Press.

Suggested Reading

Baloche, L. (1997). *The cooperative classroom: Empowering learning.* Upper Saddle River, NJ: Merrill/Prentice Hall.

Jacobs, G., Power, M., & Loh, W. (2002). *Teachers' sourcebook for cooperative learning: Practical techniques, basic principles, and frequently asked questions.* Thousand Oaks, CA: Corwin.

ENSURING THAT ALL STUDENTS ARE ACTIVE PARTICIPANTS IN COOPERATIVE ACTIVITIES

Making decisions about the composition of groups for cooperative group work is an important part of the process. The groups should be mixed by academic ability, ethnicity, and gender. As group work becomes more common in the classroom, students will have opportunities to work with everyone in the class as they rotate membership in the groups. Groups of four or five seem to work best (Cohen, 1994).

Students' roles in groups should be carefully planned. While some roles are necessary for almost all projects, other projects have specific needs. Teachers should make roles clear to the students, and many roles require some training.

 ## STEP BY STEP

The steps for assigning and using roles in cooperative group work:

FOCUS ON ENGLISH LEARNERS

It is vital to support English learners in understanding and performing their roles. Start them with a job like materials manager or cleanup manager so they can gain confidence and observe others who are doing the more language-based roles.

• **Determine the roles needed for a group project** Most activities need a leader or facilitator, a recorder, a materials manager, and a cleanup manager. Depending on the task assigned, the group may also need a reporter or an illustrator. As you think about the roles for the activity, write a description to help each student understand exactly what is expected of him or her. Write these descriptions on role cards for each student or on a poster that is kept on display in the classroom. Posters or role cards should include graphic illustrations depicting the role; this is a visual aid for English language learners and challenged readers. See Figure 30.1 for an example of group-work role cards.

• **Compose the groups** Determine how many members each group should have, making sure each member will have a specific role to play. Research shows that four- or five-member groups function best (Cohen, 1994), but certain tasks may require groups of two, three, or six. However, be very careful with groups of three. They often end up with

Figure 30.1   Group-Work Task Cards

Facilitator	Recorder
1. Reads the task assignment to the group 2. Makes sure that everyone knows what to do 3. Makes sure that everyone gets to talk and participate	1. Records the group actions and decisions 2. Keeps track of the progress of the group 3. Writes a brief summary of the group solution or report with input from the entire group
Materials manager	Cleanup manager
1. Obtains any needed materials 2. Makes sure that everyone has the materials needed to do his or her jobs 3. Collects and returns leftover materials to their proper storage place	1. Assigns cleanup duties to other members of the group 2. Checks to make sure that all tables and desks are clean after the project 3. Gets the trash can and supervises the floor cleanup
Reporter	Illustrator
1. Takes directions from the group about what he or she will report to the whole class 2. Creates a brief oral report for the class 3. Summarizes the group's work using the summary written by the group and recorded by the recorder	1. Creates a visual to represent the work of the group, with the input of the entire group 2. Takes direction from the group for the visual but puts their ideas into the visual format 3. May enlist others to draw or print

a pair working and the third member being left out (Cohen, 1994). Arrange the groups to include a range of academic achievers, a mix of diversity, and genders. Plan to rearrange the groups for each different group-work activity. Be sure to keep track of the assignments to allow for thorough mixing with new activities.

• **Assign and explain the roles**   As you assign the roles, give each student in the group a role card or point out his or her duties on the roles poster. Emphasize the importance of everyone doing his or her job to keep the group working well together. Give some examples of things that might occur while the group is working and who is responsible for taking care of it. For example, if two people disagree, the facilitator must provide some conflict-resolution intervention. If something gets spilled, the cleanup manager must make sure that it gets cleaned up.

• **Train students to perform their roles**   In the beginning, you will want to meet with the facilitators to train them in strategies for keeping the group working together well. You may want to give them some ideas about questions they can ask to get the group thinking or respectful ways to remind someone to perform his or her job. Some activities may require a step-by-step action plan to divide the labor and move through the task in a timely manner.

Sometimes a solution sheet or a task checklist is helpful to the group. Meet with the facilitators and recorders to clarify the use of these tools to help them do their jobs more efficiently.

If you do a thorough job of explaining the roles, the students should be able to follow through on their duties. But if you see a problem, don't hesitate to gather together the students who have a specific role to clarify their tasks.

• **Monitor the role performance**   Circulate as the groups are working to make sure everyone is doing his or her job. However, do not intervene unless the group asks for help. If you see a group floundering, approach the members and ask how they might solve the problem. For example, you might approach a group that doesn't seem to be working and ask, "I notice you're not getting much done. Is there a problem?" Depending on the response you get, you may want to suggest that the facilitator should remind the students of their roles or direct the materials manager to get certain materials so they can get started.

• **Evaluate the process**   Be sure to take notes on students who do a particularly effective job of performing their roles. After the activity, have each group evaluate the group dynamics. When they report their evaluation to the class, provide positive feedback to those students who really worked well, being very specific about what they did. For example, "Robert did a great job as illustrator. He had everyone in the group contribute a drawing to the visual they created."

Applications and Examples

Mrs. Gonzalez's third-graders have been studying the solar system. So far they have looked at the planet Earth and its moon. Mrs. Gonzalez wants the students to begin some basic research, so she introduces a data chart as a research tool. Because the students have just completed a study of Earth, she uses the information they have gathered about Earth to demonstrate the use of the data chart. See Figure 30.2 for the data chart that Mrs. Gonzalez and her students complete.

Once the class has finished the data about Earth, Mrs. Gonzalez introduces their next study. "We are going to be studying the other eight planets in our galaxy. You will work in groups to complete a data chart about your assigned planet. You will also make a model of your planet to place on our bulletin board. We already have the Sun, Earth, and our moon represented on the bulletin board. You will have to figure out how big to make your planet in relation to the Sun and Earth. Your group will then present your data chart to the class and teach us all about your planet. Each of you will have a special role to play in your group."

Mrs. Gonzalez has divided the class into eight groups of four students. She distributes their role cards and explains exactly what their jobs will entail. As she gives out the eight facilitator cards to the group leaders, she explains, "The facilitator is responsible for keeping the group on task, for making sure that everyone has a chance to contribute, and for leading the discussions and planning."

She then passes out role cards for a materials manager, a recorder, and a reporter for each group. She explains that the group will work collaboratively on collecting the data but that each student must contribute some information to the data chart. She distributes a list of websites for them to explore and a schedule for computer use. Since there are four computers with Internet access in the classroom, they will all have enough time to do research. She then asks the materials managers to come to the front of the room to get the resource books she has collected on each of the planets and a blank transparency containing the data-chart form for their group to use.

"I have posted your assigned roles on the pocket chart," Mrs. Gonzalez explains. "In the future, we will be changing the roles and groups frequently, so this will help you remember your assignments each time." See Figure 30.3 for an example of this chart.

Figure 30.2   A Data Chart About the Planet Earth

	Questions					
	How Large?	**Pattern around the Sun?**	**Special Features?**	**Signs of Life?**	**Distance from the Sun?**	**Other Interesting Facts?**
Sources nineplanets. com	5th-largest planet	Elliptical	71% of surface is covered with water Atmosphere Is 77% nitrogen, 12% oxygen	Supports both plant and animal life	3rd planet from the sun	Composed of iron core; crust is iron, calcium, aluminum Core may be as hot as 7,500 K (hotter than the surface of the Sun)
enchanted learning.com	12,756.3 km in diameter				149,600,000 km from Sun	Only planet whose name does not come from Greek/Roman mythology

Mr. Clark's eighth-grade social science class is studying the struggle for racial and gender equality and the civil rights movement. He decides to use cooperative groups to enable his students to research some important events and present them in dramatic reenactments. His students will research background information leading up to the event, create an informational presentation for the class, and then reenact the event with a reader's theatre, dramatic scenes, or mime presentations.

He plans to have them research the *Brown v. Board of Education* ruling, the influence of Martin Luther King, Jr. and the "freedom rides," regional issues regarding the disabled and women's rights, the emergence of the National Organization for Women, the Warren court's decisions regarding civil rights, and the role of the NAACP.

He introduces the assignment by talking about his expectations for the study: "You will be working with a group of students to research some important events or issues in the civil right movement. Your group will have five members, and each of you will have a specific role to play in the group. You will all work on researching your topic and contribute to the report that your group will give to the class. In addition to the report, your group will be responsible for preparing a dramatic reenactment that helps us all understand the event or issue.

"For this assignment, each group will have a facilitator, a recorder, a reporter, a materials manager, a cleanup manager, and a drama director. I will assign the roles and explain a little about each person's responsibility. The one role that is different for this project is the drama director. This person will have responsibility for helping the group practice the

Figure 30.3   Group-Work Assignments Using a Pocket Chart

Group	Facilitator	Recorder	Materials	Cleanup
1	Name	Name	Name	Name
2	Name	Name	Name	Name
3	Name	Name	Name	Name
4	Name	Name	Name	Name
5	Name	Name	Name	Name
6	Name	Name	Name	Name
7	Name	Name	Name	Name
8	Name	Name	Name	Name

dramatic reenactment, helping them learn lines, and generally directing the production. The scripts and reports should be group projects, with everyone helping. The recorder will write down the words the group decides are appropriate. Materials managers will need to get materials and costumes from the closet. I have brought in some clothes for you to use, but you may have to find some additional things."

Mr. Clark carefully explains the responsibilities for each role as he passes out role cards. He also talks about the grading procedure: "You will each get two grades for this project. One grade will be based on the quality of work done by the group. Each person in the group will get the same grade depending on how well your group completes the assignment. Individual grades will be based on your self-assessment of your contributions to the project. Of course, you will have to document exactly what you do to contribute to the project, so keep notes for yourself."

The material managers come up to the teacher's desk to get the packets of materials Mr. Clark has found for each issue. They also get a list of websites and the computer schedule. The class breaks up into small groups and begins its research.

 CONCLUSION

One of the most important parts of cooperative group work is making sure that students understand their roles. Explaining the roles is time-consuming in the beginning but gets much easier as the students work in groups more frequently. It is important to give all students an opportunity to serve in leadership roles. If you have students who need support in performing these roles, provide some training before getting the groups started. Many teachers regularly work with all facilitators for a project, reinforcing their understanding of what is expected of them and how to do the job.

References

Cohen, E. (1994). *Designing groupwork: Strategies for the heterogeneous classroom* (2nd ed.). New York: Teachers College Press.

Suggested Reading

Cohen, E. (1992). *Restructuring the classroom: Conditions for productive small groups.* Madison: University of Wisconsin—Madison, Center on the Organization and Restructuring of Schools.

Sharan, Y., & Sahan, S. (1992). *Expanding cooperative learning through group investigation.* New York: Teachers College Press.

INTERVENING TO SUPPORT TOTAL PARTICIPATION BY ALL MEMBERS OF THE GROUPS

No matter how much training you provide in cooperative behaviors and role performance, you will still notice some students who either remove themselves from the interactions or get left out (Cohen, 1994). Therefore, the teacher must observe the group interactions and be prepared to intervene to ensure that all students become engaged in the activity.

Because one of the goals of cooperative group work is to support students in learning to maximize social interactions in the pursuit of learning, teachers must be careful not to become controlling but to provide instruction or modeling. There are several proven interventions that can both give students opportunities to interact and teach them how to gain access to social interaction (Cohen, 1994).

STEP BY STEP

The steps for gaining full participation for students in cooperative group work:

• **Treat expectations for competence** You will probably know from having observed your students which of them is likely to have lower-status or nonparticipating behaviors in group-work situations. To convince those students of their competence to perform well in interactive assignments, you may have to do some expectation training. To do this, you actually teach the students a skill that they, in turn, will teach to their groups. When they feel competent about teaching something to the group, their expectations for success for themselves and the group's expectations of their competence will improve, and their group interactions should also increase (Cohen & Sharan, 1980).

FOCUS ON ENGLISH LEARNERS

Part of treating competence for English learners is preparing them with the English vocabulary they will need to present their skills to the class.

There are several things to be very careful about in this approach. It is absolutely vital that the students be thoroughly prepared to succeed. To put already low-status students in a position to fail will increase their feelings of incompetence and lessen their abilities to interact in group situations. Because this training is time-consuming, some teachers do it before or after school or during times when the other students are actively involved in another pursuit. If you are successful in training competence, the students will gain status in the eyes of their peers as well as self-confidence (Cohen & Roper, 1972).

• **Validate student expertise** Since all students have areas of expertise, one of your jobs as teacher is to identify those areas. When you have low-status students who are struggling to be active participants in group-work activities, validating their special areas of expertise by having the student teach others in the class how to perform some unique skill or activity serves this purpose. It may be a nonacademic skill such as riding a unicycle or juggling, but it will raise the student's status in some way. Although the status may not transfer to more academic tasks (Cohen, 1994), the opportu-

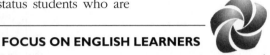

FOCUS ON ENGLISH LEARNERS

English learners often need support and status treatment from the teacher in order to become active members of a cooperative group.

nity to demonstrate competence does help raise such students' self-esteem and perceptions of their competence in the eyes of their fellow students.

• **Provide multiple-abilities treatment:** Multiple-abilities treatment involves introducing students to the concept of multiple ways of being smart. They are taught about Gardner's (1999) multiple intelligences theory and the importance of recognizing the different abilities available for working together in group-work projects. The mantra "No one is good at everything, but everyone is good at something" is repeated frequently, and students are engaged in activities that require new ways of approaching a problem such as using visualization skills, reasoning, or intuitive thinking. Group-training tasks must involve activities in which everyone contributes a unique approach to find an innovative answer to the problem. It is also helpful to restructure the groups during these activities so that more students can observe the unique abilities necessary to approach such challenges. See Figure 31.1 for suggestions of activities for multiple-abilities training activities.

This training is best performed prior to beginning group-work activities. The purpose is twofold: (1) to convince students that many different abilities are required for any task and (2) to create a wider definition of expectations for each student (Cohen, 1994).

• **Assign competence to low-status students** After you have completed expectation and multiple-abilities training with your students, you can continue to assign competence to low-status students by publicly recognizing their abilities. As you circulate during independent work or group-work time, verbalize your recognition of abilities so that everyone in the class can hear that the students possess competence in many arenas. If you see a student being left out of a group-work activity, you might help him or her to gain access by assigning competence. For example, "You may want to ask Juan to draw a diagram for that. He's really good at diagramming." Don't push; just keep moving, but observe to see if this approach works with the group. Of course, the recognition must be truthful to be effective.

• **Avoid pitfalls** Focus on validating and recognizing abilities that are seen as intellectual or a sign of multiple intelligences. Avoid making references such as "some people are good with their heads, and others are good with their hands," as these generalized references seem to undermine nonintellectual tasks. When talking about artistic ability, try to identify the specific ability and its connection to the task at hand (Cohen, 1994).

• **Evaluate student engagement** Keep observing on a regular basis and continue to note those students who are not full participants in the activities. If necessary, return to the training exercises and find a way in which the underparticipating students can build their self-confidence and begin to be seen as more competent among their peers. Training for specific roles of leadership and recognizing competence publicly should be ongoing as well.

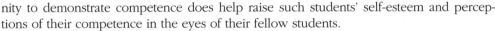

Figure 31.1   Multiple-Abilities Training Activities

Activity	Explanation
Represent it	Teacher describes a person, place, or thing without naming it. Everyone must represent what the teacher describes by drawing it, writing a paragraph describing what it is and what it does, creating and acting out a mime, or creating a song about it. Students share their creations. Two students may combine their presentations.
News reporter	The principal, librarian, coach, or someone else the students all know is brought into the classroom. The teacher begins the interview, but students are encouraged to ask questions of the person also. After the interview, each student draws a picture of the person and creates an acrostic poem about the person based on the information gained in the interview. The acrostic may use the person's name or job as the base, and descriptive words or phrases starting with the letters are added to make the poem. Example: J – Judicious O – Obviously likes her job B – Born to be a principal
Puzzles	Each student receives a small puzzle. They assemble their puzzles, create diagrams of how they solved it, and then teach the class how to solve it using their individual diagrams on a transparency film. Tangrams work well for this.

Applications and Examples

Mr. Beatty is preparing his second-graders for cooperative group work. Since he has a very diverse group of seven-year-olds whose native languages include Spanish, Hmong, and Korean, he decides to do extensive multiple-abilities training with the group before he begins the group work. He starts with an activity in which the students must listen carefully to his description of a character from a book he is reading aloud to the class. The students must then draw a picture of the character. After the pictures are drawn, Mr. Beatty asks the students to display their pictures on the bulletin board with a brief caption about the character. After school that day, he carefully labels each picture with the artist's name in bold letters. The next morning he hears the students talking about how well some of their classmates, who happen to be second-language learners, can draw. In doing this, they are in fact themselves assigning competency to their fellow students. He follows that activity with a discussion of multiple abilities and the importance of having a wide variety of strengths in a group when students are working together. He asks the students to name a few of the abilities they might need in their group if they were assigned the task of planning a party for the class. He also wants them to be specific about what each ability would add to the group project. The students come up with this list:

1. Someone who can write well, to write down all the plans and supplies needed
2. Someone who can talk well, to explain the plan to the class.
3. Someone who can draw well, to draw diagrams and pictures of the plans

4. Someone who can do math well, to figure out the budget

5. Someone who can make things, to show everyone how to make the decorations

6. Someone who can cook, to make the refreshments

After the class has created this list, Mr. Beatty asks the students to make a list of people in the class who they think would be good at each of these jobs and turn the list in to him so he can begin to plan the groups. He notes that the second-language learners are included in most of the lists as artists, decorations makers, or cooks. The cooks happen to be students who have shared food from their culture with the class in the past. Mr. Beatty feels that the group is ready to begin group work, but he knows he will have to continue with careful observation and status treatment for some of his students to ensure that their intellectual abilities are equally recognized as well.

Ms. Hemick's ninth-graders are working in cooperative groups to plan their class community project. They plan a neighborhood vegetable garden for their schoolyard. They have talked to the principal and have been given permission to use a plot of land at the back of the playground. Each group is now working on plans for tilling, planting, and managing the garden. The plan is to let anyone in the neighborhood help with maintenance and harvesting of the vegetables. Neighbors will have access to free vegetables for the entire spring and will take over the garden during the summer months. One of the local churches has volunteered to take over the project when school lets out for the summer.

As Ms. Hemick circulates during the group work, she notices one group arguing about the choice of vegetables to plant. Carlos, a native Spanish speaker, has pulled away from his group. He is listening to the discussion and making suggestions, but he is being ignored. His body language tells Ms. Hemick that he's aware of being left out. As Ms. Hemick passes the group, she hears Carlos say, "You can plant some vegetables early in the spring and others later when it's hotter." She responds by replying to Carlos, "You are exactly right, Carlos! What a good idea." She gives him a thumbs-up signal and continues walking. His group immediately turns to him, asking, "What did you say, Carlos? What was your idea?" Carlos pulls back up to the group and begins to explain that some vegetables do better in cooler weather, while others need warmer weather.

"How do you know that?" asks one of the girls.

"My dad raises vegetables," Carlos replies. "I know all about them."

"Well, help us with this plan," responds the group and hands the plot drawing over to Carlos.

Ms. Hemick smiles. "This status treatment stuff really works," she says to herself.

 # CONCLUSION

Multiple-abilities training and status treatment are powerful strategies for cooperative group work. Even more important, these approaches transfer to other activities in the classroom and tend to raise the status of all students (Cohen & Sharan, 1980). They can and should be used continuously during the day to build the confidence of all students in their abilities to be successful.

References

Cohen, E. (1994). *Designing groupwork: Strategies for the heterogeneous classroom* (2nd ed.). New York: Teachers College Press.

Cohen, E., & Roper, S. (1972). Modification of interracial interaction disability: An application of status characteristic theory. *American Sociological Review, 37,* 648–655.

Cohen, E., & Sharan, S. (1980). Modifying status relations in Israeli youth. *Journal of Cross-Cultural Psychology, 11,* 364–368.

Gardner, H. (1999). *Intelligence reframed: Multiple intelligences for the 21st century*. New York: Perseus.

Suggested Reading

Rosenholtz, S. (1985). Modeling status expectations in the traditional classroom. In J. Berger & M. Zelditch, Jr. (Eds.), *Status, rewards, and influence* (pp. 445–470). San Francisco: Jossey-Bass.

Solomon, R., Davidson, N., & Solomon, E. (1992). Some thinking skills and social skills that facilitate cooperative learning. In N. Davidson & T. Wosham (Eds.), *Enhancing thinking through cooperative learning* (pp. 101–119). New York: Teachers College Press.

BUILDING A SUPPORT SYSTEM: CELEBRATIONS AND PARENT INVOLVEMENT

In looking at the educational setting from the view of the learner, many educational theorists have emphasized the importance of student motivation on learning (Brophy, 1987; Keller, 1983.) Other educational theorists have examined the elements of motivation in classroom situations. Bandura's theory (1997) tells us that the learner must be influenced by feelings of self-efficacy. Albert Bandura defines *self-efficacy* as a combination of two components. First, the learners must believe that they are capable of learning what is being taught. Second, the learners must see that the learning will lead to desirable outcomes. For more information about Bandura's theory, see Figure VII.1

Stephen Krashen (1994) tells us that three elements are important in creating a positive learning environment. First, the learners must feel that what is being asked of them is possible for them to do. Second, they must have the self-confidence to actively participate in the learning process. And third, they must be functioning in an environment in which stress is low. In order to support learners in functioning at their best and in being able to take on the challenges of academic achievement, teachers must structure the learning environment to make sure that all three of Krashen's elements are present in the classroom on a daily basis. See Figure VII.2 for more information about Krashen's theory.

One component of a positive learning environment that contributes heavily to student motivation is the regular affirmation of abilities and progress in the form of classroom celebrations. These celebrations are not parties but regular structures built into the daily routine as a time for students and teachers to share achievements and celebrate progress. In this section of the text we will examine several ways in which to provide this affirmation of learning, increase student motivation, and use these celebrations as learning activities for all students.

Classroom celebrations support individual self-efficacy by providing immediate satisfaction for a job well done. More importantly, they provide students with feedback on their progress as well as opportunities to document achievement and set new, more challenging goals.

Our purpose here is to sequentially examine the elements of classroom celebrations to provide support to the teacher in establishing and maintaining them. Recurring celebrations are used to support and enrich student motivation and active engagement in learning. The inclusion of parents in the learning community is also important, as parents are a vital part of each student's wider circle of community.

Figure VII.1   Important Theory

Albert Bandura 1925–Present

Albert Bandura is a professor of psychology at Stanford University. He is best known for his social learning theory, a combination of cognitive and behavioral psychology that encompasses attention, memory, and motivation. Trained in traditional behaviorism, Bandura extended his beliefs to include the importance of three factors: the environment, behavior, and the person's psychological processes. These psychological processes include the ability to create images in the mind and use language.

Bandura is known as a father of the cognitivist movement largely because he recognizes the importance of imagery and language in learning. He is well known for his theory of learning from modeling, also known as observational learning. The basic principles of this type of learning consist of:

- Observational learning takes place when the learner observes a behavior and then acts it out. Behavior can be coded into words, labels, or images that add to the retention of the learning.
- People are more likely to adopt a modeled behavior if it results in outcomes they value.
- People are more likely to adopt a modeled behavior if the model is similar to the observer, has admired status, and has functional value.

Bandura maintains that observational learning requires a number of important factors.

1. *Attention*   To learn you must be paying attention. If the model is dramatic, you pay better attention. Other factors are the attractiveness, prestige, and competence of the model.
2. *Retention*   You must be able to remember what you have seen. The ability to use imagery and language supports the ability to retain.
3. *Reproduction*   You can't just sit and observe to learn. You need to be able to reproduce the behavior. For example, just watching high-level performers such as Olympic athletes will not enable you to imitate them.
4. *Motivation*   You must be motivated to actually perform the behavior. Some things such as past reinforcement, promised reinforcement, or vicarious reinforcement can serve to increase motivation. In this instance the word *reinforcement* refers to a positive reaction from another person such as a peer, parent, or teacher. There may also be several reasons explaining why you might decide not to imitate someone, such as past punishment, promised punishment, or vicarious punishment.

References

Bandura's published works include the following:

Bandura, A. (1969). *Principles of behavior modification.* New York: Holt, Rinehart, & Winston.
Bandura, A. (1977). *Social learning theory.* New York: General Learning Press.
Bandura, A. (1986). *Social foundations of thought and action.* Englewood Cliffs, NJ: Prentice Hall.
Bandura, A. (1997). *Self-efficacy: The exercise of control.* New York: Freeman.

Figure VII.2   Important Theory

Stephen Krashen 1941–Present

Stephen Krashen is a professor of linguistics at the University of Southern California. Much of his recent research has been in the area of language acquisition and the study of non-English-speaking students and bilingual education. His theory of second-language acquisition has had a major impact on teaching strategies for English learners across the United States. His theory of language acquisition consists of five main hypotheses:

Figure VII.2 Continued

- *Language acquisition versus language learning* Krashen makes a vital distinction between learning a language where the focus is on conjugating verbs and grammar rules and language acquisition, which to Krashen, means naturally acquiring a language by verbal interactions and natural communication. In language acquisition the focus is on the communicative act rather than the correctness of the speech. He does believe that language learning has a place in education but is only a way of monitoring and refining language.

- *The monitor hypothesis* This hypothesis explains the relationship between language acquisition and language learning. Learning the rules of language allows the speaker and writer to monitor language production and supports planning, editing, and correcting language production. Krashen cautions that three conditions must be present in order to use the monitoring function. The second-language learner must have time to focus on the rules and correct production, must focus on form and correctness, and must know the rules.

- *The natural order hypothesis* This hypothesis is based on research that suggests that people acquire grammatical structures in a natural order that is predictable. For any given language, some structures tend to be acquired early while others appear later, regardless of the learner's age, first language, or conditions of exposure.

- *The input hypothesis* This hypothesis is Krashen's explanation of how learners acquire a second language. His theory states that the learners progress in acquiring language when they receive input that is one step beyond their current stage of language competence. Krashen calls this communication just above the learners' current stage of development *comprehensible input* and contends that it is through this type of input that language is acquired.

- *The affective filter hypothesis* Krashen's fifth hypothesis explains the importance of the learners' motivation, self-confidence, and anxiety in learning. A low level of motivation and self-confidence combined with a high anxiety level cause learners to raise "the affective filter" and form a mental block that prevents learning from taking place. Krashen theorizes that raising motivation and self-confidence by presenting tasks that learners see as within their capabilities and keeping stress low create a more effective learning environment.

References

Krashen's published work includes the following:

Krashen, S. (1987). *Principles and practices in second language acquisition.* New York: Prentice Hall.
Krashen, S. (1988). *Second language acquisition and second language learning.* New York: Prentice Hall.

References

Bandura, A. (1997). *Self-efficacy: The exercise of control.* New York: Freeman.

Brophy, J. E. (1987). On motivating students. In D. G. Berliner & B. V. Rosenshine (Eds.), *Talks to teachers* (pp. 201–245). New York: Random House.

Keller, J. (1983). Motivational design of instruction. In C. Reigeluth (Ed.), *Instructional design theories and models: An overview of their current status.* Hillsdale, NJ: Erlbaum.

Krashen, S. (1988). *Second language acquisition and second language learning.* New York: Prentice Hall.

SCHEDULING CELEBRATIONS THROUGHOUT THE SCHOOL DAY

Many teachers complain of not having enough hours in the day. They talk about all the things they would like to do if only there were more time. Classroom celebrations are often lost in the shuffle as teachers try to satisfy all the standards for which they are responsible. Part of the problem is that the concept of celebration brings to mind a big party or major fiesta.

Classroom celebrations are most effective when they happen frequently and celebrate specific accomplishments. Teachers who find small bits of time in the schedule and celebrate in a meaningful way at the time of a child's accomplishment find them most motivating.

Teachers are by their very nature innovative and can find many unique ways of celebrating, ways that do not take time away from learning. See Figure 32.1 for suggestions of ways to celebrate children's accomplishments in the classroom.

Small recognitions are also appropriate as celebrations. The teacher can say, "I'm going to ask Joseph to lead the line to lunch today because he has learned all his addition facts. Way to go, Joseph!" This is, of course, accompanied by a big smile and a thumbs-up.

The reason for scheduling celebrations is to make sure they occur. If the teacher sets a goal to find time to celebrate and students to recognize each day, it will happen. Some teachers schedule a short celebration circle time between activities to briefly give recognition and a pat on the back to students who are working hard, behaving well, or supporting others. These celebration circles also give students a chance to talk about something they're proud of, a story they've written, math facts they've learned, etc.

 STEP BY STEP

The steps in scheduling classroom celebrations:

- **Identify the things you want to highlight** Think about the things you would like to highlight in your classroom. Do you want to begin with a focus on behavior and

Figure 32.1 Classroom Celebration Suggestions

How to Celebrate	When to Celebrate
Silent cheer—Raise your hands over your head and wave your fingers. Smile broadly as you do this.	• When the group responds well • When a student gives an outstanding verbal response • When the class moves to a new activity quickly and quietly
Give thumbs up … with a big smile.	• When a student gives a correct response
Author's chair—Student who has completed a piece of writing gets to come up, sit in the author's chair, and read the original work to the class.	• Whenever a student has completed an outstanding piece of writing • After each writing period, choosing one student to share; give all students a turn as they complete assignment (over time)
Publication of a student's writing—Using a word processor and simple binding, publish student work and add it to the class library. Announce the publication to the class and have the student paste his or her picture into the back cover and autograph the "first edition."	• When a student completes a piece of writing.
Atta boys and atta girls—Make stickers or buttons that say "atta boy" and "atta girl" and give them to students. Simply smile and say, "Here's an atta boy for Tony for his good behavior this morning. He's been working hard all morning."	• To recognize unusually good work habits, behavior, kindness to others, remembering to use words of encouragement
Student-led conferences—Parents are invited for a student-led conference. The student leads the discussion, sharing work from the work folder or portfolio and focusing on academic and behavioral growth.	• Periodically throughout the year; more than one conference can be scheduled at the same time, in the same room, with the teacher circulating among the conferences

following rules and routines? Will you then move to more academic-related celebrations? Or do you think you want to celebrate both? Are your students having problems with being supportive of one another? This might be the place to start, then, with a focused approach.

FOCUS ON ENGLISH LEARNERS

Modeling celebrations helps support English learners in using appropriate words when complimenting others.

- **Model the use of positive words**   Model verbal celebrations by recognizing individual accomplishments and progress. During this phase take a few minutes each day to recognize students who are using their time wisely, who have accomplished a new skill, or have done something to support another student in the learning process. Students should be encouraged to use positive words to recognize one another as well. In order for this modeling to be effective, you must take care to recognize student progress at all levels, not singling out the high-level students.

- **Think of some natural times for celebrations**   Are there natural transition times in your classroom just made for celebration? If so, think of a way you can use that time for quick recognition. Do your students change classes every hour? Then you need to take a few minutes for celebration at the end of each period. Those brief moments spent getting ready for recess and lunch provide great opportunities for small celebrations and fill the time with meaningful activity. Do you want your students to leave on a positive note? If so, dismissal time is another great celebration opportunity.

- **Teach celebration signals**   Introduce your students to some signals of celebration such as "thumbs-up" or "silent cheer." Make eye contact with the student you're targeting, smile, and give him the signal. After students have learned the signals, encourage them to signal one another when they see something that is worthy of celebration.

FOCUS ON ENGLISH LEARNERS

Signals used to celebrate accomplishments or appropriate behaviors help English learners recognize when their actions are acceptable.

- **Bring parents into the act**   Share your celebration signals with parents and encourage them to use them at home. Making a classroom video to show at open house is an excellent way to help parents see how the signals are used in the classroom and how positively the children react to them.

- **Support students who are working on goals**   After you have individual conferences with students and set goals, establish a private signal that you will use with that student to recognize his effort toward meeting his goals. Make eye contact and pull on your ear or touch your nose. Any signal works as long as the student gets the idea that "My effort is recognized!"

- **Evaluate your celebrations**   Stop every now and then and make sure that you are being consistent with celebrations. Are you celebrating every day? Do some students get all the recognition? Adjust your activity to make sure the celebrations are being used effectively.

Applications and Examples

Mr. Lorenzo's third-graders are working very hard on using encouraging words. He wants to focus celebrations on this important skill. He has already instituted celebration circles after center time in the morning. Student accomplishments are frequently celebrated with a silent cheer, a chance to read from the author's chair, or a celebration button made from the class button-making machine.

Mr. Lorenzo decides to do some observations as the students are working independently. He carries a note pad with him and writes down encouraging words he hears as the students are working. He uses the words he hears to conduct a lesson on quotation marks. He gathers his students together at the front of the room and introduces the use of quotation marks in the regular way. The difference is that instead of making up examples, he uses actual words he has heard spoken in the classroom that morning. His examples include

Mario said, "That was a good try, Jacob," when Jacob tried to throw beanbags through the math fact clown's mouth.

"Your cursive writing is really good," said Beatriz to Lauren.

"I wish I was as good at reading as you are," said Henry to Juan.

Kay said, "Wow! That looks great!" when Yvette made a puppet.

For the next few days, Mr. Lorenzo heard encouraging words much more frequently. The students were asked to become detectives and write down any they heard. They then wrote the sentences, using quotation marks correctly, and posted them on the bulletin board along with the ones Mr. Lorenzo had written.

Mrs. White is working with a group of high school seniors who have not yet passed their exit exam. Some of them are very discouraged since they're worried about graduating and have several standards to pass. They work diligently on standards all week, and on Friday Mrs. White gives them a practice test on the standards they've been practicing. At the end of the period on Friday Mrs. White has a short celebration where she hands back their practice tests wrapped in ribbons as if they were diplomas: green if they passed the practice test, orange if they improved their score from the week before, and yellow if they still have work to do. She makes a big show of the presentation, saying, "I am proud to present a green ribbon test to Manuel who has passed his fourth standard today. Congratulations, Manuel. I knew you could do it." The students practice walking across the front of the room, accepting their "diplomas," and shaking Mrs. White's hand.

"These are students who don't receive much recognition in school," says Mrs. White. "They work very hard in this class, and I think it's the words of encouragement they hear and the silly little celebrations we have that make the difference."

 ## CONCLUSION

Both Mr. Lorenzo and Mrs. White have found simple ways to celebrate achievement in their classes. They know that recognition is an important need (Maslow, 1987) for all human beings. They also know that motivation is another vital part of effective learning (Bandura, 1997) and find ways to help their students see themselves as capable learners.

References

Bandura, A. (1997). *Self-efficacy: The exercise of control.* New York: Freeman.
Maslow, A. (1987). *Motivation and personality* (3rd ed.). New York: Addison-Wesley.

Suggested Reading

Fisher, B. (1991). *Joyful learning.* Portsmouth, NH: Heinemann.
Kenkel, S., Hoelscher, S., & West, T. (2006). Leading adolescents to mastery. *Educational leadership, 63*(7), 33–37.

33

USING SPACE IN THE ROOM TO CELEBRATE LEARNING

Classroom celebrations can take place in many ways. Teachers have traditionally used bulletin boards to display student work, but they don't always use the opportunity to give recognition to the students whose work is displayed. In order to provide motivation for learning and an additional teaching opportunity, displaying student work should be accompanied by a brief celebration. The teacher takes time to recognize the student's accomplishments and, very specifically, explains to the class why this work is outstanding. This review of standards and expectations for excellence helps other students understand what they need to do in order to meet the standards.

Standards-based education is accepted in all 50 states in the United States. Teachers are being held accountable for addressing standards in all major curricular areas. The display of student work, celebrating the meeting of standards, and carefully documenting the standards being met support students' understanding of what is expected of them (Glasser, 2001). It also serves to inform visitors to the classroom, telling them exactly what is being studied and how the students are progressing.

Greenberg Elementary School in Fresno, California, displays student work on "standards boards." These are bulletin boards in the classrooms and hallways containing examples of student work. They are labeled with the standard addressed by the work that is displayed. The principal and leadership team do weekly walk-throughs to visit the classrooms, observe the teaching and learning that is taking place, and examine the standards boards. A very important part of these visits is the celebration of learning with the students that takes place as the team walks through the classrooms.

 STEP BY STEP

The steps for using classroom space to celebrate learning:

• **Identify areas in the classroom available for celebration displays** Examine your classroom carefully. Do you have bulletin boards, counter spaces, display cases, or bookshelves that could be used to display student work? If your space is limited, can you improvise by attaching cork strips from which to hang displays? Can student work be suspended from the ceiling? Some teachers have even created celebration areas by using large cardboard boxes, covering the cardboard with wallpaper, and displaying student work on all four sides.

• **Discuss the purpose of the display areas with the students**   Talk to your students about the work that will be displayed in the classroom. Help them to understand the standards that are being taught and how their work is demonstrating their achievement of those standards. Select an example of work to be displayed and explain why it was chosen. Encourage them to strive for display-quality work. Be sure to tell them that you believe they can succeed in doing this, and you will be supporting them in creating work that meets the standards.

• **Involve students in the process**   Ask students who are good at art to design the standards boards: colors, borders, and layout. Ask students whose writing is exemplary to create the labels. Ask others to serve as the mounting committee, putting up the work once it is chosen. Every now and then, have students share their work and allow the class to decide whose work should be displayed. When you do this, however, make sure the standards for the assignment are made very clear and that it doesn't turn into a popularity contest.

• **Label the standards boards**   The wording of the labels should be extremely clear so that visitors to the classroom can see exactly what the expectations are. For example, "good writing" doesn't convey the purpose of the assignment. "This work shows that we have met the language arts standard *'The student uses descriptive writing to create a visual image'*" helps students and visitors understand why the work was chosen. Try to avoid jargon that might confuse the reader.

FOCUS ON ENGLISH LEARNERS

Displaying and reviewing standards helps English learners understand what is expected of them.

• **Find other celebration space in the classroom**   While bulletin boards are among the most obvious places in the classroom for displaying student accomplishments, there are numerous other possibilities. See Figure 33.1 for suggestions.

• **Support students in meeting the standards**   If you notice students whose work is not being displayed, meet with the students individually, review the work they've done, and give them specific feedback and suggestions to help them meet the standards.

Figure 33.1   Classroom Celebration Spaces

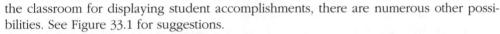

Space	Celebration Use
Class library	Publish and bind student writing. After the student shares the book from the author's chair, place the student's picture and a brief biography of the author in the inside back cover.
TV and VCR	Have students who read a lot choose their favorite books. Videotape them giving a brief review of the books and leave the TV monitor and VCR available close to the class library so others can view the tape to help them select good books to read. Make sure you make it clear *how* the students are chosen to make book commercials
Countertops	Display three-dimensional projects, clearly labeled, on countertops.
Quilt displays	When bulletin board space is limited, quilt displays serve well. Place a strip of cord across a wall and hang student work, backed by colorful construction paper and tied together with yarn. Only the top row of the quilt needs to be attached.

The work that is displayed does not have to be final-draft work. Conferencing and rewriting support learning also. It's important that all children see the value of meeting the standards and have the opportunity to see their work on display.

• **Evaluate the classroom celebrations**   Observe your students carefully to make sure the celebrations are serving to motivate. Be very cautious if you see students becoming competitive or nonsupportive of one another. Review the concept of supporting one another as a community on a regular basis.

Applications and Examples

Mrs. Nyberg's first-graders are studying the life cycle of a butterfly. She wants her students to learn to read and write about the science concepts they are learning, so she designs an integrated science/language arts unit. The students are involved in many active-learning experiences and enjoying writing about what they are doing. To celebrate their learning and give them recognition for their wonderful work, Mrs. Nyberg plans many classroom displays to highlight their accomplishments.

Because her school is focusing on standards in writing this year, Mrs. Nyberg displays a lot of writing in the classroom. She has many big books on display that are written by her students. Each big book is labeled on the cover with the standard it addresses. She always spends a few minutes talking about the quality of the work that is displayed and how proud she is of her students. Her favorite sentence is "I can't believe how smart you are!"

After her students have completed a writing assignment that meets the standard *"Students write complete sentences,"* Mrs. Nyberg displays the students' writing in a sentence quilt. She chose the quilt format because she had writing samples for 16 of her 20 students to display. See Figure 33.2 for the quilt plan.

Mrs. Nyberg constructs the quilt from construction paper in bright colors. She ties the construction paper squares together with red yarn. In each of the 16 quilt blocks, she glues one of her student's illustrated sentences.

Mrs. Nyberg is extremely pleased with the progress her students are making in reading, writing, and science, but she is most excited when she overhears one of her students say to another, "You are so smart!"

Figure 33.2   Mrs. Nyberg's Quilt Display Plan

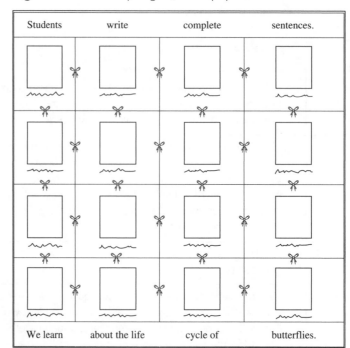

Mr. Osterberg's ninth-graders are constructing a neighborhood resources guide for their community. His school has adopted a block scheduling plan, and his classes meet for 2 hours each day. He is responsible for teaching both English and social studies. Since geography is a focus during this grading period, Mr. Osterberg decides to combine interviewing, writing, and map construction. The culminating project for the 6-week period is a three-dimensional map of the school neighborhood. The map displays local businesses and homes, and locations on the map are linked to student writing about people they have interviewed.

The principal is so impressed with the students' project that he agrees to display it on a raised platform in the center courtyard of the school. Yarn connects the writing displayed along the outside edge of the platform to the location of the person's home or business that is the topic of the writing.

The day the display is assembled, the class gathers in the courtyard around the map. They attach one end of their yarn strip to the correct location on the map and then use tape to attach their writing to the platform edge.

As the students attach their contributions to the project, they tell one important thing they learned about their community through the project. The students share things about people's native countries, their reasons for moving to the community, and special gifts they possess.

Many of the local merchants take the time to come and view the display, and the local newspaper prints a picture of the students mounting their contributions. One student says, "This was the most fun I've ever had in school."

 # CONCLUSION

Teachers have always displayed student work, but they haven't always linked the display to the expectations and accomplishments of the students. Classroom displays and celebrations of excellence can contribute to a community pride in the classroom. In order to serve this purpose, they need to be changed frequently, be directly related to the goals of the curriculum, and provide genuine incentives for students.

STRATEGY ON VIDEO
Celebrating Learning

Approaches to celebrating learning are demonstrated on segment 12 of the DVD that accompanies this text. You will see the school principal and a first-grade teacher explain ways to celebrate student learning and examples of approaches. As you view this segment, think about the following:

- How do the bulletin boards become a part of the learning process at this school?
- What is the difference between a display board and a learning board?
- What additional ways can you think of to celebrate student learning?

References

Glasser, W. (2001). *Every student can succeed.* Los Angeles: William Glasser Institute.

Suggested Reading

Bafile, C. (2004). From "pretty" to practical: Using bulletin boards to teach. *Education World: Professional Development Center.* www.educationworld.com

SETTING UP CLASS WEB PAGES, NEWSLETTERS, AND NEWSPAPERS TO DOCUMENT AND CELEBRATE LEARNING

Learning communities have lots of news and celebrations to share. To keep parents informed of the classroom events and to share good news, teachers are involving the students in the publishing of web pages, newsletters, and newspapers. These communications provide another avenue for sharing student writing and accomplishments. Parents can also be kept informed of special event schedules, items needed for the classroom, and topics being studied.

Depending on the ages of the students, they can become responsible for much of the production of classroom publications. Some class newsletters are completely written, edited, and produced by students. The teacher simply facilitates the process and may contribute a guest column.

Keeping the parents informed of the curriculum and events enables them to be more involved in their child's schooling, a factor that has been shown to enhance academic success (Henderson & Berla, 1994). Because many homes now have computers and Internet connections, teachers are using that mode to facilitate communication. Keep in mind, however, that families without Internet must also be kept up to date. If you have families who speak another language at home, you may also want to consider finding someone in the school or community to translate your newsletter if you cannot do it yourself.

FOCUS ON ENGLISH LEARNERS

Translations for non-English-speaking parents help them become part of the learning support team for their children.

 STEP BY STEP

The steps for creating a classroom website, newsletter, or newspaper:

• **Start simple** Teachers have used photocopied newsletters for many years. They are effective communication tools and are a great way to communicate with the parents and community. Using a word-processing program, set up a standard format for the piece and gradually add elements such as graphics, student art, and classroom photos. Simply

Figure 34.1   An Example of a Class Newsletter Using Microsoft Word

---

The Cougar Roar

Published by Mrs. Clark's Third Grade   September 12, 2005

Special Events this week:
Field trip Thursday, September 15, 2005—We still need a parent volunteer. We will be walking a lot, so be sure to wear comfortable shoes on Thursday.

Classroom needs: **Egg cartons, yarn scraps**

My Kitten by Melissa Fox
Kitten
Soft and sweet
Purring, stretching, licking
My kitten loves to sit in my lap.

Sneakers by Jim Treadwell
Sneakers
Torn, stinky, old
Running, jumping, racing
My sneakers look bad, but they go fast.

Teacher's Corner

We have four students who have published books this week:
   John Grey
   Rebecca Brown
   Carlos Lopez
   Didi Sommers
Come by the classroom to read their books. Those students will be having lunch with Mr. Frederic, the principal, at his weekly authors' luncheon on Friday, September 16. Their parents are invited to join the party at 11:45 in the principal's conference room.
Congratulations!
Mrs. Clark

Class News

The following students have moved up a level in reading this week:
   Henri Korda
   Gloria Goode
   Maria Sanchez
   Joey Howard
   Lewis Thomas

Kelly Taylor has a new baby sister. Her name is Faith.

Robbie Greene has been selected for baseball all-star team and will play at the high school field on Saturday at 2 PM. Let's all come out to cheer him on!

---

take pictures with a digital camera and download the pictures onto the computer. With a simple photo-processing program, the pictures can then be resized, cropped as necessary, and moved into the newsletter. Student art can be photographed or scanned using a flat-bed scanner and copied into the newsletter. See Figure 34.1 for an example of a newsletter done in this way.

• **Find resources**   As you get more confident, you may want to find a different way to publish the newsletter. You may want to expand it to several pages in order to include more student writing. There are many resources available for even the most technologically challenged. For sources of information about creating web pages, electronic newsletters, and e-zines (a web-based magazine), see Figure 34.2.

• **Set up the process**   In order to collect materials for the newsletters and make sure that a newsletter goes home on a regular basis, an organizational structure is a necessity. There should be a clearly marked location in the classroom where students may place any material they wish to have published in the newsletter. If you plan to send home a newsletter each Monday, set a deadline that allows you to complete the newsletter before you leave for the weekend. Students need to understand that late submissions will be considered for the following week. Make an attempt to publish work by as many

Figure 34.2 Resources on the Internet for Classroom Publishing

Examples of school newsletters:
http://norwood.epsb.ca/classroom_newsletters.htm

Directions for publishing online newsletters:
http://www.go-ezines.com/1/creating-classroom-newsletters.html

Online newsletter writing tutorial using AppleWorks:
http://www.k12.hi.us/-gfujimur/trng%20module/newstitle.htm

For additional sites, search using the words "classroom newsletters."

Step-by-step instructions for building a website:
www.graphicwebdesign.net/easy-website-creation.html

www.mwelot.com/

www.web-site-tools.com/webmake.htm

For additional website resources, search using the words "website creation."

different students as possible. This necessitates keeping track of exactly whose work is published each week. Let parents know when they can expect the newsletters to come home. To help parents to get into the habit of reading the newsletter, print it on the same brightly colored paper each week. This will help them locate it in crowded backpacks.

• **Gradually turn production over to the students** As the year progresses, gradually turn over the production of the newsletter to the students. Form a committee to select the student work to be included. Have students do the typing and layout. This will take some instruction in the beginning. Eventually all you should need to do is review the content and write the "Teacher's Corner" items. Once you have a core group of students trained in the process, give them the responsibility of training additional journalists. If you want to get more complex and add a web page or electronic newsletter, check with the parents to see if you can locate a volunteer. Many parents use computers at work and have valuable computer skills. They may even be willing to train students in the web-page production process. Some of your more computer-savvy students might even be capable of creating it themselves. Older students could be brought into classrooms with younger students to assist in the process.

• **Keep a class scrapbook** Be sure to keep copies of all the newsletters you send home. Use them to create a class scrapbook, adding student work that was not published each week as well. Students enjoy reading through these types of publications, so place the scrapbook in the classroom so that it's accessible to the students and any visiting adults.

• **Add bells and whistles** Don't feel that you need to start with all the bells and whistles in place. Start with a simple format and, as you get more comfortable with the technology, add features. As you add features, be sure to train your students in the process so the responsibility can become theirs.

• **Get feedback from parents and administrators** Never send home a newsletter without sharing it with your building administrator. Principals may be comfortable about your newsletter going home without their having read it each week, but get permission before you do this. No matter what, be sure to share the newsletter with your principal each week so that he or she knows what's happening in your classroom. Ask parents for feedback also, determining which features they enjoy and what they would like to see added.

Applications and Examples

Miss Hunt's second grade starts the year with a simple, one-page photocopied newsletter that goes home each Friday. As the year progresses, the students are submitting more writing, art, and photos of projects to be published. Miss Hunt decides to expand her newsletter into a newspaper. Using the same technology she used for the newsletter, Microsoft Word and PhotoShop, she simply expands the newsletter into a four-page newspaper. She enlists two parents to assist her in the project.

The students know that any work they want to see published must be submitted before they leave school on Wednesday afternoon. Miss Hunt's two helpers arrive after school to choose the materials to include in the weekly edition of the "Hunt Herald." They keep careful track of the students who are published each week and try to make sure everyone is published at least once a month. This translates into eight pieces of student work in each issue. Sometimes, if the pieces are short, they manage to include work from more students. The newspaper is published on bright orange paper that another parent has donated.

Miss Hunt gets a lot of positive feedback from the parents and her principal, and she's very careful to make sure she recognizes the hard work of the two parents who work on the paper. Gradually, students sign up to work on the paper and stay after school to help publish. By the end of the year the students are doing all the selection of items for the paper and the layout. They've learned to use the scanner to include student art. The third-grade teacher is thrilled that these students are ready to work on a newspaper because she plans to publish one next year.

Ms. Meadows's eighth-graders publish their own classroom anthology online, using work written for Ms. Meadows's language arts class. Since the students are older, they submit their writing by e-mail so nothing has to be retyped. A rotating group of students makes the selections for the anthology.

The students learned to create the web page by walking through the steps from a website resource (www.web-site-tools.com/webmake.htm). One of the fathers helped them get started and volunteered to pay the $10 monthly fee to the hosting service (TruePath.com). The students keep the web page up to date. Ms. Meadows and their principal must approve all content before she makes the page visible to the public.

They are gradually including more art, graphics, color, and photos to make their web page more dynamic. Several of the students have now created their own personal web pages as a result of their involvement in Ms. Meadows's project.

 ## CONCLUSION

Teachers have used newsletters to communicate and celebrate with parents for many years. The process is becoming easier and more exciting each year with the new technology that is available in almost every home and school. Parents appreciate this type of communication and say that it helps them to stay in touch with their children's school and teacher (Henderson & Berla, 1994). The newsletter can also be used as a method for locating parents with specific skills to volunteer in the classroom. Publishing a newsletter proves very motivational to budding authors and provides a rich creative outlet for all students as well.

References

Henderson, A., & Berla, N. (Eds.). (1994). *A new generation of evidence: The family is critical to student achievement*. Washington, DC: Center for Law and Education.

Suggested Reading

Epstein, J. (1995). School/family/community partnerships: Caring for the children we have. *Phi Delta Kappan, 76*(9), 701–712.

Moles, O. (1996). *Reaching all families: Creating family-friendly schools*. Available at http:www.ed.gov/pubs/Reachfam/index/htm

INVOLVING PARENTS IN THEIR CHILDREN'S EDUCATION

Many researchers have documented the importance of parent involvement in their children's education (Henderson & Berla, 1994; Oldstead & Rubin, 1983). When children see their parents actively involved in the educational process, they begin to better understand the importance of the process and the commitment that their parents and significant others are willing to invest in their future. The presence of other adults in the classroom can help create the feeling of an extended community in the classroom that reinforces the importance of education in students' lives. In the previous chapter the importance of communication with parents was explored, but there are many ways for parents to be involved. When both parents are employed outside of the home, they may not feel that they have the time or opportunity to be involved in the school activities. Teachers hold the key to parent involvement. Through regular communication with the parents, invitations to be involved in many different ways, and an openness to parental involvement, teachers help parents to find ways to be a part of the learning team (Ames, 1995).

Parents may have preconceived notions about parental involvement, thinking that it means being available to volunteer in the classroom. The teacher's job is to widen these concepts, making some type of involvement open to all parents. For suggestions of ways in which parents can be involved, see Figure 35.1. While this list is not exhaustive, it will provide ideas for parents who may want to help but aren't available during the school day.

 STEP BY STEP

The steps for encouraging parental involvement:

• **Issue invitations** Using notes to the parents or a class newsletter, make parents aware of opportunities to become involved. Let them know when you need simple recycled items such as newspapers, toilet-paper tubes, or yogurt cups for projects. Don't be shy about asking parents to sew or create learning materials at home. Just be willing to provide the materials necessary. Always thank the child for bringing things into the class

Figure 35.1   Ways in Which Parents Can Become Involved in Their Child's Education

Involvement	Description
Setting up a study area and monitoring homework	Parents work collaboratively with the student to establish a quiet place for study. They also set a specific homework time each day. They check over the homework once it is complete and help when the child requests help. They communicate with the teacher if there are any problems.
Attending school functions	Parents attend meetings, open houses, and programs that are presented in the evening. They talk to their child about what was learned at the meetings and show interest in the child's participation in school events.
Reading and responding to all communications from school	Parents ask the child for any newsletters or notes each day. They discuss the content of the communications with the child. They respond to requests for supplies and help whenever they are able to do so. They talk to their child about school events.
Preparing teaching materials at home	Parents volunteer to prepare teaching materials for the teacher. These types of materials can usually be done at home. They talk to the child about the materials being prepared and ask about their use after they are sent to the teacher.
Offering special expertise to the teacher	Parents talk to the teacher to determine areas in which they can be helpful (computer work, videotaping, video editing, newsletter preparation, word-processing of student writing, cooking and hobby demonstrations).
Constructing classroom materials	Parents build bookshelves, lofts, storage cabinets. They can also sew curtains, chair covers, costumes. The project should be done collaboratively with the child whenever possible.
Planning and coordinating parent-help days	Parents volunteer to plan and coordinate parent-help days for projects such as play-ground construction and landscaping. They can also gather parents together for a social-work day to make teaching materials.
Coordinating fund-raising events to raise money for special school projects	Parents work with the school to determine needs and find ways to raise funds. Children are involved whenever it is appropriate.
Reading to children	Parents who can spare an hour during the day can coordinate with the teacher to provide read-alouds for students who need them.

and follow up with a short note to the parents as well. Some teachers have groups of students take turns writing thank-you notes for donated items. If a child is going to be honored for publishing a book or memorizing math facts, invite the parents to share in the celebration. Survey the parents to find out if they have any interesting hobbies to share with the class. If some of the parents drop their children off at school in the morning, ask them for a half hour of their time to help you prepare art materials or read to a child. Make the parents feel welcome by offering invitations as often as possible, but be sure that you have tasks for them to do when they volunteer their time.

FOCUS ON ENGLISH LEARNERS

Invitations to non-English-speaking parents should be conveyed in their native language and focus on ways that they can demonstrate special skills or culture-related activities in the classroom. Providing a translator for their demonstrations helps them be more comfortable.

• **Plan for the parents' time** Before you issue blanket invitations for parents to come to the classroom to help, organize the tasks you can ask them to do. Some teachers have constructed a parent-volunteer file with directions for common classroom tasks so that orienting the parents doesn't take time away from the students. See Figure 35.2 for an example of a volunteer task file.

Be sure to recognize that some parents have small children at home and can't come into the classroom. Encourage them to volunteer by performing tasks at home. You can write out task cards for home projects as you think of them and then give them to parents when they ask, "Is there anything I can do at home?" You might place the materials for the project in a resealable plastic bag, along with the task card, for ease of transportation.

Figure 35.2   Parent-Volunteer Task File

Monday and Wednesday Task Fill the paint cups in the easel tray. Use the tempura paint under the sink and fill cups to half full. If paint colors have become mixed or muddy, rinse cups and fill with fresh paint.	**Tuesday and Thursday Task** Chart student books read. Look through the reading logs in red basket on the counter and place a stick on the chart next to the student's name for each book read. Once book has been charted, place a large check in the upper-right corner of the page in the log. Only chart books on pages without checks.
Everyday Task File papers in workfolders. The graded papers are in the green basket on teacher's desk. Portfolios are in hanging file next to teacher's desk. File by placing papers into the *front* of the folder so most current papers are in front.	**Monday and Wednesday Task** Sit in rocking chair by the back door. Once you are seated children will bring a book to you. Read the book to the children once and then ask them to read it to you. Encourage them to figure out words, but if they can't, supply the word for them.
Friday Task Sit at teacher's desk and call students to you, one at a time. Go through the child's portfolio with him or her and encourage the child to choose papers completed this week to keep in the portfolio. Other papers from this week go into backpacks to be taken home. Remind students to put the papers into their green folders and to take a newsletter too.	**Tuesday and Thursday Task** Sit at the back table with the multiplication fact games. They are in the second drawer to the right of the sink. Call students from the multiplication list on the chalkboard over to the table three or four at a time. Play one of the multiplication fact games with them for about 20 minutes. If a child is at reading group when you call, he or she will tell you that. Just call the child with the next group.

These cards are cut apart and filed by Monday and Wednesday, Tuesday and Thursday, Friday only, and every day. Parent volunteers choose a card and follow the directions.

Some schools have appointed a parent-volunteer coordinator who schedules parent volunteers into the classroom and assigns tasks. One innovative parent volunteer organized a mother's morning out with a babysitter and a project for the parents to complete that involved preparing teaching materials. She made a big pot of coffee and brought in cookies for the parents and preschoolers. This eventually became a schoolwide weekly event with the cafeteria full of moms and dads making teaching aids for 2 hours every Wednesday morning.

• **Recognize parental efforts**   Parents will continue to volunteer as long as they feel that they are performing valuable tasks and that their time is appreciated (Epstein, 1983). Write a brief note or have the students write a note thanking parents who volunteer. Give recognition to parents who are helping by publicly thanking them in the class newsletter. You might even consider having an informal luncheon at the conclusion of the year to express your appreciation.

• **Ask for feedback**   Parents are often comfortable with some tasks and not with others. Have a variety of tasks available to them and be sure to make it clear that they have choices. Ask for periodic feedback from volunteers about their experiences. Be sure to ask if they feel their contributions were appreciated and valuable. Ask for suggestions on how their time could be used more effectively. You may have some credentialed teachers as parents. They may want to actually teach some small groups or individuals.

• **Continue to expand**   Once you make it clear to parents that their help is wanted and appreciated, you may have to expand your thinking and use their help in more innovative ways. Do you have class projects that you would like to capture on video? You may have some parents who can do this for you. Do you have any parents who are artists or musicians? Maybe they can volunteer with groups of students working on projects to integrate these areas. Do you have parents from other cultures? Maybe they can share some of the customs and foods from their cultures with the class.

• **Establish schoolwide efforts**   Some of the most effective parent-involvement projects are schoolwide efforts. Schools with parents who speak languages other than English often hire liaison personnel or use volunteers to translate written communications and provide support during meetings. Many schools are organizing parent-education programs to help parents understand how best to help their children succeed in school.

Schools in poor neighborhoods have provided bus service and babysitting for evening meetings in order to encourage parent participation. In multiethnic neighborhoods, schools start the school year with a covered-dish dinner and encourage parents to bring and share their native delicacies. Others invite everyone, provide games, and cook for the entire group. Issuing an invitation to come and help with the cooking is a wonderful way to get a number of parents involved. In one school the principal serves as the chief cook and wears a chef's hat as he serves the parents in a cafeteria-style line. The parents love it!

Applications and Examples

Mrs. Nabors always issues an open invitation to the parents of her first-graders. She says on the first evening parent meeting, "Children love to see their parents involved in their classroom. I know many of you work outside the home, but there are many ways that you can be involved. Some of the parents have helped with field trips and holiday celebrations. Other have come into the classroom to help on days when they've taken time off from work for dentist appointments. I had a group last year who came in on the mornings they drove as a car pool and listened to children read. Other parents have done sewing or worked on the class newsletter at home. If you are interested in getting involved, there's a way for you to do it. I have a questionnaire I'd like you to complete so I know who to call when I need some help. If you have any other way that you'd like to be involved, please feel free to write it in on the form." Then she passes out a form for the parents to complete and return while they are there. See Figure 35.3 for an example of the type of form Mrs. Nabors uses.

Mrs. Nabors uses the information she gathers from the forms to ask parents to perform specific tasks. She also invites them to class for special occasions and to share in

Figure 35.3 A Parent-Volunteer Information Form

Name _____ Phone number _____

When are you available for volunteer work?

    Mornings   Afternoons   At-home assignments, please

Days of the week available _____

Would you be comfortable:

Working with individual children
    Listening to them read _____ Helping them with math facts _____

Working with small groups
    Playing learning games _____ Working on an art project _____

Please check any tasks you feel you could do to help our class.

    Word processing _____ Preparing teaching materials _____

    Monitoring a learning center _____ Supervising a small-group project _____

    Videotaping class activities _____ Chaperoning field trips _____

Do you have any hobbies or interests you would be willing to demonstrate for our class?
_____

Do you speak any languages other than English _____

Would you be available to translate written material? _____

Please share anything else you would like to do for our class:

celebrations. They are invited to come for lunch any day they're free to do so. Mrs. Nabors also lets them know if she needs any special materials that they might have at home. She often sends projects home for parents to complete. Her parents feel welcome in her classroom, and they come to volunteer frequently, many of them for just an hour at a time.

In Mrs. Nabors's school one of the parents serves as a projects coordinator and assembles work parties of parents to complete tasks such as making math manipulative kits for an entire grade level. This parent volunteer has her helpers spray-paint dry beans to use as colorful math counters. They then assemble kits using the beans and props. Some of the beans become eggs to be counted into small birds' nests made of paper strips glued onto cardboard. Other beans are made to look like different colors of frogs, and they are combined in small ponds drawn on cardboard and laminated. The parents enjoy participating in the work days, and the cafeteria supplies coffee and homemade cookies.

Another parent, an artist, arranges for some of her colleagues to come and set up shop in the school courtyard so the students can observe an actual artist in the process of painting or sculpting or working with a potter's wheel. The artists have learned to answer questions appropriately, and the students are gaining an appreciation of the unique talents required to become artists.

Parents of middle- and high school students are often at a loss as to how they can support their children's education. They often complain that the students don't really want them to come to school anymore. Teachers at this level try to reassure the parents that their interest and involvement is still needed; it just has to grow and change as their children have. One middle school sends home a list of ways in which parents can be supportive. It reads:

Middle-school students still need to know that their parents are concerned about them and interested in their activities. Here are some ways that you, as parents, can provide that support:

- Talk with your child about events at school each day. Try to ask open-ended questions and encourage your child to talk.
- Keep abreast of school events by visiting the school website at ———. Offer to help with fund-raisers or social activities.
- Set up a quiet place for your children to do homework. Provide necessary materials and show an interest in their assignments.
- Get to know your child's teachers. Schedule regular conferences.

Many parents at the secondary level stay involved through booster clubs for band, competitive academic groups, or athletics. Others work on schoolwide committees. The idea for sober graduation activities was a result of parent committees and has spread across the nation rapidly. Parents of older students still make a big difference in the success of their children.

 ## CONCLUSION

Parental involvement is a positive factor is children's success in school. The key to this involvement continues to be the teacher's commitment to including parents in the process (Ames, 1995). Although beginning teachers are sometimes reluctant to add parents to the classroom mix, they frequently find that additional adults in the classroom can improve their teaching effectiveness if their participation is well planned and teachers use their services well. This, of course, takes a commitment to planning and organization. School-wide efforts have been extremely successful and take some of the responsibility off the teacher's shoulders.

References

Ames, C. (1995). *Teachers' school-to-home communications and parent involvement: The role of parent perceptions and beliefs* (Report No. 28). East Lansing: Michigan State University, Center on Families, Communities, Schools, and Children's Learning.

Epstein, J. (1983). *Effects on parents of teacher practices in parent involvement.* Baltimore: Johns Hopkins University, Center for Social Organization of Schools.

Henderson, A., & Berla, N. (1994). *A new generation of evidence: The family is crucial to student achievement.* St. Louis, MO: Danforth Foundation; and Flint, MI: C. S. Mott Foundation.

Olmstead, P., & Rubin, R. (1983). Linking parent behaviors to child achievement: Four evaluation studies from the parent education follow-through programs. *Studies in Educational Evaluation, 8,* 317–325.

Suggested Reading

Rich, D. (1993). Building the bridge to reach minority parents: Educational infrastructure supporting success for all children. In N. Chavkin (Ed.), *Families and schools in a pluralistic society* (pp. 235–244). Albany: State University of New York Press.

SUPPORTING ONE ANOTHER: SCHOOLWIDE STRUCTURES TO ENCOURAGE INTERACTION AND COLLABORATION

Establishing a schoolwide paradigm for collaboration supports the classroom teacher's efforts in moving students away from the "every man for himself" mentality, but collaboration among teachers is very often the exception rather than the rule (Inger, 1993). One of the major factors cited by teachers who drop out of the teaching profession is a feeling of isolation from colleagues (Inger, 1993).

Collaboration among administrators, faculty, and community is defined as "a shared partnership working on behalf of student learning" (Montague & Warger, 2001). But collaborative approaches to building meaningful curriculum and schoolwide reform are not a short-term project. Teachers, administrators, and parents must commit to long-term goals in order to make these types of collaborations successful (Risko & Bromley, 2001).

As teachers begin to introduce students to collaboration in the classroom, set up their furniture and time periods to support collaboration, and enlist students in the planning of collaborative projects, they also need to engage colleagues in the process. Collaborative planning among teachers can boost the creative energy and lower the responsibility levels for gathering materials and resources, since these activities can be shared.

Some of the important elements of a collaborative teaching environment require support from the administration for shared decision-making. Many of the decisions involve systemic changes such as scheduling, time and opportunity for participants to meet together, and possibly even released time from teaching duties to observe other teachers or visit other school sites (Allington & Cunningham, 2002).

Much of the change from isolated teaching of skills to integrated learning takes a shift in thinking, and it's the same process in professional collaboration. When teachers collaborate in planning and brainstorming, everyone wins, including the students (Farr & Tone, 2004).

 STEP BY STEP

The steps for implementing collaborative planning:

• **Identify a core group of teachers to approach the topic**   In many cases, one teacher, who sees the benefit of collaboration, is the initiator of this step. Because this teacher sees some barriers to collaboration in the current school structure, a movement for change is begun. Teachers who are interesting in beginning to collaborate may meet together to establish their wish list and approach the administrators for support. In other cases, the principal may approach a group of teachers and form an ad hoc committee to examine the ways in which collaboration can be encouraged.

• **Identify small steps with which to begin**   Some schools have begun by eliminating bells and other interruptions such as intercom announcements that steal time from the instructional day. Others have begun with after-school in-service programs to introduce the concept of shared responsibility and collaborative planning.

• **Conduct a needs assessment**   Making changes in education is extremely difficult. Many teachers are comfortable doing things the way they have always done them. In order to encourage ownership of a new approach, all teachers at the school should be given an opportunity to express their views. See Figure VIII.1 for an example of a schoolwide needs assessment.

• **Form a planning committee**   Once the needs assessments are collected, members of the core committee meet together to examine the responses. If additional teachers have volunteered to serve on the planning committee, they should be invited to join the group. Support for the collaboration project may not be widespread, as evidenced by the responses on the needs survey. If this is the case, the core group and supporters may decide to use a partial implementation plan with only those who actively support the process involved. If there are only a few dissenters, the principal may decide to stage a schoolwide implementation and use further in-service training and encouragement to bring everyone on board.

• **Develop a plan**   The planning committee develops a plan for the implementation, meets with the principal for approval, and brings it back to the entire faculty. If there are elements of the plan that require further training, in-service is scheduled. The process is the same for a partial implementation if fewer teachers are involved. See Figure VIII.2 for an example of one school's implementation plan.

• **Provide training**   As the plan is implemented, a need for further training in such areas as collaborative planning, cooperative learning, project learning, or classroom management may be evident. Local universities are often a good source for workshop leaders

Figure VIII.1   Collaboration Needs Assessment

1. How often do you plan with colleagues?
2. What do you see as the barriers to collaborative planning?
3. Are you willing to participate in collaborative planning if the barriers can be eliminated or lessened?
4. Which of the following would you support?

     Block scheduling, giving more time to in-depth exploration
     Grade-level or subject-discipline joint planning
     Team teaching
     Partner teaching
     After-school remedial teaching

5. Do you have any other needs you would like to see addressed by the planning committee?
6. Would you be willing to serve on the planning committee? If so, please sign this form and indicate days and times when you could meet.

Thank you for your help!

Figure VIII.2   One School's Collaboration Plan

In order to make more time for teaching:

- Nonemergency intercom announcements will be eliminated.
- Teachers will get daily announcements on their e-mail.
- No assemblies or fund-raising events will take place during the week.
- Assemblies, when deemed appropriate by a vote of the faculty, will be held on Friday during the last hour of the day.

In order to facilitate grade-level planning:

- Library, art, music, lunch, and physical education will be scheduled according to grade level so that all teachers at a grade level will have 1 hour of planning time at the same time each day.
- PTA officers have agreed to provide funds for roaming substitutes to be used to release teachers to observe in another class or at another school for the purpose of researching collaborative learning projects.
- Saturday, summer, and after-school planning sessions will be supported by school improvement funds, and teachers who participate will be given a stipend (to be determined by the number of teachers wishing to be involved).

for these types of in-service activities, but teachers themselves can often be enlisted to provide training for other teachers.

- **Establish communication and sharing of ideas**   Teachers are encouraged to share ideas, either in the form of lesson plans, grade-level meetings, presentations at faculty meetings, or e-mail exchanges. The principal can set the tone for these interactions by asking teachers to share at meetings, taking classroom photos and sharing them at faculty meetings, or just recognizing the teachers' efforts and suggesting that others pay a visit to the classrooms where the innovations are taking place. See Figure 26.2 for websites that support teacher idea exchange.

- **Involve parents**   Parents can also support the process by serving on the planning committee. They can provide support by celebrating the activities in newsletters and websites explaining the innovations and containing progress reports. If the collaboration is to be successful, parents must understand the reasons for the movement and the benefits they can expect for their children.

Applications and Examples

Mrs. Walden is a second-grade teacher at a rural school in a very poor area. This is her first year of teaching, and she is discouraged by the poor progress her students are making. One day in the faculty lounge, she asks Mrs. Black, her colleague, "How can we begin to help our students make better progress? Not one of my students is reading on the second-grade level. I'm very discouraged."

Mrs. Black responds with a wry smile, "I know. Many of the parents don't read at all. We need to do something very different if these kids are going to stand a chance."

Mrs. Carten, the principal, has overheard this exchange and stops by the table. "I'm glad to hear your concern," she says. "Maybe we can work on a plan to give the students more reading instruction."

"You know, that's a great idea," responds Mrs. Walden. "Last year my master teacher had one group of students with whom she met twice a day. They had a formal reading group in the morning and then again in the afternoon. They really made progress that way."

"If the second-grade teachers want to give it a try, I'm all for it," responds Mrs. Carten. "Just let me know how I can help you."

Mrs. Walden and Mrs. Brown meet with their teammate that afternoon to tell her about their conversation with the principal. They devise a plan in which they will have reading groups morning and afternoon, integrating science and social studies content into their oral reading and writing instruction to free up time. They approach Mrs. Carten the next morning with their plan.

"I think this may work," says Mrs. Carten, "but I will need to get school board approval to adapt the adopted science and social studies program. Let's write up a formal proposal, and I'll take it to the board next week. What else are you going to need to do this?"

"We want to teach our own PE in the afternoon instead of interrupting the morning. Right now, we have PE at 9:30, right in the middle of the morning," says Mrs. Walden.

"I'll talk to the PE teacher to see if there's any time in the afternoon available," responds Mrs. Carten. "I think he has planning time scheduled in the afternoon because it's so hot. Maybe we can work something out."

"There is one other thing," suggests Mrs. Brown timidly. "Can you monitor the use of the intercom, please? Announcements are being made all day long, and they really interrupt the flow of our lessons."

"Well, we certainly can do that," says Mrs. Carten with a smile. "I'll send e-mail messages and make sure the secretary does too. But you're going to have to remember to check your e-mail. We can have a schoolwide announcement ban during the instructional day. You're not the first ones I've heard complaining about that. In return, I want you to keep very good records on the progress of your students this year. If this approach works, we may adopt it schoolwide for next year."

The second-grade teachers are very pleased with their solution. They work together to gather materials to infuse science and social studies into the language arts program. At the end of the first semester their students are doing better. Other teachers are beginning to notice their collaboration because they stay a little later in the afternoon, working together. Mrs. Carten is very supportive and often gives the second-grade team recognition in faculty meetings. Near the end of the school year the school board appropriates funding for a week-long summer planning institute for the whole school. The second-grade teachers serve as group leaders, sharing their successful collaboration. The entire faculty is feeling positive about the prospect of making a difference for their students.

The City Heights project in San Diego is a perfect example of a successful collaboration. San Diego State faculty collaborate with teachers at three schools in the City Heights section of the city. Rosa Parks Elementary, Clark Middle School, and Hoover High School teachers are mentored by university faculty, who provide in-service training, classroom demonstrations, and even an on-site master's program.

The teachers work collaboratively with university faculty to supervise student teachers. The administrators are actively involved as well. Dr. Doug Fisher has written grants for funding and located a local corporate sponsor who underwrites a number of the projects. This is especially valuable in this neighborhood because most of the students are learning English as a second language.

The grant and corporate funding have allowed this collaborative to make exciting innovations at the school. Literacy coaches are hired and regularly teach demonstration lessons in the classrooms. Guest speakers are brought in to conduct workshops in areas identified by the teachers as needs.

The high school, as a whole, chooses to implement seven strategies schoolwide. The purpose for adopting a schoolwide implementation of specific strategies is to support all teachers in mastering the strategy use but also to teach study and learning skills to the students. (The results of this implementation have been published in *Educational Leadership*. See "Seven Literacy Strategies That Work" in the November 2002 issue.)

CONCLUSION

Making systemic changes in education is not an easy task. It is often done with impetus from one teacher or a small group of teachers who recognize a need and work together to devise a solution. It is important to get support from administrators and parents for an implementation to have lasting effects. Teachers all over the nation have found success in this way.

References

Allington, R., & Cunningham, P. (2002). *Schools that work: Where all children read and write* (2nd ed.). Boston: Allyn & Bacon.

Farr, R. & Tone, B. (2004) *Portfolio and performance assessment: Helping students evaluate their progress as readers and writers* (2nd ed.). New York: Wadsworth.

Fisher, D., Frey, N., & Williams, D. (2002, November). Seven literacy strategies that work. *Educational Leadership,* pp. 70–73.

Inger, M. (1993, December). Teacher collaboration in secondary schools. In *Centerfocus* (pp. 17–19). Berkeley, CA: National Association for Research in Vocational Education.

Montague, M., & Warger, C. (2001). Getting started with collaboration. In V. Risko & K. Bromley (Eds.), *Collaboration for diverse learners: Viewpoints and practices* (pp. 20–31). Newark, DE: International Reading Association.

Risko, V., & Bromley, K. (Eds.). (2001). *Collaboration for diverse learners: Viewpoints and practices.* Newark, DE: International Reading Association.

TEACHER RESOURCES

Antibullying Pledge Form

Name of School

SCHOOLWIDE "LET'S STOP BULLING NOW" CAMPAIGN

I, _____, pledge that I will help stop bullying at my

school, _____. I will not participate in any physical or verbal bully-

ing. If I see any bullying, I will report it immediately through the _____

anonymous bully line or by telling a teacher or school administrator.

I, _____, will not stand by and let any other student be bul-

lied. I will speak up by stating loudly, "Bullying is a crime at this school! Stop it now!"

_____   _____

signature   date

BASIC PARAGRAPH CHECKLIST

Names					
Writes complete sentences					
Begins with a topic sentence					
Builds on the topic sentence					
Stays on the topic					
Ends with a concluding sentence					
Uses punctuation correctly					
Uses capitalization correctly					
Uses a variety of sentence structures					
Uses connectives and segues					

Class Meeting Item Form

Name _____ Date _____

Class meeting agenda item _____

_____

_____

If this is a problem with another student, how have you tried to work it out?

_____

_____

Conference and Goal-Setting Report Form

Student's name _____ Date of conference _____

Academic topics: _____

Behavior topics: _____

Responsibility topics: _____

Academic goals set: _____

Behavioral goals set: _____

Responsibility goals set: _____

Other goals set: _____

Student's signature _____

Teacher's signature: _____

Approximate date of next conference: _____

Comments:

Data Chart

Topic _____	Student name(s) _____			
Sources (Book and Author)	**Question 1**	**Question 2**	**Question 3**	**Other Interesting Information**

Field Trip Data-Collection Chart

What I Saw (Draw a Picture)	**What I Learned**

Group Work Self-Evaluation Form

Name _____ Date _____

My role in the group _____

What I contributed to the group _____

I encouraged others in the group by _____

I helped the group achieve its goal by _____

I remember to use respectful words

    Sometimes   Most of the time   Always

I do my share of the work

    Sometimes   Most of the time   Always

I am cooperative with others

    Sometimes   Most of the time   Always

Signed _____

My goal for improvement in group work is to _____

_____

Homework Journal Form

Name _____ Week of _____

Date	Time Started	Time Completed	Assignments	Parent's Signature Any Problems?

Learning Center Record Sheet

Student's name _____ Week of _____

Center	Monday	Tuesday	Wednesday	Thursday	Friday
Verbal-linguistic					
Logical-mathematical					
Visual-spatial					
Body-kinesthetic					
Musical-rhythmic					
Interpersonal					
Intrapersonal					
Naturalistic					

Mediation Report

Mediator's name _____ Date _____

Participants _____

_____

What was the problem? (be brief)

Did both participants follow the mediation rules? If not, what was the problem?

What solution was agreed on?

Parent-Volunteer Information Form

Name _____ Phone number _____

When are you available for volunteer work?

 Mornings   Afternoons   At-home assignments, please

Days of the week available _____

Would you be comfortable:

Working with individual children
    Listening to them read _____ Helping them with math facts _____

Working with small groups
    Playing learning games _____ Working on an art project _____

Please check any tasks you feel you could do to help our class.

 Word processing _____   Preparing teaching materials _____

 Monitoring a learning center _____   Supervising a small-group project _____

 Videotaping class activities _____   Chaperoning field trips _____

Do you have any hobbies or interests you would be willing to demonstrate for our class?
_____

Do you speak any languages other than English _____

Would you be available to translate written material? _____

Please share anything else you would like to do for our class:

Oral Report Scoring Rubric

Name _____ Project Title _____

Quality of research

1	2	3	4	5
Incomplete	Minimal	Adequate	Strong	Outstanding

Quality of visuals

1	2	3	4	5
Missing	Minimal	Adequate but doesn't represent all components well	Strong	Outstanding

Standards met

1	2	3	4	5
A few	Most in one area, others missing	Most met in all areas	All met	Went beyond what was required

Reading and Writing Workshop Record Form

Student's name _____ Month of _____

Date Begun/ Date Published	Project	Prewriting	Drafting	Conference	Revising	Editing

Books Read	Author	Title	Begun	Completed	Project	Date

Status-of-the-Class Chart

Dates												
Names												

PW = prewriting   D = draft   C = conference   R = revising   E = editing   P = publishing